CW00890186

THE SEA TRAVELLER

A ROUND-THE-YEAR-GUIDE
TO EUROPE'S BEST
VACATIONS

Carol Wright

CHRISTOPHER HELM
London

© 1989 Carol Wright

Line illustrations by Lynn Armstrong
Christopher Helm (Publishers) Ltd, Imperial House,
21–25 North Street, Bromley, Kent, BR1 1SD

ISBN 0-7470-3402-8

A CIP catalogue record for this book
is available from the British Library

Typeset by Florencetype Ltd, Kewstoke, Avon
Printed and bound in Great Britain by Billing & Sons Ltd, Worcester

CONTENTS

ACKNOWLEDGEMENTS

The author would like to thank the many tourist offices and travel organisations which have helped supply information on events for this book, and in particular the London Tourist Board and their publication *Traditional London*, and husband, Michael Geare who kept the reviving cuppas coming during the writing.

INTRODUCTION:

THE TRAVELLER'S CALENDAR

T HOUGH travel companies still like everyone to book vacations in January, holidays are now taken year round. Jet travel has enabled winter sun to be pursued southwards and the growth of the leisure industry has brought into being short breaks around Europe at most seasons of the year. Unless restricted by school holidays, the traveller can choose the time of year to go seeking sun, snow, sport or other interests. Sun is no longer the only motivation in travel and surveys have shown that the more affluent take up to four different kinds and lengths of holiday a year.

Too often, as I have discovered over my travel-writing years, the first words one hears on arrival, usually from a travel agency or tourist office representative, are 'you should have been here last week'; a title I may use when I come to write my globe-trotting autobiography. 'Last week' is always hotter, less stormy, snowier (if one is an ardent skier), the celebration of the decade – everything that the rain-leaden, closed-down time you are there never is.

This book will help to guide the traveller in choosing the right time to be anywhere in Europe for the warmest beach, the first fruits or vegetables of the year, and the best weather. The latter, of course, cannot in any way be guaranteed. I crossed the Moroccan Sahara fringe one March, assuredly the best season to see the desert, but it snowed steadily, occasionally lightening to sleet, the tracks churned to mud. Guests at my New Year Cotswold parties often sip champagne in the garden; in August we huddle round an open fire indoors. But this book tries to supply a guide to the earliest and latest warm sun and sea in Europe and to the cooler escape spots in summer. I will add a disclaimer here on the weather notes: they are what experience indicates it *should* be, not always what it is. The skiing season is changing subtly (see page 250) and the sun is even more perverse in its appearances.

1

Introduction

'Just in time for the folklore' is another tourist board phrase that brings a chill to my heart, detesting, as I do, the contrived dancing only kept going by an influx of tourists to once pleasant peasant areas. But true customs and feasts, from carnivals to crayfish festivals, are a way of learning more about, and getting closer to, the local people. *The Seasoned Traveller* lists highlight events that travellers can join or, if they are quiet, solitude-seeking people, avoid like the plague. The book's selection is somewhat subjective, omitting events like bull-fighting fiestas (though I have included a note on the bull running in Pamplona), and choosing to highlight events in different countries' 'seasons', whether sporting or social, together with some more esoteric and offbeat events to intrigue and lure the traveller to such occasions as the Ball of the Dead Rat.

Where appropriate I have noted holiday possibilities and tours set around events; tour operators are increasingly arranging packages to events abroad, not just sporting but carnival or Christmas in other countries. Addresses for more general information and dates of annual events are given at the end of the book in addition to local addresses where useful in the text.

Both holidaymakers and businessmen should note the main festivals and public holidays listed at the end of each chapter. While they may add some colour and jollity to a holiday, they can also result in shortages of money, food and shopping when facilities are shut for days on end and roads, restaurants and beaches crammed with holidaying locals. Hints on the holiday habits of different countries can help the traveller to avoid crowds or 'dead cities'. It may be more peaceful visiting Paris or Vienna in August, when everyone is away, but many of the attractions may be closed and it is not till the winter that major European cities come into their cultural own. Nothing is more depressing than a seaside resort out of season, as any travel writer knows. Part of the enjoyment of any visit abroad is table travel and I have included, where appropriate, details of seasonal local foods and drinks. A happy memory is of the late sun in the Neckar valley in Germany sitting under chestnut trees in front of a wine producer's cave sipping the new wines and eating the traditional onion flan, or in Venice tasting the first asparagus or strawberries of the season. Flowering trees, shrubs, colourful flower beds in parks or cool water gardens in which to walk are soothing to any sightseer and to the keen gardener sources of inspiration and a delight to see.

This traveller's calendar must be a flexible guide. It should start in December not January; more logical in the traveller's diary. The travelling season often begins with holidays taken over the Christmas and New Year break and the turkey is hardly

2

cool before one is poring over the latest brochures (many of which now appear in November) planning and trying to break up winter with short excursions.

I have put leading events in the month in which they most usually occur. But dates vary and Easter is a particularly moveable feast. I have merely indicated events roughly, for example 'second week in August' and it would be wise for the traveller to check year by year as needed with the national tourist offices of the country concerned. Occasionally, where local tourist offices are particularly helpful or where tickets can be obtained, I have added their addresses as well as relevant tour operators arranging packages to various events and festivals.

JANUARY

IS HAVING A BALL

J ANUARY is named for the Roman two-faced god, Janus. January for the traveller is also two-faced; a choice of snow in Europe or sun further away. It is the month of travel brochures' dreams of summer escapes to come and the best time for armchair travel with favourite authors.

Dance your way into the New Year in Vienna at one of their series of splendid and elegant balls. At least 300 are listed, starting in January and running through till March. Vienna is the last city to preserve so many of these elaborate affairs and in January the entire city gives itself up to waltzing and enjoying itself.

What is more, the Viennese are hospitable about their events and the very efficient tourist office (Kinderspitalgasse 5, A–1095 Vienna, tel. (222) 435974) issues leaflets in different languages listing the balls and detailing how to get tickets, what to wear, etc.

For those, like me, who have tried the tricky left-handed waltz (the fleckerl) on the stage of the opera house at the famous Opera Ball, and found my rhythm wanting, the Viennese run waltz courses. Courses at several dancing schools 'can be attended by the hour at short notice and without tedious registration formalities'. Tuition is available in English on request and a 50-minute lesson costs about £5 (AS100). Locations of waltz teachers are found in a brochure 'Walzertansen in Wien' from the Viennese Association of Dancing Teachers, Gusshausstrasse 15, A–1040 Vienna, tel. (222) 650612. The traditional Viennese dancing school of Elmayer-Vestenbrugg offers Viennese waltz courses specially designed for vistors with only a short time to spare. Without registering, visitors can attend the course in the Palais Pallavicini, Braunerstrasse 13, A–1010, Vienna, on Tuesday and Saturday afternoons with 50-minute lessons at AS100. After three lessons you get a certificate. Couples or individuals can take part, and tuition is in English, French, German and Italian.

Sure-footed locals have plenty to get waltzed up about. Though now the initial ball of the season is the Champagne Ball, held at the Intercontinental on the second Friday of November, the traditional dance series kicks off with the first of the fasching celebrations, calling for evening dress or fancy dress at dances known as gschnas. The first grand ball on New Year's Eve is the Kaiser Ball at the Hofburg Palace where the officers of the Austrian Army and the Pharmacists also hold their dances.

The Vienna Philharmonic is one of the most spectacular balls held in the Golden Hall of the Musikvereign. Others to note are the Flower Ball, Confectionery, Coffee-house Owners, Chemistry and Economy Balls and the Green Cross Ball at which evening dress is replaced by hunting suits and dirndls.

The dance sequence moves on into February with the Masked Ball which turns the clock back at the Hofburg with eighteenth-century dress, liveried footmen, rococo orchestra and masked processions. At the Rudolfina Redoute it is ladies choice of dancing partner until midnight; ladies must wear masks. The Artists' Ball is more bohemian in character, taking place at the Hilton Hotel. The Opera Ball in February, started by the Emperor Franz Josef, is considered the highlight by many. The ladies mostly wear white. Tickets cost anything up to £1,500 for seats in the various tiers of the theatre and central room. The ball opens with a parade of girls in white dresses and tiny coronets who lead their black-tailed partners into the left-handed waltz. The corps de ballet then show how a Strauss waltz can achieve classic grace to the lead of a dancing master. And then everyone waltzes, all 7,000; gowns and jewels whirl under the tiers of boxes garlanded with flowers and under the massive round chandelier. The waltzing continues till dawn, followed by a drift to hotels like the Bristol next door to the Opera House for sustaining goulaschen soup and light wine.

These are the stately yesteryear occasions when one can catch at the elegance of the Hapsburg court. But there are many informal dances; the Nearly Bare Ball at the Metropol culture centre at the end of January is an 'anything goes' affair as far as costumes are concerned. One can also design an unusual costume for the Okista Gschnas organised by youth travel groups at the Sofiensale in February.

All the events are listed in the leaflet 'Have a Ball in Vienna' from the Austrian National Tourist Offices or Vienna tourist board. Even if you are like Cinderella and don't go to the ball, you can catch much of the flavour at dinner, along with the ballgoers in restaurants where special ball dinner menus are often put on. Those going to a ball eat at a restaurant near the ball venue. They hurry away in order not to miss the opening ceremony, a centuries-old ritual in which there is usually a fanfare from the orchestra and the ceremonial entry of the young committee to the strains of the 'Fan Polonaise'. The opening ceremony ends with the left-handed waltz. Another dance highlight of a Viennese ball, usually performed after midnight, is the Fledermaus Quadrille by Johann Strauss. The dancers form up in columns and follow the instructions of the dancing master, whose authority diminishes as the dance wears on and dancers become confused and tangled up. The main dance is inevitably the Viennese waltz plus polka and 'galop'. Happily there are refreshment bars in all the ballrooms and table service. Oyster bars and splendid buffets abound and the wonderful sweet pastries are often served.

After it all, the dancers make for an early opening coffee house for chicken or goulash soup with freshly baked rolls. Or more informal, a snack from a street sausage stall. About lunch time the dancers meet for a 'hair of the dog' breakfast to gossip over the night's events. Buffet breakfasts are served in most of the main hotels. That of the Bristol is considered the best, but its sister hotel the Imperial has everything in its about £10 price from champagne and kipferl, Vienna's croissant, to country cream cheeses and the Imperial torte, layers of almond paste coated in marzipan and milk chocolate, from a recipe dating back to 1873. At this time of year a special doughnut called a krapfen is made, filled with apricot jam and often also with cream; ten million of these were said to have been made for the Congress of Vienna in 1815.

Coffee houses are Vienna's delight, whether you have been to a ball or a concert the night before or not. Demel's is the classy one, where tourists go rather as one goes to the Ritz in London for tea, where a hundred cakes and sweetmeats are served by waitresses in black dresses and white aprons. Other excellent spots for the coffee cult include Cafe Central in the Palais Ferstel, below the old Stock Exchange, where Trotsky took coffee; Cafe Landtmann near the Hofburg Gardens, decorated in Beidermeier period inlaid wood and, on Saturday afternoons, Landtmann organises walking tours of cafes and pastry shops for a small fee; Mozart or Tirolerhof are more for tourists, locals favour Heine or Kur Condoterie Oberlaa, and artists go to Hawelka near the Spanish riding school, where the nicotine-stained walls are hung with valuable paintings once donated by their creators in exchange for food. Music with the pastries comes at the Konzertcafes listed by the tourist office. The *Johan Strauss* is an old Danube passenger boat moored on the Danube canal where live concerts are given in the afternoon and evening. Later at night one can go underground to cellar taverns for food, drinks and music. The Piaristenkeller has zither music in the baroque setting of a former monastery; classical music is the backing at the Antiquitaten Keller, slightly off the city centre. In summer, the Viennese go out by tram or city railway to the Vienna woods to drink and snack at the Heurigen (wine inns) which are open most of the year.

Having picked a coffee house, one cannot just ask for 'coffee'. There are at least 30 to 40 variations, in addition to those with added alcohol. Coffee is mostly taken with a shlag heap of whipped cream. 'Melange' coffee is common, either with hot milky cream or whipped cream on the side. Kaiser Melange has egg yolk in it, possibly a morning-after stabiliser. Other options include Einspanner, coffee in tall glasses with lots of whipped cream and powdered sugar; kaffe creme, with cream in a separate jug; doppel mocca, black and served in a big cup; teeshall, with milk served in a tea cup; kapuziner, a small cup of black coffee mixed with cream to the colour of a capucine monk's robe; and Lauf, coffee with whipped cream mixed in and served in a tall glass. A platter of varied sugars comes with the coffee, a small glass of water and possibly a 'submarine', a small chocolate case filled with cream to melt into the coffee. Less formal are the palatschinken cafes where thin freshly-made pancakes are served with varieties of fillings.

All good fare for mornings after the dance night before. A ball visit at the weekend can be packaged to include three nights accommodation and buffet breakfast at a central four star hotel. Also included are two dinners, one at a heuriger wine tavern, gala dinner and champagne breakfast after the ball. Among the balls included in this packaging are the Flower, Bakers, Chemists, Doctors, Furriers, and Electricians. Details from Hotel Alba, Margaretenstrasse 53, A–1050, Vienna, tel. (222) 58850. Austro Tours, 5 St Peter's Street, St Albans, Herts AL1 3DJ (02727 38191) arrange a special package to take in the New Year Ball at the Hilton and a New Year's day concert.

Climate and Place

Snow is the scene, with seasonal discounts for the month of January known as 'white weeks' when ski resorts offer special inclusive packages at reduced rates. The Aosta valley has an annual booklet listing white-week offers for its resorts available from the Swiss Tourist Offices.

Austria offers some more off-beat ideas for New Year winter enjoyment. In Carinthia, the Obervallach area has farm holidays from 80AS for bed and breakfast. Mallnitz has winter walking tours for non-skiers on 30 km of cleared paths to inns, cabins or restaurants. Details from the area tourist board, Kaufmanngasse 13, A9121; Klagenfurt tel. (042 22) 56 4860.

Non-skiers can also boast of January recreations such as ice-diving at the school in Hallstatt in Upper Austria. There is ice-surfing at Feld am See. Staying under cover one can play tennis, swim or ride in Austria's 98 covered stables. The more daredevil can try the world's fastest downhill slope in Planai/Schladming in Styria: the average speed is about 70 mph.

Switzerland is the home of the chic winter sports scene and offers weather forecasts on 162 on the Swiss phone system; dial 163 for information on roads and alpine pass conditions.

The place to be

In January it is St Moritz. In 1864 Johannes Badrutts proved to some British guests that winter in a snowy place was sunnier and much more fun than misty, murky Northern Europe. St Moritz offers much much more than just slithering around on the ski slopes. Though its initial attraction to visitors was as a spa, the little Engadine Valley town has always provided a wide list of sports to suit every muscular talent down to wrist movements for bridge and backgammon. It took only 20 years from that first visit for a group of Britains in 1884 to tie together two small American tobaggans to make a snow descent in pairs; the ancestor of the bobsleigh. Kings and princesses then bobbed down the roads to Celerina. Ladies, now banned from the Cresta run, made the descent in large hats skewered on with yard-long hat pins.

An afternoon taxi ride takes on a whole new meaning in St Moritz. Here a taxi ride is as a passenger wedged between two experts down the world's only natural ice run in a bobsleigh. It costs about 100 Swiss francs, lasts about 1½ minutes (the record is 1 minute 10 seconds) and is a life-long conversation stopper. A souvenir photo is included in the price as proof positive. The steel bobs skim an ice canal of sixteen curves that takes eight days and thirteen million litres of water to create each year and which pulls the body with four times the force of gravity. But the worst is the last zigzag of curves, when the limbs feel as if they are about to leave their sockets.

You can, of course, just watch from the refreshment terrace by the Dracula Club bar or, if you know a member, watch the Cresta run in the mornings. The season for the Cresta starts a week before Christmas and ends on 1 March. Only during this time is it cold enough, with not too little or too much snow. There are races every weekend and most Wednesdays and the rest of the time is practice or discussion, on the Kulm Hotel's Sunny Terrace, of times taken to complete the 1,328-yard track past the horrors of Shuttlecock, Battledore and Stream Corner, the most difficult banks. The Sunny Terrace looks down over the Palace Hotel and town to the frozen lake below. It is a good vantage point to watch another of St Moritz's adventures, hang gliding. Launched from the slopes above the town, the bat-winged aviators soar out over the Kulm Hotel and down to land on the frozen lake. A gentler art, taken no less seriously than the Cresta run, is curling, with rinks at the Kulm, Palace and Suvretta House hotels. The St Moritz curling club has its own curling school for beginners. Skating of course is also available but another way of covering the snow surface is on horse back, with daily excursion rides offered. The less hearty can take horse-drawn sleigh rides along the valley or watch international dog sleigh races.

An unusual winter sport is polo on the ice, at St Moritz

At the end of January and the beginning of February there are the St Moritz horse races, on the frozen lake polo and jumping competitions. Coloured golf balls are used for the rounds taken on the golf course set up on the frozen lake. There is skiing – 200 miles of slopes – but a glance at the St Moritz tourist office and Palace Hotel's list of winter events shows it is not an evident or essential pastime. The slopes are above the town at Corviglia, where there is also a covered tennis complex. Cross-country skiing in the Engadine Valley is on 50 miles of trails. Most spend the day pottering around the designer shops in the little town preparing for the apres ski life with dancing at the Kulm's Sunny Bar or Palace King's Club disco. A new beauty spa with regimes of walking and calorie controlled diets or a three-day fitness package including sports are alternatives.

It is, however, a pity to opt out of St Moritz's eating scene. The Chesa Veglia, a seventeenth-century farmhouse, is the place for fondues and local food at night. There is formal dining at the Kulm or Palace, afternoon tea in the rather ecclesiastical decor of the Palace lobby – *the* place for off the slopes, pre-apres ski meetings, or for mornings, with coffee, hot chocolate piled with cream and Kirsch-soaked cakes, at Condoterie Hauselman in the town centre.

The Hauselman is opposite the active and helpful tourist office, whose windows have press button audio visuals giving the visitor yet more ideas of how to pass the time (address: CH–7500, St Moritz, Switzerland). One can bus or taxi along the valley to Sils to walk in a typical Engadine village with the deep-set windows edged with a decoration the locals call grafitti. The Pension Andreola, a family run place, is a pleasantly rustic spot to stay. The same family owns the Chesa Marchetta restaurant with two small stove-dominated rooms where local dishes like plain in pigna, potato gratin with home made sausages and vegetables are served. In the cellars below, air-dried beef, home-made cheeses, sausages and home-cured hams hang above the wine casks.

Finally, if you find skiing too tame, you can snow surf on skate boards without the rollers, swooping through the snow gates of the giant slalom run.

Natural Inclinations

Gale watching is the most exhilarating experience on a rough winter day, watching waves crash on rocks and cliffs from a snug niche well above. The British Isles get some spectacular bashings in January and some spots for viewing the best include Land's End in Cornwall, when the mass of summer visitors eroding the cliff tops are absent; Hartland Point in Devon, 350 feet of strataed cliffs and jagged reefs; Portland Bill in Dorset for Europe's fiercest rip tides and 13 miles of shingle beach at Chesil Beach. In Scotland, go to Duncansby Head, Easter Ross near Wick for 200-foot cliffs and isolated single rock stacks. Near here are the Whaligoe steps that go mysteriously down to the water through small abandoned cottages of what was once a fishing village; their terracing gives excellent viewpoints for watching the waves. Other wind watch points are the south coast of the Isle of Wight near the Needles; St Goran's head, Dyfed, Pembrokeshire, which has a chapel in a cliff cleft; the

National Trust owned cliff area around Wheel Coates near Bude, with ruined mine houses for wind shelter. In Devon, one can watch the weather whip across Torbay from the comfort of the Imperial Hotel or walk the cliffs of the South Hams near Thurlestone, switchbacking over the curling cliffs looking out to Burgh Island with its little white hotel (often closed in January); a site for some of the best seascapes from every window of the hotel or just for a day visit thawing out in the tiny stone Pilchard Inn with its log fires. In Northern Ireland there's the Giant's Causeway, now with its own visitor centre.

The Atlantic coasts of the Continent provide further excitements, the long promontories of Brittany stretching westward with spots like the Pot des Pois rocks, as dramatic as Land's End. Portugal has some of the best breaker beaches. In the north, south of Viana, there's Ofir, with huge sweeps of sand beaten by booming white-crested waves. Near Lisbon, beyond Cascais, is Guincho, sand again, with breakers and little storm-protected beach restaurants. Above towers Cabo da Roca, the most westerly point of Europe once known as Fim del Mundo, the end of the world; medieval sailors believing if you sailed west from here you eventually fell off the edge of the earth. In the south's Algarve, the furthest point west is Cape St Vincent, a squared-off cliff plateau around which ships struggle to enter European waters. The cliffs have neat natural niches in which to sit in shelter and watch the Atlantic's might.

Old Customs die Hard

Swallow a grape, throw out household junk, kiss the first footer – all ways of seeing in the New Year around Europe.

Package tours are available that include taking in New Year celebrations in major cities.

Madrid   Warm up first with sherry and tapas (bar snacks that are mini versions of full dishes) in a bar near the Plaza Mayor, the old square. Take along with you twelve grapes and swallow one on each stroke of midnight. This brings good luck, they say, and is not as easy as it sounds. Laughter induced by the sherry does not help.

Rome   Most Romans dine at home, eating smoked loin of pork and lentils. At midnight any old household junk is thrown – literally – out of the window into the street, so take special care when parking and walking on New Year's Eve and get up early on 1 January to collect any bargains.

Vienna Locals gather in the pedestrian-only square around St Stephen's Cathedral. The bells ring out at midnight; then chimney sweeps tour the square as the crowd kisses them for good luck. Next day everyone listens to the New Year's Day concert given by the Vienna Symphony Orchestra, always broadcast and always including Beethoven's Ninth Symphony. The Hofburg Orchestra also gives a concert of operetta music in the big hall of the music society and this is also covered worldwide by TV and radio. Tickets from Wiener Konzerthaus-gesellschaft, Lothringerstrasse 20, A–1030, Vienna tel. (222 721 211).

Copenhagen The Danes go for humour. They dine first with the family with games, fireworks and the last lighting of the Christmas tree candles at midnight. Practical jokes are played; bikes end up on the roofs of houses; garden gates are hung on flagpoles.

Paris Paris goes out on reveillon, New Year's Eve. They have a luxury meal and restaurants are booked a long way ahead. Oysters, goose stuffed with sausage and lots of marron glacés are traditional fare. Each restaurant competes to produce the best menu, especially in country areas of France. Florists and confectioners stay open late on New Year's Eve so presents can be bought.

Amsterdam The Dutch capital celebrates with a bang, lots of fireworks; livening up from the middle of New Year's Eve afternoon with Chinese restaurants joining in and letting off firecrackers.

Madeira This is the place for the European area's best New Year firework display and cruise ship itineraries are planned to stay in that port for two days to watch.

Geneva This city also explodes into the New Year, firing cannons and giving concerts and musical events. Hotels hold gala dinners and dances.

Germany At midnight, the whole country bursts into colour and light with everyone letting off fireworks. The sight is especially stunning if you can book a flight that crosses the country at midnight as I once did. Tradition has it that the noise drove away evil spirits. At midnight church bells also toll and in some small towns trombonists play in the church towers. The evening is spent at home or in restaurants or at New Year balls.

In Bavaria, house lights are turned out just before midnight and on again as the clock begins to strike. In the Alps, as much noise as possible is made. In Oberammagau there is a 'star singer procession' with a band that plays for the Passion Play. Krapfen, doughnuts, are made and eaten with punch. The Germans also like jokes at this time, such as chocolates filled with mustard, sugar lumps that contain spiders, plastic sausages and dog figures which emit long strings of black sausage-like polystyrene; all these can be seen on sale in the days preceding the festival.

Greece celebrate the feast of St Basil on 1 January and a New Year cake (*vassilopitta*) is sliced as it has been since Byzantine times. The person in whose slice a coin is found is the year's lucky person. St Basil overshadows the day with good wishes and blessings in his name. As on Christmas Eve (see page 249), the children go from house to house singing the kalanda songs, carrying a green rod from a tree and tapping the master of the house on the back with it while singing their good wishes. This is also done on New Year's Day as well as Eve and the children are rewarded with sweetmeats, nuts or coins. It is important to choose the right person to be the first to enter the house on 1 January. Rituals are carefully observed at their entrance and accompanied by a lot of well-wishing. The New Year's Day dinner table must be richly laden to warrant abundance the year round. As well as cold and hot dishes, the table is piled with fruit, fresh or dried, honey, olive branches and on Lemnos pomegranates are added to the table. The table remains fully laden all day. The main dish is the Vassilopitta, St Basil's cake, with its hidden coin. In Athens and larger towns this cake is bought at a confectioner and is made of milk, eggs, butter and sugar, shaped into a round; the New Year date is made on top in dough. In villages the cake has more spices and it is more elaborately decorated, and a coin, a leaf or a piece of straw may be added; the leaf finder will inherit the vineyard, the straw indicates a future farmer. The head of the household cuts the cake with great solemnity; a slice is first cut for St Basil and then Christ, then one for the house and only then for each member of the household. After this the cattle and the poor get a slice. In some parts of Greece, windows and doors are left open all day so anyone, stranger or not, can come and receive a share of the cake.

In Northern Greece masquerades and mumming is a custom between New Year's Day and Epiphany. Mummers dress as animals or particular humans such as bride and groom, old granny, the Moorish sea captain. The dramas were originally enacted to rouse the fertilising powers of nature. One ritual is to ensure the 'renewal of water' and on New Year's Day all pitchers and jugs in the house must be replenished with new water, St Basil's water, with offerings to the spirit dwelling in the well or fountain.

Scotland   New Year's Eve, or Hogmanay is welcomed communally round a clock tower with kissing for luck and the traditional drink is Het Pint, hot mulled ale spiced with nutmeg and whisky. First-footing means visiting in the early hours of New Year's morning bearing gifts of coal, bread and salt; whisky and shortbread are offered by the head of the household in return. The first footer is the first person not a member of the family to cross the threshold in the New Year. As Big Ben chimes in the New Year from London, the whole country sings 'Auld Lang Syne'.

If you want an unusual New Year, take a Scanscape holiday to Rovaniemi on the Arctic circle to celebrate with the Lapps. The tour leaves on 30 December and gets back on 3 January, with a night in Helsinki on the way up and the return. The New Year will start for you with sauna, swim, buffet breakfast and a snowmobile safari to a reindeer farm to take your reindeer driving test. Details from Scanscape, 197–199 City Road, London EC1V 1JN, 01 251 2500.

6 January

Epiphany, or the Three Kings Day, is still an important day in the eastern orthodox church calendar. In London in the Chapel Royal of St James's Palace there is a special 11.30 am service with a procession of choir and clergy followed by a detachment of the Yeomen of the Guard. The service proceeds to the anthem, at which point two gentlemen ushers to the Queen bring traditional gifts of gold, frankincense and myrrh, dedicating them on the altar with a Yeoman escort. Admission for this service is by ticket only, available by writing to Serjeant of the Vestry, St James's Palace, London SW1.

The day is particularly celebrated in Germany and Austria, often with bonfires and Christmas trees lit outside the houses. There is much ringing of bells and processions bearing burning torches. A Bean King and Queen are chosen on 6 January and a large black bean is baked in the Three Kings' Cake. The finder becomes the Bean King and plays master of ceremonies at the Twelfth Night party. Christmas trees are taken down and the social emphasis moves into the carnival season (see February).

Cologne Cathedral, which contains the relics of the Magi in the golden shrine of the Three Kings which prompted the building of the cathedral, has high mass to celebrate Epiphany. The beginning of the service is marked by sounding the Emperor's bell (Kaiserglocke), the largest bell in Germany. 'Star singers', three boys dressed as kings, carry a star on the end of a pole through the streets and sing 'star carols'. Sometimes all the men of a village will take part and money is raised for charity.

In Salzburg, Austria, the Perchten run on the eve of 6 January. Perchten can be good or evil figures, beautiful or ugly. In Salzburg they are called 'Schnabel perchten' (perchten with beaks) and wear old skirts and jackets, straw hats, scarves and huge cloth beaks. They carry a broom for cleaning, scissors (threatening to cut open the slovenly and let the dirt in) and a crate for taking away wrongdoers. The ugly perchten have devils' masks with horns and wear skins. Originally the male perchten were thought to be superhumans who could influence fertility and bring well-being.

From 6 January in the Voralberg till the end of the carnival season, skiing races are held with racers in disguise. In Upper Austria's Salzkammergut, the Glocklerlaufen are groups of masked men wearing huge wooden structures on their heads covered with opaque paper decorated and covered with coloured tissue paper with lights placed inside, creating a stained glass effect. The men run through the towns carrying these strange lanterns.

In Rome, Twelfth Night begins on the evening before with the Epiphany fair held in the Piazza Navona selling toys, sweets and presents. The fair among the fountains is open till dawn. In Greece, 6 January is celebrated by the blessing of the waters. A cross is immersed in the sea or in lakes and rivers. At Piraeus, the port of Athens, there is a special ceremony.

Burns Night (25 January)

This is a Scottish celebration which has spread through the world wherever the Scots congregate. A dinner in honour of the poet Robert Burns is held at which the haggis is served with tatties and neeps (potatoes and swedes). The haggis is brought in ceremoniously accompanied by a piper, it is 'addressed' with the reading of Burns' poem 'to a haggis', a skean dhu is used to cut it open, and a toast in whisky is given. During the evening, traditional speeches, songs, a reading of Burns' poems and piped music form the entertainment. Those with any claim to the clans wear kilts and Highland dress and women decorate their dresses with a sash of tartan. If you are searching for a haggis to eat, Edinburgh is a good source. Butcher Alex Crombie, 97 Broughton Street, has won awards for his haggis and runs a postal service throughout the UK and Europe, which takes about three days. He also runs a sampling for the un-initiated, for a small charge, of haggis, tatties and neeps. The Scottish Tourist Board (tel. 031 332 2433) can give more details.

Food

Winter is hardly considered prime picnic time but in Austria's TurracherHohe the larger guesthouses and hotels in this area organise snow picnics for their guests. At 6,500 feet up in the mountains they serve hot soups, sausages, cabbage, speck (an Austrian bacon speciality), bread and cakes. The food, together with plates and cutlery, is taken up the mountain and the spread consumed to a background of harmonica music. To end the meal, there is a shot of mountain pine schnapps to warm everyone up for the return to the villages.

Scottish salmon, traditionally considered a summer dish for the June season's events, is in plentiful supply in January and cooked the traditional Scottish way is poached lightly in salted water and served hot with melted butter or cold with mayonnaise.

Truffles Known as black diamonds (for their cost), or the daughters of thunder (from what was thought to cause their growth in Roman times), truffles are considered, in the Perigord area of France, to be at their choicest in January. The hard, barren soil of Perigord, 100 miles east of Bordeaux, is ideal terrain for this mysterious fungus, black and about the size of a walnut. The Romans and later the French court considered the truffle to be an aphrodisiac. Truffles are graded into four qualities, finest, extra, high grade and pieces and peelings. In Paris there are specialist shops in which they can be bought, such as La Maison de la Truffe, Place de la Madeleine, though many will buy them from a favourite restaurant. In London, Fortnum and Mason in Piccadilly will fly in fresh supplies and they can be tasted in varied ways on the breakfast menu (and others) of Truffles Restaurant in the Portman Hotel, Portman Square.

Arts

In Britain, pantomime runs in many theatres from Christmas through January. This is a topsy-turvey fantasy theatre world, where penniless kings and queens are afraid of their servants. The principal boy is a girl, the comic dame is played by a man, and leading artists take part in tenuous fairy tales extended with music, dancing, conjuring and topical jokes.

Politics have always been part of pantomime. In the eighteenth century Sir Robert Walpole was enraged enough to go backstage and beat the clown with his stick. Panto itself began in ancient Rome, where a single man played all the roles in a myth story in mime. He wore a mask and expression was principally conveyed by hands and fingers. In the second century women became pantomimes and often appeared naked. Pantomime popularity pleased Augustus, angered Tiberius, was back in favour under Caligula, while Nero himself played pantomime. The Comedia dell'arte from Italy toured Europe with mimed plays, coming to Britain in the mid sixteenth century. The first English pantomime is marked as John Weaver's *The Tavern Bilkers*, performed at Drury Lane in 1702 and based on a Goldoni Harlequin sequence from Italy. In 1758 the Grimaldi family came to Britain and performed *Mother Goose* in London. Joseph Grimaldi, a brilliant comic, developed the British panto clown and dame figures.

Until about 70 years ago, panto plots were original each year. Now panto is a swift moving melange of part story, part revue and part music hall and variety show. Mid nineteenth-century titles were a lot longer than those today; 'Harlequin Cinderella or the Little Fairy with the Large Glass Slipper' or 'Harlequin Sinbad the Sailor or the Great Roc of the Diamond Valley and the Seven Wonders of the World' were titles used to pull the crowds then. Great music hall artists played roles early in this century; now TV and film stars take roles. Dames like George Robey were so good that people came just to watch one act. The Royal Shakespeare Company have not been above playing panto. George Robey may have bewailed 'panto's are going out because people have been pampered too much', but they still survive and flourish.

The Annual Circus Festival, Monte Carlo, in late January, is where the big top acts gather, along with 20,000 circus fans from all over the world. The festival, founded by Prince Rainier, has around 24 circus acts from different countries of which the best win prizes. The festival ends with a gala ball at one of the principality's hotels. Loews Hotel, the usual venue, is also used by the celebrities and performers attending the festival. Special packages are available including circus performance tickets and transfers to the circus grounds. Lights blaze around the circus area, especially near the huge new permanent big top that takes 4,200 spectators. Film stars often act as festival judges; the late Cary Grant, once an acrobat and stilt walker, was a popular and frequent judge.

Horticultural

A hot spot to go on cold days is a hot house in a botanical garden. Less known than Kew, but with plenty to see in winter, is the Birmingham Botanical Gardens, Westbourne Road, Edgbaston (021 454 1860). Open every day except Christmas Day, the 17-acre garden is over 150 years old. Mature trees cut the garden off from the world and its Victorian lines lead from a central band stand. The hot houses are well stocked with palms, tree ferns, water lilies and tropical plants. In the grounds are large rock pools and a long rhododendron walk. Facilities include restaurant, shop and garden centre.

Sports

Switzerland runs the Inferno, that country's longest ski race. It begins at Murren, 10,000 feet up the summit of the Schilthorn, and ends 7½ miles and 7,000 feet lower at Lauterbrunnen.

Seckau, in the Austrian province of Styria, is Europe's centre for dogsleigh races, held early in January. Teams race for £2,000 of prizes and the programme includes country music, a Fire Brigade ball and prize-giving.

Wales has its season of international rugby matches running through the month. The matches are held at Cardiff Arms Park, which is in the centre of the city. Fans gather at the Royal Hotel, the Barbarian team's home bar, or at Spanghero's, a restaurant in an old warehouse near the ground and named for a French rugby star; book well ahead and aim to eat in a continuous party atmosphere that day. When the Welsh play the French, the French supporters tour the streets with bands.

In mid January there is the Dee River race held at Llangollen, Clwyd, which is part of the British championship wild water races.

Shopping

UK The January sales actually start in late December, as soon as the Christmas public holidays are over. The sales in big

London stores like Harrods, Liberty's, Selfridges and Harvey Nichols attract many visitors hunting for bargains. Harrods, for example, gets about 250,000 shoppers each sales day and takes many millions of pounds daily, with cashmere, china and crystal the top sellers with overseas shoppers. If you have a Harrods credit card you get advance details and their catalogue, which can save a lot of fighting through the throngs when you go. After the initial invasion, Mondays are the slowest days and it's wise to get a map of the store to guide you straight to which of the 230 departments you want. If queueing and watching the scrum is part of the attraction of the sales, then stores offering sustenance while waiting include Harrods with tea, coffee and biscuits, and in-queue entertainment; in 1988 the sales were opened by Charlton Heston. Hilditch and Key, 37 and 73 Jermyn Street, have given out doughnuts and tea, entertaining at number 37 with music and at 73 with a performing dog. Lillywhites on Piccadilly Circus provide hot drinks.

The hunt is part of the fun of finding a bargain which can be as simple as a buyer's mistake that the store just wants to see the back of. Harrods, ever in the lead with sales statistics, offered a discount of £97,500 off in their 1988 January sale. You still needed another £97,000 to buy the bargain in question, a diamond-encrusted watch offered at half price. Or you could have opted for a £29,995 chinchilla coat for a mere £14,995, though the bargain of the year would appear to be a £1,787 Bonsack bath decorated with gold fleur de lis for only £179.

Sale goods are covered by law and must have been on sale for four weeks at non sale prices within the previous six months and be of good quality. Fashion seekers should go early though at the end of the sale period, clothes come down to half price but the choice of sizes is smaller (usually larger!) Narrowing down what you want to get, a round the London stores basic guide is Harrods for bone china; Selfridges for household and fashions; Harvey Nichols for designer fashion; Hilditch and Key for shirts; John Lewis with 30 per cent discounts on its own brands; Fortnum and Mason for food and children's clothes; Liberty, fabrics, scarves and cashmere for men; Lillywhites for sports goods; the White House for linens and bathrobes; and Jaeger for fashion. Be early for the best.

At Selfridges, where the enthusiastic bargain-hunters camp out days before the sale starts, brass bands play to the waiting queues for an hour before the doors open. At Burberry's in the Haymarket, queues of around 400 people wait for the 25 per cent discounts off trench coats. The store's manager and his staff serve hot coffee and shortbread to those waiting.

The January sales usually last about three weeks to a month

and include shops of all sizes all over the country. Some London hotels, for example the Embassy Group, 34 Queens Gate, London SW7 5JA (tel. 01–584 8222), offer saletime discounts till the end of February with offers of unlimited travel on London transport included.

Those who are big spending and get a thrill from it, can save the street and store struggles and go for a big spend weekend at the Armanthwaite Hall hotel on Lake Bassenthwaite near Keswick in the Lake District. In 1988, the hotel was offering, naturally to a limited number of takers, a £1,000 a day stay with the most expensive of foods like caviar, truffles and pate de foie gras, return helicopter travel from up to 200 miles away, self drive or chauffeured Rolls, a luxury suite with spa bath and sunbathing tower, a case of champagne per person, pick of the winecellar, a personal chef to cook whatever you like, two sheepskin coats and personalised crystal decanter and glasses as souvenirs.

Denmark   Copenhagen's January sales begin around 5 January, but in other towns, sales start as in the UK between Christmas and the New Year.

Germany   Sales last from the end of January until mid February with the prices down by 50 per cent in some cases, especially on textiles and leather goods. Try shopping streets such as Berlin's Ku-damm, Dusseldorf's Konigsallee, Frankfurt's Zell or Munich's Maxmilianstrasse (you can get refunds of the 14 per cent VAT paid if taking articles out of the country).

Paris   The sales start around 6 January and continue until the end of the month.

Shows

London, Earls Court, the London Boat Show – to which crowds in thick sweaters, trousers and deck shoes make their way. The exhibition hall is a forest of tall masts of exhibits set up by the British Marine Industries Federation. The show lasts twelve days and exhibitors often virtually live on the premises in order to cut expenses. There are sightseers as well as sailing enthusiasts and buyers, 350,000 people in all, many of whom get converted to life (or rather weekends) on the ocean wave while in the middle of London. Much of the attraction is the ingenuity with which the depressing exhibition hall is converted, in bleak January, into a Mediterranean harbour, a Channel Islands port or a Tudor village. Even designer oilskins will be there and there are displays and competitions from the navy, coastguard and lifeboat services.

Summer sailing dreams start in January at London's Boat Show

Public Holidays

1 January, New Year's Day, Belgium, Denmark, France, Germany, Italy, Luxembourg, Netherlands, Norway, Portugal, Ireland, Spain, Sweden, UK.
2 January, Scotland.
6 January, Epiphany, Germany, Spain, Sweden.
10 January, Finland.

2
FEBRUARY
IS FAREWELL TO THE FLESH

FEBRUARY, also known as 'fill dyke', is usually the lowest
weather point of the northern European year, with snow,
sleet, rain and bleakness. Human jollity counters this with
fun and feasting. Carnival carries on this month in the more
Catholic countries, while St Valentine's Day on 14 February
gives an excuse for romance and celebration.

Catholic countries such as Italy, Germany, Austria, Belgium,
Spain, Malta, and Portugal – and also non-Catholic Holland –
have a carnival season that may start on the eleventh hour of the
eleventh day of the eleventh month but really gets going after
New Year and swings along to Shrove Tuesday, usually involving a lot of noisy, colourful feasting, saying farewell to the
delights of the flesh before Lenten fasting and abstinence
begins.

The most elegant emanation of European carnivals is that of
Venice. It dates back to the Middle Ages and reached its full
splendour in the eighteenth century when even the poorest of
its inhabitants enjoyed the freedom of the mask and disguise.
The 'bamba', a black and white mask, and the Venetian-style
tricorn hat were the cheapest and most common apparel, used
by both sexes and all classes. The nobles frequently dressed as
peasants or fishermen; men dressed as women; and even the
mask of the plague doctor was employed – a figure well known
in the sea port over the centuries.

The Venice carnival declined after 1797, when Napoleon
abolished the Venetian republic, and was only revived in 1979
when the mayor resurrected it by official decree. In the past
decade, the carnival has gradually blossomed into a haunting
and beautiful spectacle; the old mascari (mask) shops have
reopened, and costumes are elaborate. Everyone has a chance to
perform on this urban stage; portly middle-aged men don masks
for an evening stroll; even dogs may be seen in costume.
Visitors and locals alike retreat behind the mask: wearing
flowing robes, the plague doctor with his beaked nose walks
again; harlequin – the link with the Comedia dell'arte – is
much seen, along with clowns and Puchinellas, pantaloons and
Columbines. Some visitors arrive with different costumes for
every night of the posing and parading.

At the weekend, the throngs gather in St Mark's Square trying
to squeeze into Florian's cafe. Foreigners, particularly the English speakers, group around Harry's Bar. There are parties in
every square, concerts in the churches, private balls in the
palaces; Vivaldi's music fills the air and a band plays – as
always – in St Mark's.

Events are organised by the city, based on an annual theme.
The Goldoni and Fenice theatres offer opera and drama.

Museums and galleries have special displays. Local community organisations create special events. Street entertainers roam the alleyways and gondoliers raise their prices and sing more loudly during carnival, poling their way through the misty, chill canals.

Apart from St Mark's Square, which in carnival time more then ever lives up to Napoleon's description of it as 'the drawing room of Europe', the Rialto Bridge is a centre of carnival activity with street artists, pizzérias and, for children, parades, acrobats, puppet shows, games and costume contests.

During carnival, the city moves out onto the streets. There are workshops where the face can be made up to carnival whites or patterns and painted by professional make up artists and their students. In the final evenings, there are splendid costume balls, also held in St Mark's Square. The carnival ends with the burning of the carnival king's symbol tied to a post, as fireworks explode over the Guidecca Canal.

Joining in . . . you can plan a swirling silk cape or kaftan to cover warm clothing and buy a delicate or exotic mask in Venice to take part anonymously – a delight for inhibited Anglo-Saxons. Tour companies make arrangements to visit Venice at carnival time but book well ahead. Ciga Hotels, which own the Danieli, a fourteenth-century palace with its canal-side view of the action, as well as the Europe and Regina hotels on the Grand Canal near St Mark's, have carnival packages of four nights' bed and breakfast with free casino and ducal palace entrance and discount shopping card. You can travel in style on the Venice Simplon Orient Express (though the same company's Cipriani Hotel is not open during carnival). Carnival spirit starts back in London as passengers are given a Vivaldi Concertante welcome at Victoria Station. Once on the continental section of the train, passengers find mask, corsage, champagne and commemorative glasses in their berths. Dinner takes place with everyone wearing feathered carnival masks. (Practice in advance with knife, fork, spoon and jiggling train might be wise.)

In Germany, they call carnival, the year's 'fifth season' reaching its climax in the last three days in mid February to mid March. It certainly enlivens the dull days of February with colour, noise, tradition and strange costumes. Against a backdrop of forest villages and snow the most traditional carnival with pagan undertones can be seen in Swabia where haunting processions of furry devils bearing flaming torches converge on the villages from the forests. Other highlight spots are Cologne, Dusseldorf, Aachen, Mainz and Munich. In Bavaria carnival is known as 'fasching' where there are over 100 costume balls, street dances and ski processions in the mountains. Elsewhere, carnival spreads to the smallest communities with processions, bands, fancy dress parties. People wear false noses, elect carnival kings and queens and make political and satirical speeches.

In Cologne, the highlight is the Sunday before Shrove Tuesday, with a massive children's fancy dress parade. On Rose Monday, the following day, there is a four-mile procession of decorated floats, brass bands, walking caricatures of well-known people, masked fools and jesters. This is watched by a 1½ million-strong carnival crowd. Mainz is another good carnival spot, with a big riverside fair and towering ferris wheels on which to whisk up late at night chewing on a sausage and whirling with the fireworks. Invited one year to the Hilton Hotel carnival ball, I packed my best evening dress, but soon slunk away to change to jeans and tee shirt. On Rose Monday there is an elaborate and hours-long procession of floats and figures with massive heads, and a commentary, often crude, and politically taunting. The crowds eat sausages in crusty bread rolls and drink plenty of beer and wine. Booking for German carnival places can be made through the DER Travel Service, 18 Conduit Street, London WIR 9TD (01–408 0111).

Organising a German carnival is almost an exercise in lifestyle. In Cologne, for example, where the celebrations go back 150 years, the 'fools' who organise the event formed an association in 1823 so that a unified celebration could be planned. Now about 40 clubs make up the carnival committee which organises the 'sessions' and balls. The sessions (originally council meetings to stimulate the spirit of carnival) now consist of humorous and satirical speeches, a fun commentary on world events. The speeches are given from upturned halved barrels. The sessions also include special carnival songs, dancing girls, clowns and comic acts, drag artists, and communal crowd sing-alongs. The Cologne carnival culminates in the three mad days (*3 Tollen Tage*) which start with the women's carnival, started by washerwomen as a protest against men having all the fun at carnival. Any man wearing a tie that day has it cut off below the knot. Police and others attempting to exert authority are kissed and offered a sweet from a basket the women carry (along with their scissors). Men can join in these celebrations but have to pay for the women's drinks. The children's parade on the Sunday afternoon before Shrove Tuesday precedes the major Rose Monday parade of Hollywood style floats, with huge walking dummies, regiments of masked fools, guilds in uniform, brass bands and horses, all watched by 1½ million people. Bars of chocolate and carnations flown in from the South of France are thrown to the crowds. After the procession, carnival winds down with dances and parties in local bars, where only full bottles of wine, served deliberately without glasses, are available. Cushions are supplied. The three crazy days in Cologne are offered as a package break by GTF Tours, 182–186 Kensington Church Street, London W8 4OP (01–229 2474).

Munich is influenced by the Venetian carnival, Vienna's balls and the Nice Battle of Flowers. In 1893, the first *fasching* society was founded in Munich to plan the balls and parades. The Narrhalla is a prince's household, with a princess in baroque costume recalling the Viennese balls. The Munich dances vary from year to year, but the best known are the Chrysanthemum, Press and Artists with the black and white balls early in January progressing to livelier fancy dress balls (*redouten*) towards the end of the season. The stores sell bright fabrics for costume-making, with wigs, false noses and appropriate sewing patterns.

Fasching masks, Germany

For those who cannot afford the balls, cafes, restaurants and bars put on special *fasching* parties. On the Sunday before Lent begins there used to be a procession akin to Nice's Battle of

Flowers but it has not been held recently, probably because of cold weather. However thousands of people crowd the streets between Karlstor and the Marienplatz in the afternoon dressed warmly or in costume as clowns, red Indians or sheiks. They drink schnapps from booths along the street and dance to brass bands and pop groups.

The more countrified and pre-Christian German 'fasnet' has terrifying figures as well as the fools of fun. At Rottweil in the Black Forest fools jump through the town's Blackgate and in Alzach, also in the Black Forest, the fools dress in red fringed clothes, wooden masks and large hats covered with snail shells and run through the town beating people with a blown-up pig's bladder.

Some of the most traditional and haunting carnival scenes can be enjoyed in Swabia, the agricultural area stretching the length of the Black Forest from Frankfurt to the Swiss border. The villages have A-frame timbered houses, baroque churches and cosy inns. Here carnival covers the six days just before Lent, but with characters that do not owe their ancestry to Christianity: witches, goblins, wild animals and mythical forest creatures.

But the most distinctive and disturbing sign is the carnival mask, a wooden sculpture worn by the official participants in the ceremonies. Each village has its own design of costumes and masks, monsters, witches, jesters: some of the most startling can be seen in the Black Forest museum at Triberg. Here are witches with big hooked noses and stringy hair who batter spectators with broomsticks and untie shoelaces. Village character is displayed. Tettnang is noted for its beer hops so for carnival inhabitants dress as the red spiders that infest the hops, the pigs who eat hop silage and the hop monsters, who are covered with leaves and dried cones. The official costumed carnival characters are the 'Narren', fools, who begin by liberating children from school, occupy the Rathaus (town hall), declaring themselves lords of the town and celebrate by dancing round bonfires and attending a carnival ball. This happens on Fat Thursday, named for the special pastries cooked in hot fat that are traditionally eaten.

In some villages there is a Nightshirt Parade, to which people wear night attire and lingerie, the idea being to resemble a corpse and to fool the Reaper, so that bad spirits will stay away from the carnival. Soot Friday in which boys try to smear black ash on girls, follows Fat Thursday. For adults, this is Hangover Day, after the night before's celebration. The weekend brings more balls and parties, with the Monday parade at which fools from other villages perform the Fool's Jump, hopping around, capturing spectators and creating chaos.

Carnival ends on Ash Wednesday with a symbolic funeral procession at which, in some places, a real coffin is carried to the cemetery before the last songs and drinks at the inns and bars. By midnight on Shrove Tuesday, the town is quiet.

Austria's ski villages are fun places to be in carnival time with torchlight processions, dances and costumed ski races. The Tyrol is the region for big celebrations, with elaborate masks and bell-belted figures wearing tinselled floral head dresses with glass feathers, balls and mirrors. Among the many types of masks are those of the *Wampeler* (plump clumsy person) who about every four years at Axams sneak around using cover to avoid being attacked and beaten by the Riders. If the *Wampeler* get through the village without being thrown on their backs, a good year is forecast. In Vienna, the main accent is on the ball season (see *January*). At the end of the carnival season disguised groups move around on the Ring and other streets. In the shops, assistants wear disguise and waiters in restaurants and inns are masked.

Portugal has a minor carnival with parties and fireworks in Lisbon, though most Latin countries reserve their celebrations for Easter. Italy has local town carnivals, including a charming one at Frascati, the wine town south of Rome, where the streets are decorated below the baroque palaces, and fairs and street stalls sell food and wine.

Holland's southern provinces of Limburg and Brabant have three-day carnivals ruled by princes. Maastricht's seems to be a never-ending pub-crawl, with singing and dancing along the way. Songs are specially written and floats constructed for processions. People wear costume, dance and sing and tour the taverns, and housewives don't cook during the three days. The idea is slowly spreading in the Netherlands and Amsterdam has its own carnival procession. In Belgium, the best-known carnival spot is Binche, a town in the centre of Hainault still surrounded by its old walls with 27 towers. Binche has an international Carnival and Mask Museum in a former Augustinian college containing objects evoking carnival throughout the world. The Binche carnival starts on Quinquagessima Sunday at 10am with costumed dancing. In the afternoon the dancers take part in a procession. The 'Gilles' walk the streets, from dawn onwards on Shrove Tuesday. These figures dance slowly through the town to a background of drum beats and meet up at the Grand Place at 10 am. In the afternoon they walk with the population through the town and back to the Grand Place. In the evening the procession is repeated, by the light of lanterns and the day ends with fireworks.

In Malta in mid February, carnival days are celebrated with

processions of grotesque masked figures and decorated floats. There are open-air dancing competitions and while various villages hold their own celebrations, the main events take place in Valletta and in Victoria, on sister island Gozo.

The Place to Be

Nowhere is it going to be very warm and welcoming in February, though in Madeira the weather is about the same as it is in May in England. One might as well go far north and know there is going to be no sun. 'Kaamos' is the period of polar night that begins on 24 November and lasts till 20 January: the sun doesn't rise above the Lapland horizon and during the day a pale violet light is shed by the moon. February and March are known as the second winter season and are the best months here for skiing and touring. This is the time for traditional sleigh and ski races, with the pulling power coming from reindeer. As the sun increases, excursions can be made sleeping in bell tents.

South into Europe there are warm pockets with stirrings of spring around them – Portugal's Algarve, Majorca and the Greek islands can be warm enough to dine outside. The French Riviera has gentle sun sheltered from the north by the Maritime Alps. Following this curve of coast south and into Italy, the Genoa area can be warm and welcoming at this time of year. To the south of the city are towering olive-capped mountains curving protectively round tiny resorts fringing the great seaport and excluding mist and snow; the indented rocks and coves soak up the sun and retain it to warm the night air.

Nervi is only six miles from Genoa's centre and an ideal February spot, with average 53°F winter temperature and lower hotel rates. On mountain slopes sweeping down into Nervi in early spring, mimosa bobs among bitter oranges and orchids, and palms plume in the subtropical gardens. Lacking a beach, the rock shoreline has been shaped by a circuitous promenade path with restaurants, concrete dive decks and seats set in the warm rock embrasures to capture the sun.

The eighteenth-century Villa Serra acts as a museum for the Ligurian modern art collection of eighteenth- and nineteenth-century works donated by the Prince of Savoy. Between the two main roads shaving the hillside, traffic-free hotels are reached by stone-stepped alleyways hung with ferns and shrubs. Here can be found small hotels, once elegant villas from the time in the 1860s when Nervi was a fashionable wintering spot and family villas were built there. Next to the tourist office is a Visitors' Club in an eighteenth-century villa where foreign visitors can meet to read the papers, drink in the bar, use the library and generally enjoy a bad-weather bolt hole.

In the perhaps too fashionable Rapallo, Santa Margerita and Portofino peninsula nearby, Camogli is a paint-peeling, harbour-hearted town with the Hotel Cenobio dei dogi, once the residence of the Venetian doges. It has a tennis court, solarium, terrace pool and grounds descending through rock-sheltered sun ledges to a private beach. From Camogli, boat trips can be made along the coast to Rapallo or Chiavari, where fringed Arab cotton towels, chairs and lace are made.

For exercise, tracks circle up from mountain villages and on from the little villages through olive groves. A late afternoon walk can be taken from San Rocco along a narrow ledge path which drops down to the sea on one side, with creepers and flowers on the other. Seats are set in grottos along the walk and there are little bars for Camparis or ice cream.

Sightseeing in winter, especially round churches and chateaux, can be so cold the chill sears the bones. One of February's warmer sports is to go pot holing; the deeper the caves the warmer, say the experts. Some of Britain's biggest caves are found in Dentdale where the National Caving Centre is also located. Going underground elsewhere also has its protection factor. On a sub zero mid-February day, when the fountains froze in Rome and breath hung in the air, I discovered an unlikely place in which to be warm and enchanted. Icicles hung in Viterbo's spindle shaped fountains and snow lay in handfuls among crumpled chestnut leaves of the mountain passes of this land of the Etruscans. In Tarquinia, stone courts and terraces and the Etruscan museum housed in high arched stone rooms of a gothic Renaissance palace were numbingly cold. Around Tarquinia are about 6,000 Etruscan tombs of which 300 are opened to view, but each year only 3 to 4 are opened in order to preserve the frescoes. Spread over a breezy hill side, the tombs resemble a town in readiness for a nuclear attack, with little grassed mounds with an entrance door. The doors lead down steep steps to small square rooms below.

Incredibly these are warm, light and lively, not a place of tearful death. It is a place to thaw out happily and in February enjoy the frescoes without the claustrophobic crowds that gather later in the season. From the sixth century BC the colours are russet, green and red. Dancing girls' skirts swirl, musicians bang drums, stylised trees twirl up walls, and men and women are seen enjoying a funeral banquet. The fifth-century tombs are just as warm with ribbons, belts, and garlands decorating the panels.

Stay warm afterwards at the D. Ciro restaurant in the

sixteenth-century Via Cardinal la Fontaine in Viterbo, where a big log fire burns on which the proprietor prepares grills to order, plump local sausages, sucking pig, beef or lamb eaten after a dish of lombrichelli pasta, named for its shapes resembling local worms much prized for the natural work of land fertilisation they do. While menu studying, and choosing local wines, try bruschetta, an antipasto of olive oil and garlic soaked fried bread. Staying in the area, in the sixteenth-century hill village of San Martino just south of Viterbo, dominated by its Doria Pamphili palace, is the Balleti Palace Hotel, a modern building looking down over the plain. As well as the tombs, this is a good base for visiting the Lake Bolseno area to the north with its strong red Cannaiola wines and Montefiascone with its Est Est Est wine.

Natural Attractions

In Central Switzerland in mid February there is an annual Swiss snow sculpture competition at Hoch-Ybrig. Participants get free youth hostel dormitory accommodation, and free cableway

Ice sculpture, Finland

transport. Groups of three to four at most can participate together with a time limit of three days. Only snow and water can be used to create their sculpture. Tools are available for a deposit. The winners, judged by a jury according to quality, originality and interpretation of the annually announced theme, are offered a free holiday in Switzerland. The competition is run by the Swiss National Tourist Office. Details and registration (by early January) is made to Hoch-Ybrig, AG 8842, Switzerland (tel. 055 5617 17).

Finland also puts on a snow sculpture championship at Savonlinna towards the end of the month. The competition is held within the walls and on the surrounding islands of the castle of Olavnlinna. Over a three-day period about twenty teams with a maximum of two per country work to mould a 30 cubic metre block of snow in a 100 square metre area assigned to each team. The entire amount of snow should be used for the sculptures, which must be only of ice and water. Equipment is provided and the results are judged by a jury which includes a child. As well as artistic quality, the sculptures must have functionality for children's games.

Old Customs

Chinese New Year: you don't have to go to Hong Kong or China to experience the Chinese New Year celebrations. Chinatown in London's Gerrard Street, Lisle Street, Newport Place area sees a moveable New Year date from late January to early to middle of February. Decorations, streamers and garlands festoon the streets and crowds come to watch the Lion Dances in which young men put on a costume resembling a lengthy lion and dance through the streets from 11.30 till dusk, receiving gifts of money and food from restaurants and residents as they go. Chinese businesses virtually close down for a couple of weeks during the New Year celebrations that herald the influence of a different traditional animal symbol for the year. In the next five years, 1989 will see New Year on 6 February and the year of the serpent; 1990, 27 January and the horse; 1991, 15 January and sheep/goat; 1992, 4 February and the monkey; and 1993, 3 January and chicken/cock. On New Year's Eve Chinese families, even the smallest children, stay up all night and after the New Year has arrived the head of the family presents everyone with red packets (lai see) to ensure good fortune for the year. Festive treats served include peanuts, melon seeds and preserved fruits; two traditional foods specially made for New Year are chin duy, a mixture of peanuts, sesame, popcorn and molasses rolled into a ball before frying, and yau kok, glutinous rice flour in a triangle stuffed with crushed peanuts, coconut shreds and sesame seeds. The traditional New Year greeting is Kung hay fat choi, 'wishing you prosperity'. On the fifteenth day of the celebration, a three-day lantern festival begins with lanterns displayed in homes and salted or sweetened dumplings served to mark the end to the festivities.

St Valentine's Day, 14 February   Revived more recently as another way of coping with the month's greyness. Red hearts and lovers' symbols greet the day, loving or funny cards – about 16 million in the UK – are sent, usually anonymously, kissograms are booked well in advance and special romantic menus are planned. British Airways puts a special St Valentine's day menu on its flights with romantic poems on it. Lovers exchange special messages in the personal columns of the papers, particularly *The Times*.

Food and Drink

In certain parts of Germany local snails are eaten at carnival time and in the Swabia area carnival time beers and wines are prepared along with kase schpetzle, a rich cream and noodle dish. The German carnival doughnuts are thought to be a variation on the Anglo-Saxon tradition of pancakes for Shrove Tuesday, using up all fat and eggs before the Lenten fast. A translated Bavarian verse shows how important krapfen are considered. 'Carnival is fun, when the farmer's wife bakes doughnuts. But if she doesn't bake any, I couldn't care less about carnival.'

Lent comes from the Anglo-Saxon, meaning lengthening of days, and commemorates the 40 days Christ spent in the wilderness. Weddings during Lent are still considered unlucky by many. Lent starts with Ash Wednesday, when bishops once sprinkled ash over penitents' heads. Now Shrove Tuesday is the occasion for pancake races and eating. In Lichfield there is a Shrovetide Fair which has been held for over 300 years. The mayor opens the fair and wine and simnel cake is served in the Guildhall. Details from City Council, Guildhall, Lichfield (tel. 05432 54031).

London, like several other places, holds pancake races with a changing venue. Currently there are races at Covent Garden on Shrove Tuesday in which anyone can take part. The races are run from noon on, and followed by a concert.

A Fountain in February In Spain, San Blas day in early February is celebrated at Burriana in Castile by the opening of a wine fountain in the street named for him. Anyone may drink from it according to a tradition going back to 1854, when the local city heads decided the fountain should be the means of distributing the abundant quantities of wine to locals and visitors at a time when most of the municipality was under vines. A wine fountain also features in the carnival of Cebreros in Avila.

The Arts

Operetta in Vienna: for a week at the beginning of February, operetta is performed at the State Opera, Volksoper and Raimund Theatre. Strauss, Lehar, Kalman and Millocker are among the composers whose works are performed. Operetta's golden age began in Vienna in 1874 with *Die Fledermaus*; the *Merry Widow* in 1907 covered a disintegrating society with a musical veneer of confidence and gaiety. Many people were tempted to write operetta, inspiring Zola to say 'operetta is a public evil and should have been throttled at birth like a dangerous animal'. But the best are shown at the operetta week along with historical displays and a masked ball evening at the Imperial Court at the Hofburg. Packages are arranged to cover accommodation and tickets. Between performances one can follow a Strauss trail from his grave in the musicians' section in Vienna's cemetery to statues in the park and the flat where he composed the Blue Danube, now a museum (2 Praterstrasse 54). Hotels also put on operetta snacks with the Vienna Ladies Orchestra playing operetta medleys in the late afternoon as a background to coffee and cakes. For dinner, themed operetta menus are served. A special Vienna Tourist Board leaflet outlines the annual programme.

Berlin: in mid February to the beginning of March, there is the film festival, with 4,000 films judged and 200 films from 25 countries screened and open to the public to see. The festival is a meeting place for both the movie people and their fans. Films are shown round the clock, there are retrospective shows and fringe events and a children's film festival. As a finale, there is the presentation of the Golden Bear award for the best film. Information from Berlin Festivals, Budapest strasse 50 (tel. 030 254890).

Sports

February is the month for skiing; the hearty can enter the 75 km ski marathon in Finland that runs from Hameenlainna to Lahti in southern Finland's lakeland. Over 6,000 competitors from 14 countries take part in the 8 am departure from Hamleenlinna, the birthplace of Sibelius, and food, a ski service and a nine-point check are provided along the route. Details from Finlandia hiihto, Urheilukeskus, SF–15110 Lahti 11, Finland (918 49811).

Another all-out effort can be made in Finland in the 38-day 'Finland on Skis' race that runs through to mid March. This is a 1,660 km (1,031 miles) relay race and details are available from Suoman Latu ry, Fabianinkatu 7 00130, Helsinki (tel. 90 170101). Near Helsinki, *pikki*, fishing through the ice, can be practised.

Less predictable because of weather variations is the eleven cities race in Friesland in the north of Holland. The Elfsteden-tocht is a 200 km (124 mile) event that began in 1890 when a sports journalist, Pim Mulier, skated to eleven towns; to prove he had not missed any, he got people to sign a notebook. It is necessary for the freeze to last several weeks before the race can be held. It was held in 1985 and 1986 after a gap of over 20 years. About 16,000 people, including many overseas visitors, registered for the race. As a spectator sport it rates a visit, with the frozen waterway lined with crowds drinking hot chocolate, Dutch gin and pea soup and encouraging the skaters.

Those less fortunate need not miss out on winter sports. In the first half of February, Norway holds winter olympics for the deaf and the Swiss ski school offers skiing to the blind or visually handicapped, with specially trained instructors, using a ski helmet with inbuilt headphones. Information from Kur-und Verkehrsverein, Via Maistra, 7500 St Moritz (tel. 082 33147).

Shopping

For most of us window shopping for ideas for the fashion trends are the nearest we'll get to owning an outfit from Dior or Balmain. But it is possible to go and see the haute couture collections when in Paris. The press shows for autumn/winter take place at the end of January and the spring/summer collections at the end of July. These are strictly by ticket only, but during the following two months the public can be admitted and the use of video now means people have more of a chance of seeing the collection without the need to use live models. Any day one can see videos of couture collections at the Galeries Lafayette. The fashion freak can also get a look at the home of fashion at the National Museum of Fashion Arts, Pavillon de Marsan, 109 Rue de Rivoli, 75001 Paris (tel. 260 32 14) with permanent collections and changing exhibitions. Clothes, including historical costumes, furnishings and accessories are on show.

General information on the haute couture shows and member houses can be obtained from La Chambre syndicale de la Couture Parisienne, 100 Rue du Faubourg Saint Honore, 75008 Paris (tel. 226 64 44). From the list of leading houses below, it is best to write for an appointment or information on the public showings and facilities they offer.

Balmain, 44 Rue Francois Ier, 75008 Paris (tel. 720 35 34); live shows for 1½ months after the collections; make arrangements about a week in advance.

Pierre Cardin, 27 Avenue de Marigny, 75008 Paris (tel. 266 92 25), has videotaped shows and appointments can be made the same day.

Carven, 6 Bond Point des Champs Elysees, 75008 Paris (tel. 359 17 52); shows on Tuesdays and Thursdays through to mid March.

Chanel, 31 Rue Cambon, 75001 Paris (tel. 261 54 55) shows on Tuesdays and Thursday afternoons, make reservations 15 days in advance.

Christian Dior, 30 Avenue Montaigne, 75008 Paris (tel. 723 54 44) video show of collection every afternoon except Saturdays and Sundays.

Givenchy, 3 Avenue Georges V, 75008 Paris (tel. 723 81 36) showings every day.

Guy Laroche, 29 Avenue Montaigne, 75008 Paris (tel. 723 78 72) live shows Tuesdays and Thursday afternoons; say they don't receive tourist groups but will welcome groups of 'motivated women'.

Jean-Louis Scherrer, 51 Avenue Montaigne, 75008 Paris (tel. 359 55 39) only gives shows for private clientele.

Lanvin, 22 rue du Faubourg Saint-Honoré, 75008 Paris (tel. 265 14 40), give a video presentation every Tuesday and Thursday at 15.30.

Christian Lacroix, 73 Rue du Faubourg Saint-Honoré, 75008 Paris (tel. 266 79 08), the newest fashion house, gives video shows by appointment only.

Nina Ricci, 39 Avenue Montaigne, 75008 Paris (tel. 723 78 88): initially live shows, then videos. Phone for entrance 24 hours ahead for individuals.

Yves Saint Laurent, 5 Avenue Marceau, 75116 Paris (tel. 723 72 71): video shows on a large screen every day in February (and September); small groups also accepted.

Each year in mid-February one of the most important jewellery auctions takes place in St Moritz when complete collections of precious stones are exhibited and auctioned. Those on exhibit which are not sold are later auctioned in New York in April, and in Geneva in May.

Bonham's hold a specialist sale of dog and cat paintings during Cruft's dog show week in London (see below). Held in a viewing room near Olympia, there are prints and paintings of canines and felines of every size and shape, though never enough of sporting dogs to meet demand. Prices run from £50.

The first flowers

For almond blossom go to Sicily for the blossom festival in the valley of the temples at Agrigento or to Portugal's Algarve. In Nice they have the famous Battle of Flowers with decorated floats and masses of carnations. Britain has little to show except drifts of snowdrops, but Aberdeen in the far north-east stages its spring flower show in February.

Show time

In Perth, Scotland, there are the Aberdeen Angus bull sales and in London Cruft's dog show, founded almost a century ago by a manufacturer of dog food, Charles Cruft, is held. It is the country's leading canine event, with fierce competition for championships, and the breeders often as colourful and fascinating as their dogs (some 15,557 dogs competed in 1988).

In Germany, Nurnberg holds its toy fair in good time for the following Christmas. Nurnberg has no less that 400 toy factories employing 25,000 people and a delightful toy museum in an old private house near the main square. It is the world's toy capital and the fair attracts buyers from all over the globe.

Miscellaneous

Clowns may be more associated with Christmas and circuses, but they too have an occasional solemn moment. On the first Sunday in February the clown's service is held, usually at Holy Trinity Church in London's Dalston E8 area (check with the London Tourist Office, 26 Grosvenor Gardens, London SW1W 0DU (tel. 01–730 3488) for exact date and location). Many members of the Clowns International Club, whose church this is, attend the service in full costume and traditional makeup. The service begins at 1600 and begins with a memorial wreath placed on the monument to Grimaldi who originated the clown character and costume as it is now known and had his memoirs edited by Charles Dickens. Afterwards in the church hall a free clown show is put on and visitors are welcome. A clown pilgrimage can be made to the churchyard (the church is no longer in existence) of St James's, Pentonville Road, London N1, where Grimaldi is buried. It is now known as Grimaldi Park and there is a plaque marking where the clown was buried in 1837.

Public Holidays

Chinese New Year for Chinese Communities (see page 33).
Germany: Rosemontag (Rose Monday), 42 days before Easter, is an unofficial holiday in carnival centres particularly in the Rhineland region.

3

MARCH

IS FLOWERS THAT BLOOM
IN THE SPRING

T HE month that in Northern Europe at least is supposed to come in like a lion and exit like a lamb, weather wise, certainly does not have a lion-hearted appetite, with many people still observing Lent for varied reasons and abstinences. It is however a time when the first spring flowers, particularly bulbs, come into bloom relieving the gloom of winter. Primroses and aconites make their appearance along with daffodils and tulips in Holland. In warmer western and southern areas violets and celadines also bloom. The spring equinox is celebrated by druids in London on Primrose Hill, marking the season of planting and renewal with the symbolic sowing of seeds.

Holland calls its springtime 'the bulb season' or 'tulip time'. It usually gets under way at the end of March though does not reach the full glory of great carpets of colour over the bulb fields until mid April.

Tulips, in particular, fascinate. The Americans tend to like the tall dramatically coloured ones; the British the shorter, dwarf varieties. Tulips came to Europe from Turkey in 1559 and were imported into the Netherlands by 1561. The tulip became the flower of fashion in the seventeenth century and the rich calculated each other's wealth in terms of possession of tulips. In 1634–7 there was what became known as the 'foolish tulip trade' of speculation, when bulbs were sold at incredible prices. Striped tulips were valued the highest, and a brown tulip with yellow stripes known as 'Semper Augustus' was sold for 30,000 Dutch florins per three bulbs. These striped tulips can be seen in Rembrandt's paintings and are called Rembrandt tulips today. In 1637 the States of Holland ended the tulip speculation and cultivation then developed at a more normal pace. The first cultivation started around Haarlem and Overveen. Mary – of William and Mary – loved tulips and in her little corner cabinet rooms at Het Loo palace near Apeldoorn would place a few in the special Delft vases, much as the palace flower arranger does today for the benefit of visitors. Mary brought a collection of such vases to Britain when she became Queen there in 1688. The formal gardens of her days at Het Loo have recently been restored to their original form and style, at a considerable cost. They are now laid out in baroque formality, with fountains, parterres, terraces and statuary.

The best place to learn about the varieties of tulips and gain advice on selection for garden displays is at the bulb producer Franz Roozen's display area and bulb fields at Vogelenzangse-weg 49, 2114 BB Vogelenzang (tel. 02502 7245). This is just south of Haarlem, a delightful canal city to explore, and not far from Schipliol Airport. In fact, with only an hour or two stopover between planes at the airport one can easily slip across to

Roozen or to the Keukenhof gardens in season and companies like Travelscene, St Ann's Road, Harrow (tel. 01–427 4445) and Tailor Made Holland, 35 Eyre Street Hill, London EC1R 5ET (tel. 01–278 5319) run special bulb field tours from the end of March. Travelscene include visits to Franz Roozen's huge conservatory display and bulb fields.

The Lisse/Sassenheim area of Holland has ideal soil and conditions for bulb-growing. Roozen opens his display at the end of March till the end of May and again in July till the end of September for summer bulbs, dahlias and begonias.

Celebrating 50 years of growing in 1982, Franz Roozen, in his eighties, is still active, though his son runs the business. It was Franz's idea, between the world wars, to show the public how to grow tulips and display rare varieties. Then it was an innovation and the Keukenhof show was a later development. Now Roozen displays 200,000 to 300,000 bulbs each year in a show garden, plus 60,000 in a greenhouse area. His bulb fields bloom from the beginning of April though he says the best time is from 20 April to 5 May for the best and busiest time, with opening hours from 0800 to 1800. There are some 5,000 to 6,000 varieties of tulips and it takes 10 to 15 years to create a new variety. But visitors can see the new varieties – over 1,000 on show – and order from multilingual hostesses or from a catalogue and have them delivered home. Roozen's son says there is no such thing as a black tulip, just very dark blue. Roozen varieties have been named for figures like Hilton, Neil Armstrong and Arthur Rubinstein and the Aga Khan comes for advice for his Swiss garden. When seeking individual advice, remember that lunchtime is quieter (there is a cafe opposite). The most expensive and rarer varieties of tulip cost up to 15 guilder a bulb, and the British are Roozens' most frequent visitors.

Dutch bulb producers compete to get displays in the Keukenhof gardens which are only open each year from the end of March to the end of May. From Holland's 10,000 bulb growers only 100 are selected to donate bulbs for the fabulous displays in the Keukenhof park, Postbox 66, 2160 AB Lisse (tel. 02521 19034). This show originated in 1949 when bulb growers decided to exhibit flowering bulbs in natural surroundings in contrast to the rectangular slabs of field colour.

Getting the Keukenhof display together and dismantling it and designing next year's arrangements takes all year. A fifth of the display is changed each year and plants are arranged in English, French, Dutch and German garden areas and around a lake with swans, ducks, and flamingoes in what was dune land. There is a 1892 Groningen corn mill and an old canal bridge in the park and tall beech trees 240 years old. Six and a half million bulbs are hand planted each year with 12,000 varieties of tulips, hyacinths, narcissus, muscari (including the rarer white variety). It takes 2½ months just to remove these bulbs after the show. The 850,000 visitors can order bulbs and watch flower arrangement demonstrations and eat at the three self service restaurants in the 30 acres; Monday and Tuesday are usually the quietest days to visit.

The climate and soil conditions here are perfect for bulbs. The name means 'kitchen garden', from the days when the park formed a countess's castle garden. The Keukenhof area includes a 5,000 square metre greenhouse to create an indoors spring garden where over 500 different tulip varieties are shown; a bonus in late flowering seasons or if the day is wet. One greenhouse has a collection of Royal Dutch Amaryllis. The ardent bulb enthusiast can cover 10 miles on paths around the display beds. As a guide to what flowers to see in bloom, tulips are from mid April to end of May, daffodils from the beginning to end of April and hyacinths from mid April to the end of April.

Tickets to the Keukenhof, by rail or bus, are sold at many Dutch railway stations. By train to Haarlem or Leiden one can then get a bus to the Keukenhof and there is plentiful parking on the 50 acres. Wheelchairs are available free of charge, with special toilets and showers for the handicapped. The Dutch tourist offices have information and brochures about the Keukenhof.

At any time of the year one can see flowers in Holland – millions of them comfortably indoors on the coldest day. This is at the world's largest flower market, the Aalsmeer flower auction held every weekday at the World Flower Centre, Legmeerdijk 313, Postbus 1000, 1430 BA Aalsmeer (tel. 02977 34567).

Each day about 11 million flowers and 1 million pot plants are sold, amounting annually to 3 billion flowers and 273 million pot plants. In the huge modern building, which has ample roof parking and clear directions for visitors, a workforce of 8,000 including exporters and buyers move the flowers in and out from all over the world with 2,000 lorries leaving the building every day; 80 per cent of the flowers are exported.

The centre welcomes visitors and has extensive facilities for them, including a restaurant and a souvenir shop that attract some 200,000 people each year. Galleries, half a mile long, run through the 50,000 square feet of space, filled with truck loads of colour and scent. From the gallery visitors can see the trains of trucks loaded with flowers snaking their way from auction to dispatch. Visitors can also drop into the back of the six auction rooms. These start work on Monday to Friday at around 07.30

and each seats over 300 buyers. Buyers have to be registered and have a red buyer's plate with a number which is inserted into a slot on the seat; this registers the buyer in the computer. Then by a switch on the seat he can choose which of two auction clocks and flowers he wants to bid for. The system is unique: a Dutch auction of course. The pointer of the clocks turns backwards from 100 to 1 and can be stopped at any time for a buy. The lots are entered on the clock via computer and the auctioneer calls out the flowers and their origin and reads out remarks recorded by the inspectors. This is relayed to the buyers via a microphone on each desk. The buyer presses a button to stop the clock at the price he wants to pay. The first person to stop the clock is the highest bidder and gets the flowers or plants. He can then say if he wants the entire lot or a part. The computer invoices the buyer and produces a distribution slip placed on the flowers which are transferred to the buyer's trailer which, when full, goes to the packing area. Only 15 minutes separate the auctioneering and delivery to the buyer. Flowers sold at Aalsmeer in the morning are on sale at florists in America, Australia or elsewhere the same evening or the following morning. Holland has 63 per cent of the world's exports of cut flowers and 51 per cent of pot plants as well as the highest per capita consumption of flowers at home; the UK is well down the list.

Each auction room deals mainly with a different type of flower or potted plant. Roses, in fact, not tulips are the most important over the year with 926 million sold each year of 150 varieties; tulips are next with 287 million, then chrysanthemums and carnations. When new varieties are introduced this is indicated by a sign on the trolleys and special displays are made in the warehouse. Tulips are important for Christmas and from February to April but May is the busiest month, with Mother's Day in several countries. Christmas and Easter are also hectic times.

Every lot of flowers received is inspected with ten specifications for flowers checked out. By 11.00 all are sold (any not sold are destroyed) and 10 million to 12 million guilders banked each day. Flowers from Israel, France, Spain, Zimbabwe (for protea) and early daffodils from England are also sent in. The halls are closed on Saturdays and Sundays and an entrance fee is charged to adult visitors.

Otherwise, the place to see early flowers in Holland is in greenhouses and botanical gardens around the country. There is an orchid garden at Valkenburg, in the south of Holland in Limburg province near Maastricht, which is reached by easy train connections from Schipliol or by direct flights to Maastricht from London Gatwick.

Valkenburg is a charming small town cut by a river and has parkland walks and little coffee houses by the water. It also has a knack of keeping warm and dry in winter. It is built on soft marl limestone, which the Romans first started to quarry for building. Over the centuries the quarries have become 45 miles and 280 acres of tunnels with 200 cave chambers and a nuclear shelter. In the nineteenth century the grottoes, as they are called, were opened to the public in winter to walk in as the caves maintain a temperature around 13°C. Now guided tours are taken round the passages of about 1½ miles (there is a little train for the less active) showing the rooms, 28 acres of underground lake, the nuclear shelter, the charcoal wall drawings and carvings of huge fish, and the oldest Roman part where an amphitheatre is the setting, guided in by lines of candles, for a Christmas play.

A new and ideal winter way of keeping warm is Thermae 2000, which is being described as 'a modern version of the visit to the ancient Roman baths'. Set on the Cauberg hill outside the town, an ultra modern pyramid glass style building is being terraced over recently discovered thermal springs. As well as all kinds of pools there will be a therapeutic centre, sauna landscape, botanical garden, gym, a meditation vault (in the top of the pyramid) and restaurant facilities. The complex in glass and wood is being surrounded by gardens containing more pools and a cold mineral water drinking area.

Maastricht is a delightful town in which to base a winter stay. With strong French influences (Paris is three hours drive away), French words in its dialect, a plethora of 'traiteurs' and a love of eating, Maastricht is a less serious town than many in Holland and has a lively carnival in February.

There are two excellent hotels for stays, the Derlon and the Maastricht. The latter overlooks the river and the pleasure boats that go to Liège. The former is in a little square to which on special nights locals bear candle offerings to the shrine of the Virgin in a church on the square.

Maastricht is walkable, its cobbles known as 'the heads of children'. Across the bridge the old town has restored seventeenth- and eighteenth-century streets like Stock which are now full of elegant French couture boutiques. There are tiny squares cleverly mixing old and new architecture and the whole is bounded by fortifications and ramparts containing water mills in sturdy keeps. Within the fortifications there are two large squares, with cafes on all sides, for summer sitting out. In one is the church of St Servatuus, now being restored, and housing a treasury of religious art. The market square is surrounded by nineteeth-century French houses with pictorial gable stones and

centred by a Dutch baroque town hall with its charming traditional wedding room.

Shopping delights include wonderful flower shops, food and
household stores, chocolates from Franz Stols in Smedenstraat
and wines from G. Thiessen right in the centre of town with a
tiny vineyard at the back of the shop where wine tastings are
held in summer and cellars fingering under the town contain
350,000 bottles. Local wine can be tasted along with pungent
local cheese and bread in Den Ouden Vogelstrup, the 1730 'old
ostrich' pub with its murals of carnival scenes. One can take
coffee and slices of Limburg pie filled with fruit and topped with
cream in the numerous cake shops and coffee can also be taken
beneath the Derlon Hotel while viewing a recently excavated
Roman ruin.

Maastricht loves to eat, there are many excellent restaurants
and just outside the town, in what locals proudly refer to as
their 'mountain', at 330 feet, is Chateau Neercanne, a terraced
chateau with excellent food and a deep complex of caves and
tunnels, now a wine cellar, where tastings and pre dinner
aperitifs can be enjoyed. Near Valkenburg is the Princess
Juliana, a small elegant hotel which has restaurants designed for
day and evening and excellent food. Information on Maastricht
from tourist office, Het Dinghuis, Kleine Staat 1, 6211 Ed.
Maastricht (tel. 043 252121).

Places

Cornwall is the warmest place in Britain this month, though the
March winds and high spring tides can be at their most
dramatic; a wonderful time to rent one of the National Trust's
cottages there and walk the blustery cliffs around Bude, returning to snug stone walls and fires. In Europe, Greece by mid
month is warm, but in contrast skiing is still possible in France,
Austria and Switzerland, the more so with the change in climate
and later arrival of the snow (see the note in the December
chapter).

Lapland has no snow problems (or rather no lack of it) in
March, and one can ski here until mid May. But in March so
called 'springtime adventure packages' are available for Finnish
Lapland. The *kaamos* 'dark and cold' ends in February. In March
what the Finns call the 'spring winter' begins, as the light comes
more strongly though the dazzling Northern Lights and stars
may still be seen, especially at the beginning of the month. In
the March night, frosts harden the snow cover to tempt the skier
to make longer expeditions. A prepared trail is not necessary at

this period as the hard snow supports the skier and there are vast unpeopled wastes to explore. The further north one goes, the longer the skiing lasts and the brighter the nights are as the snow picks up every glimmer of moonlight. At full moon one can ski without floodlights.

The holiday centres in Lapland offer several trails from 1 to 15 km in length. Some are lit so one can still ski on dark nights. Guided ski treks or ski expeditions which last several days are popular and a superb way for the fit to see more of the countryside. In the 'spring winter' there are several ski events such as long distance contests attracting hundreds of skiers. These are organised with a network of aid stations. As well as those detailed under the sports section in this chapter, there are certain centres specialising in cross country skiing for the holidaymaker. The more hardy can ski in open terrain, exposed to lashing winds, but the south of Lapland has huge sheltered forests where no special equipment is needed over short hauls. Where there are no trails, wider skis, high boots and the right bindings are needed, but many of the ski centres have equipment for hire.

Among the best Lapp ski centres are Saariselka in eastern Lapland near Inari. It is an area of fells with all types of terrain, many ski trails for cross country and numerous fell cabins in the hills where one can shelter for the night. Most of the skiing area is in the Urho Kekkonen national park, named for the late president of Finland. Ivalo airport, the most northerly in the service chain to Lapland, serves the area, and there is also a coach service from Rovaniemi, the Lapland capital. Saariselka has several hotels and ski lodges, a slalom slope and lift. One can also join snowmobile treks or a reindeer safari, though the area is best suited to the fairly experienced skier.

Kilpisjarvi is an area of treeless tundra with great fells and sheltered valleys in between stretching to the fells in Norway and Sweden to which treks can be made. There are no ski trails here, the hard snow bearing the skier anywhere and in the 'spring winter' several ski treks are arranged to the highest fells in Finland and to Sweden and Norway; this is where the midsummer ski race is held on 24 June.

Pallastunturi specialises in cross-country skiing and most of its area is in the Pallas-Ousastunturi national park. One can travel a 64-km route through treeless tundra from one felltop to the next with cabins for overnighting and places for campfires. Pallastunturi also offers a slalom centre and reindeer safaris and snowmobile expeditions are arranged from Hetta, the other end of the long trail, where one can also learn about Lapp culture based on reindeer herding.

More suitable for beginners are Yllastunturi, and Levitunturi. The latter is in central Lapland near Kittila airport; one trekking route leads to the Yllastunturi centre and there is a varied and well-maintained trail network in the area offering guided ski trips all winter. There is plenty of forest in the area. A hotel on the slopes of Levitunturi offers spa facilities and there are ski holiday villages.

At Naruska, a wilderness area in eastern Lapland close to the Russian border, the scenery is magnificent, with sheltered forest and treeless tundra in which two holiday villages offer ski trekking packages. During the 'ten fell conquest', a one week ski trek, one spends the nights in fell cabins and at reindeer herders' camps. The ten fells covered include some near the Finland/Russian border with sweeping views over Russian wilds. Naruska also provides snowmobile trips, reindeer drives and winter ice fishing, but it is not recommended as a place for ski beginners.

One of the few areas retaining the feel of Lapland of the past is around Muotkatunturi in the north, with a few holiday villages near Muotkatunturi itself and a hotel in Ivalo with its airport. The holiday villages can be used by beginners, though the surrounding area is for the more experienced. Most of Lapland's ski centres will arrange instruction for various levels as well as beginners. Details can be obtained from the Finnish Tourist Office, Finnair offices or a travel agency in Finland specialising in the area: Lapin Matkailu, Pohjanpuisto 1, 96200 Rovaniemi, Finland. Sporting Travel Services, 9 Teasdale Close, Royston, Herts SG8 5TD (tel. 0763 42867) has two-week spring-time adventure packages in March and April with ferry transport to Gothenburg from Harwich, using Muonio for cross-country skiing, reindeer sledging, snow scooter excursions, fishing through the ice, igloo making and offering accommodation in log cabins. Later in the year (May/June) the company runs a similar midsummer adventure holiday with activities such as canoeing, rafting, walking; mountain huts as well as log cabins are used for accommodation.

Doing the Duchy

With the weather not at its best, it is pleasant to visit a small country with varied sightseeing possibilities that can be absorbing whatever the weather. Luxembourg fulfils this criterion and though its winter weather is often wet – it rained heavily when I took a weekend visit there early one March – it can be enjoyable none the less. A good base is the Intercontinental

Hotel in a new housing complex just outside Luxembourg city but a quick drive through the woods from the airport. In winter the hotel offers very reasonably priced Relaxembourg weekend packages when the bankers and Eurocrats have gone home. The packages include use of the hotel's indoor pool and spa facilities, so even if the weather is bad there is a chance to get some exercise. But it would be a pity to miss the walks that lead through mighty tall-treed woods immediately behind the hotel. Mapped fitness paths and jogging tracks run from the hotel and bicycles can be borrowed. Almost immediately one is in tall beech forests, quiet and sheltered, with tracks running up to openings into small fields. Hiring a car one can see a lot of Luxembourg in a very short time. One can follow the tourist office's wine route map along the banks of the Moselle about 15 minutes from the hotel. Starting from Remich one can follow the river through Greiveldange, Ehnen and Wormeldage to Grevenmacher and Wasserbillig, sampling wines at producers' cellars along the way.

Weekend car hire rates are reasonable and a lovely half day drive is up to Echternach to see the formal centre with arcaded market, turreted hotel de ville eleventh-century basilica backed by a huge abbey founded in 698 by St Willlibrord, an early Anglican visitor from Ripon. The banks of the River Our can be followed from here with glimpses on the opposite bank of Germany. One passes through craggy hill country known as Luxembourg's Little Switzerland. At Diekirch is a museum commemorating the Second World War Battle of the Bulge, but the most fairy tale place in this area of castle-topped crags and villages snuggled in thick forest is Vianden, north of Diekirch. Coming down the steep hill road to Vianden, the village is slotted deeply into a rock valley, its pastel light walls contrasting with the dark rock crag in its midst bearing a stately castle on its summit. A chair lift is available to visit the castle from the little town below. Here there is a main street of old houses, shops and cafes leading down to the river with more restaurants overlooking a river fountain by an old stone bridge. Victor Hugo lived in Vianden in 1871 and his house can be visited as well as a folk art museum.

But on a March weekend visit it is not necessary to hire a car. The Intercontinental has a shuttle mini bus service free of charge to the nearby city centre and visits can be made to the Villeroy and Bosch china showroom by the factory, the Saturday flea market or to listen to open air concerts in the Place d'Armes on Sundays. Sipping a coffee by one of the big squares one can watch the after Mass parade from the cathedral or see street entertainers perform in the shop fronts of the Grande Rue on

Sundays. Walks can be made on the sturdy ramparts created by Vauban with views down into the valley.

There is plenty of choice for eating out. Luxembourg is said to have the most Michelin stars per mile in its 1,000 square miles and one can choose between sophisticated town restaurants or good country inns specialising in seasonal game. While touring, a lunch of Ardennes ham, crusty bread, butter and gherkins from a thick blue and grey pottery jar is ample enough and in winter one of the duchy's thick warming soups can be added. In the Intercontinental there is an informal bistro style all day cafe with breakfast and lunch buffets or for dinner the more formal Les Continents, where winter menus often feature foie gras with fish such as trout, or game with wild mushrooms from the forests and superb cream, nut and chocolate gateaux confections.

These can be worked off walking and if the day is fine a lunch box can be taken through the woods encountering few people even at weekends. The energetic could reach small villages like Eisenborn or Bourglinster with its magnificently sited ruined chateau. Information on the Intercontinental's weekend winter packages can be got through the London sister hotel, 1 Hamilton Place, Park Lane, London W1.

Old Customs

Belgium The Ball of the Dead Rat, held in Ostend in early March is a catchy enough title to intrigue, if not repel. The idea came in 1900 when a group of students, including art student James Ensor, went to Paris for the weekend and enjoyed a fancy dress ball at a cafe called the Rat Mort. They decided to import the idea and each year a fancy dress ball is held named for the cafe. Each year a theme is given for the ball and 6,000 guests attend at the Casino Kursaal. Half a dozen bands, four discos and carnival groups from around Europe perform in the various halls from 2100 to 0800. The fancy dress competition has prizes to a value of around £7,000. Women must wear fancy or evening dress, men ditto, but they can hire a black cape if they do not have the obligatory dress. A hot or cold buffet is available. Information from Ostend Tourist Promotion Service, Wapenplein, B–8400, Ostend (tel. 59 80 33 15/50 06 60).

Spain Fallas de San Jose, Valencia. This festival dates from the Middle Ages but only acquired its present format in the middle of the nineteenth century. Fallas are festivals of bands, processions, beauty contests, street dancing, fireworks and competitions for the best cardboard and papier mache figures which are often comical or satirical and are all burnt on the last night of the festival. During the two weeks at Valencia, public announcements, 'crida', are made by the mayor and queen of the fallas from the Torres de Serranos. There is a delightful night-time parade of the various falla committees and the procession of

The Belgian coast is lively with winter events

the Kingdom in which various towns of the old Kingdom of Valencia take part, showing off their own folklore and local produce. Flowers are offered by the 'falleras' to Our Lady of the Forsaken, the patroness of the city. Around 19 March the fiesta has one of its most important events, the Night of Fire when, at midnight, all the fallas are burnt.

Parade of the Fallas, Spain

Norway In Narvik there is a winter festival in mid month when the city is decorated in the style of the 1890s and there is a special programme of sports, opera, concerts, exhibitions and carnival events.

Luxembourg There are plenty of customs to get through into spring. There are carnival parades in Grevenmacher at the beginning of March, a carnival dance for children with a competition for the best costume and masks in Luxembourg city; on Ash Wednesday boys parade a huge straw puppet through the streets of Remich and on the Moselle bridge, the puppet is set on fire and thrown into the river. The tradition symbolises the end of carefree carnival in the region. On or around 8 March Burgsonndeg is celebrated throughout the duchy with the building of huge bonfires on hills near communities to celebrate the return of the sun to mark the end of winter. The custom dates back to pre-Christian times. At the end of the month or at mid

Lent, Bretzelsonndeg is a Sunday dedicated to lovers and is marked with folklore events in many towns mostly in the Moselle region. Young people offer a pretzel (bretzel) to their loved ones and in Remich, Grevenmacher and Wasserbillig, pretzels are sold on the market square. A parade led by a brass band marches through the streets. Petange celebrates the end of carnival with a big parade of around 2,000 people with 20 floats, 15 bands and carnival groups marching through the streets for two to three hours. Dances are held in several of the town cafes.

Vienna There is a Lenten Calvary fair with a special tree climber toy sold to children and a general market fair.

In the Voralberg area of Austria, 'sparkle' bonfires are organised by a guild. The sparkle wood pile is burnt on the Saturday before the first Sunday in Lent and is lit as it becomes dusk and ends with the explosion of a figure of a witch in the fire. Torches are often lit and hurled into the air. The day ends with a dance at the local inn.

London On the third or fourth Thursday in March, the children of St Clement Danes primary school in Drury Lane visit the church of the same name in the Strand for a short afternoon service to which visitors are welcomed. It starts at 1500 with the tune of the old rhyme 'Oranges and Lemons say the bells of St Clements' and after the service each child is given an orange and a lemon. The ceremony was started in 1920 by the vicar when a carillon was installed so the church bells would ring out the rhyme. The bells do this every days at 0990, noon 1500 and 1800.

Food

Lenten fare can be light and is intended for fasting. Days in the month to note include St David's Day, 1 March, when leeks are worn by Welshmen and St Patrick's Day on 17 March, when the shamrock is worn and Irish-style supper parties feature Irish stew and potato dishes. On Shrove Tuesday in Belgium it is a custom to swallow live fish in red wine. On Mothering Sunday, the fourth in Lent, it was the tradition for Belgian maids and servants to visit their mother, taking with them a simnel cake with almond paste filling and decorated with marzipan balls representing the apostles but lacking one for Judas.

This is the time of year to enjoy Bockbier in Munich, Germany, a specially strong beer made for two weeks in March.

Arts

Hungary   Budapest holds a spring festival on a massive scale, with over 1,000 opera and music events scattered round a hundred places. Details from 1145 Budapest, Korong utca 29, Postbox 1441 Pf 41 Hungary (tel. 36 835389).

Spain   Cuenca houses the religious music festival in its historic buildings in the third week of the month. Internationally-known performers take part and details can be obtained from Semanas de Musica Religiosa, Palafox 1, 16001 Cuenca, Spain (tel. 34 66 226911).

Switzerland   Lucerne has an Easter festival towards the end of March with opera, concerts and choral performances. International Festival of Music, PO Box 6002, Lucerne, Switzerland (tel. 41 235272).

Luxembourg   An annual spring music series of concerts of classical music held through March and into April in Luxembourg city.

Finland   Tampere has a film festival of international short films. There are competitions for documentaries, animation and fiction/experimental films from all countries. Details from Festival Office, PB 305, 33101 Tampere (tel. 9 31 35681).

Scotland   Edinburgh holds its 'other' festival this month, with folk concerts and events include harp and piping festivals, fiddle courses, songwriting forums and guitar master classes, workshops, lectures and children's events. The organisers promise dancing in the streets, a showcase for instrument-makers, a craft fair and concerts and cabaret. Details from the Edinburgh International Folk Festival, 16a Fleamarket Close, Edinburgh EH1 1BX (tel. 031 220 0464).

Holland   More an art show than a festival is the Maastricht Fair, held in the second half of March. This European Fine Art Fair is held in the new Maastricht Exhibition and Congress Centre where 100 exhibitors display works of art with dealers from around Europe attending. A new section of the fair deals with oriental carpets and textiles, in addition to established displays of antiques and paintings. This is the opportunity for museum representatives, collectors and enthusiasts to meet leading international dealers during ten days of the fair, during which 30,000 visitors will attend. Works of art, particularly Old

Masters, are set out in an informal museum-like setting. Details, from Maastricht Exhibition Centre, PO Box 1630, 6201 BP Maastricht, Netherlands (tel. 43 21 6666).

Sport

A month of icy ideas, sport in the snow and an emphasis on Scandinavian pursuits. During the month, the Aser-Nappet, Sweden's biggest jigging (fishing) through ice competition, is held in Lapland with individual and team contests. Up in Finland's side of Lapland there is the Arctic snow week and reindeer races at Rovaniemi with reindeer-driving competitions; details from Paliskuntain Yhdistys, Koskikatu 3, A–96200, Rovaniemi (tel. 9 60 22057). Also in the month there are international winter games at Lahti, the Savonia ski race of 47 miles of cross-country skiing, and an international ski jumping competition at Jyvaskyla. Kuopio hosts the ski orienteering world champions and the Kuopio ice marathon of international skating races on lake ice, some 124 miles in length. Details of the last two events from the City Tourist Office, Haapaniemenkatu 17, 70100 Kuopio (tel. 9 71 182584).

A 90-km ski race, the Pirkka, is also held from Niinnisalo to Tampere. The first and last stretch of the route was used by hunters on their treks up north and the route was also used by soldiers in the sixteenth century. This race, 'the mother of long distance ski races', is the world's longest one-day race and there is ample provision for equipment maintenance and waxing along the way at meal stops; a bonfire is lit at every post, where the entrants can wax their own skis. The race can also be undertaken as a tour competing against oneself. The route has remained unchanged since its start in the 1950s and the start and finish are about 360 feet above sea level. There are nine control points for soup, drinks and food; first aid is also available. The race has five classes: competitors, women, touring, elderly men and veterans all of which start at 0700 with a volley fired by two cannons. The minimum age for men is 18 and women 20 years. Group accommodation for entrants is arranged at the school in Niinnisalo with transportation from Tampere by bus in the morning at 0500. Skiers' belongings are transported from start to finish and bus transport runs from the finish to sauna and swimming. The entire race course is rolled with heavy equipment every year and is now very firm; the ski tracks are opened the day before the race with a track plough. The race has never been cancelled, but organisers warn that entrants should gradually build up their stamina for the event. If you decide to tour rather than race, you ski the same course as the race itself on the day before the competition. The start is at 0600. Tour entrants provide their own food and drink but halfway along there is a juice and broth service and for the tour there are no separate classes; the minimum ages remain the same. Entrants can register by writing to Pirrka Ski Race office, Box 19, SF–33101 Tampere 10, Finland. Registration begins on 1 November and ends on 31 January. Further information about the race is available from the City Tourist Office, Box 87, SF–33211 Tampere 21, Finland (tel. 9 31 26775).

Another leg stretcher is the Arctic Circle ski race with tracks of 30, 65 and 100 km held around the third week of March. The track runs along traditional routes mainly in the Ounasjoki river valley amid beautiful scenery. The starting point is at Rovaniemi at the mouth of the river and the finish is at the Hotel Pohjanhovi. The race, beginning at 0800, has been run for over 30 years and there are groups for competition series, condition series or excursion series. The entry fee covers medal and diploma, food and drink at service posts, waxing, service, skiing equipment service, first aid, transport – for those who drop out – to the finish, sauna, stickers and information. Though Rovaniemi is far to the north, and snow drifts around it still, it is a modern town designed by Finnish architect Alva Aalto and there is no problem getting there for the race via daily air, rail and road connections. Information from Ounsavaaran Hühtoseura, Pekankatu 3, 96200 Rovaniemi (tel. 9 60 312 956).

Norway also has plenty of hearty snow sorties this month. There is the Holmenkollen ski festival in Oslo, featuring all kinds of skiing, with the Holmenkollen ski jumping the highlight. There is also a slalom race for the disabled, children's Holmenkoll day, giant slalom race, military race, cross country and events for all ages.

There are also international cross-country ski races like the Maihaugen, held at Lillehammer, with 6-mile races for men and 3-mile competitions for women. At the beginning of the month there is the Donald Duck ski jumping and cross country championships for boys and girls at Kongsberg. The most northerly ski race in the world, the Nordvagenrennet, is held at Honningsvag in mid March; at about the same time the historic 30-mile Birkebeiner ski race is held from Lillehammer to Rena. A little later, the 69-mile Raid Norvegia–Svezia, Scandinavia's only two-day cross-country ski race, takes place. The Hogasrennet, a Nordic ski jumping and alpine race, is held at Trondheim, which also hosts the Trondersvom, an annual swim involving about 600 people – strictly for those accustomed to the cold. At the end of March there is the Ridderrenet, or

Knights race, a winter sports competition for the disabled at Beitostolen.

In Britain the National Hunt festival takes place in mid month at Cheltenham, the show case for national hunt racing which has been called 'the Royal Ascot of jumping'. The racecourse is set near the city below Cleeve Hill, offering lovely views for those not admiring the horse flesh. The races here draw top runners and jockeys; packages with accommodation and admission badges are available from Keith Prowse Tours. March is also the month for international football at Wembley in London.

Otherwise London looks to its river for spectactor sport, which is often as chilly for the spectators as the participants. The Head of the River Race is an annual competition for eights rowed over the university boat race course (see below). It runs from Mortlake to Putney on the third or fourth Saturday in March and the start varies according to the state of the tides. The entry is limited to 420 crews who start consecutively at ten-second intervals; the winner is the crew with the fastest time. The record, 16 minutes 37 seconds, was established in 1987. The race has been run since 1920, when 23 crews competed. The idea came from a Cambridge oarsman and was intended to give crews a goal to work towards to make winter training more interesting. As well as clubs from all over Britain, the race attracts European crews. The race overall takes about 1½ hours and a good spectator point is the Surrey bank above Chiswick Bridge (south side of the river), about 30 minutes before the start and then walking along the path towards Putney. For information and dates call 01–940 1171, extension 4112.

The same stretch of river is used for the better-known Oxford and Cambridge university boat race which takes place on a Saturday at the end of March or beginning of April. The race started in 1829 with the water between Hambledon lock and Henley as the course. The present course has been used since 1845 and covers 4½ miles from University Stone at Putney to Mortlake and has been an annual event since 1856. The second crews for each university, Isis (Oxford) and Goldie (Cambridge), race about half an hour before the main race. The racing time varies according to the tide, but the fastest time recorded to date is Oxford's 1984 16 minutes 45 seconds. Take something to keep you warm or find a place at a riverside pub; the Dove, 19 Upper Mall, Hammersmith and the Ship Inn, Mortlake, are two possibles. The London Tourist Office (tel. 01–730 3488) can give further information and exact dates each year.

High fliers can take advantage of the winds March is noted for, at least in Britain, with gliding lessons at up to 10,000 feet over the Scottish Highlands and Islands. The Argyll and West Highland Gliding Centre is based near Oban and is one of the few schools in Scotland that offers tuition for beginners. Week-long courses are planned from late March till October. Individual tuition is given in two-seater aircraft and can progress as fast as abilities allow. Accommodation can be arranged by the centre as needed. Information from AWH Gliding Centre, Woodmarch, Kinnesswood, Kinross KY13 7HX, Scotland (tel. 059 284 288).

On Show

The world's biggest travel show, ITB, takes place in March in Berlin, but it is something of an endurance test with enormous halls and hundreds of stands, and it's best to mark down an area of the world you wish to know more about and concentrate on that; travel folk from all over the world converge on Berlin for the event, so avoid this time for a break there. In London, the Ideal Home Exhibition at Olympia is the big exhibition draw with the latest in house and household designs. In Cambridge-shire there's a shire horse show and in Birmingham there's Britain's only public golf show, which is held for three days at the beginning of the month at the National Exhibition Centre. The show includes golf clinics, driving and putting areas, displays and trade stands. Details from 021 780 4171, extension 710.

In keeping with the month's icy reputation one of the most unusual and beautiful art shows is the Kemijarvi ice-sculpting contest in Finland. Each winter a group of sculptors from around the world gathers in Kemijarvi and our old friend Rovaniemi to carve works out of snow and ice. The event begins in Kemijarvi with a three-day ice-sculpting contest. Each artist invited to be present is given two huge cubes of ice and a power saw, and is allowed three days in which to produce the sculpture. Other kinds of tools are allowed and each artist employs his own technique. There is one free day before the artists move on to the next competition in Rovaniemi, where the material for art creation is snow. Enormous cubes of packed and frozen snow are piled at the competition site for art works that have an even briefer life than the ice sculptures. In Rovaniemi the artists work as two-man teams and a jury selects the best works. Each year sculptors from all over the world accept the invitation and even eskimo artists have taken part.

Oslo, Norway holds the Sea For All international boat and engine show at Sjolyst.

Public Holidays

17 March, St Patrick's Day, Ireland.
19 March, St Joseph's Day, Spain.
25 March, Greek National Anniversary and a major religious holiday marked with military parades in the larger towns.
30 March, Maundy Thursday (moveable), Denmark, Norway, Spain.

4

APRIL

THE REBIRTH OF THE YEAR

PRIL, with its Chaucerian showers sweet, is a month of awakening; lambs bounce in fields burgeoning with young, fresh flowers; yellows and greens predominate. In southern Europe one can eat lunch out of doors and in sheltered rock niches feel the promise of searing sun to come. April is the month of Easter's death and resurrection, gloom and hope, its dates varying each year.

The places to be are Greece, Portugal, southern Spain, with temperatures into the 70s for the first tan of the year and the first flowers of southern Greece. In Cyprus the rains end, and the south of France, Sicily, Calabria in southern Italy, are good places to be. The Greek islands are already as green and warm as an English summer's day. Even so, climatically it can be a tricky time, with showers and even snow in northern Europe. Britain can be very quixotic. Bridesmaids wore ski pants under their long dresses to my cousin's wedding in London in late April. In the last week of April in 1987 I sunbathed around an outdoor swimming pool all week in Hampshire. Skiers go high this month – up above the 5,000-foot level – to find their slopes The south-facing slopes are fine early in the season, but by April they are riskier. Check out dates of Easter and school holidays to avoid crowds on the slopes.

Spain is the country to visit for Holy Week if you can get a hotel reservation. In Seville from Palm Sunday to Easter Monday, *Semana Santa* is the focus of Christian celebrations when over 50 'brotherhoods' progress along officially laid out routes from the Plaza de la Campagne to Sierpes street, past the town hall, through the vast gothic cathedral with its interior of 18 million cubic feet of space, the world's third largest church (after St Peter's, Rome and St Paul's, London) which took 100 years to build and contains the tomb of Christopher Columbus. The processions end before the Giralda tower and the baroque palace of the bishops. Especially interesting are the processions held on the Thursday afternoon and the early morning and afternoon of Friday.

The elaborate wood and silver 'pasos', carnation covered, supported on sweating shoulders, bear the richly adorned statues of the Virgins, sculpted by such artists as Roldan, Juan de Mena and Martinez Montanes. Haunting 'saetas', short ecstatic prayers or hymns, are sung and the mysterious hooded robes of many of the marchers create an eerie, compelling spectacle, rare in the modern world.

It is difficult to believe these penitent carriers of the madonna are ordinary human beings with modern everyday lives away from Holy Week. A glimpse of a besuited man with a briefcase in one hand and a crown of thorns in the other seems perfectly normal in Seville this week. Hooded figures slip through high vaulted cathedral caverns around the narrow, old streets or enjoy a sherry and a tapa snack in a bar; all seemingly a perfectly natural occurrence, not a sudden backward time warp to the Middle Ages.

The processions last a week and men from all walks of life take part. Some carry huge calvary crosses and are dressed as Christ. The streets become a religious theatre *par excellence*. As a spectator one needs almost as much stamina as the penitents. The longest parade takes twelve hours to inch its way through the 600,000 watching population doubled by visitors. There are 100 floats and 60 brotherhoods to move them.

The Virgin figures are more than just a religious symbol to Seville's people. They are local dignatories. La Macarena is one of the best known, with her single pearl 'tear'. In the Spanish Civil War she became a captain in General Franco's army. She is also the patron saint of smugglers and bullfighters, wearing widow's weeds when top toreadors are killed. She also wears jewels loaned to her by the Duchess of Alba. This Virgin even has had a hotel named for her: the Macarenas Sol.

Up at dawn on Good Friday, La Macarena and her supporters (literally) and those carrying La Esperanza Virgin converge in La Campana quarter of Seville. The crowds cheer and urge on the two groups of burdened bearers and each tries to outmanoeuvre the other till the loser eventually weakens. At night the magic heightens, as floats seem to sway past in mid air, lit by flickering candles and aided by chanting, drumbeats and the music of flamenco singers.

If you prefer your spectacles more tempered, stay around in Seville for the April Fair (*feria*) that each year seems to edge closer to Holy Week. This is the time for flamenco and fino, high-stepping Andalucian Arab horses, riders in tight black clothes with their girl friends, looking like descendants of Carmen, in flounced dresses, clinging behind them. Around 2,000 horsemen, over 100 horse-drawn carriages and crowds promenade at night lit by paper lanterns. The streets are lined with thousands of *casetas*, little tented stalls, dispensing food and drink. The *casetas* open at dusk with food and flamenco. Some are open only by invitation provided by the sherry houses or private families. Those sponsored by political parties are open to all.

The fair dates back to 1847, when it functioned mainly as a livestock market. Now the bulls charge in the ring, and from dusk to dawn flamenco, food and wine are offered in the warm air. There is plenty of time tomorrow for a siesta. The best vantage point is in the old city quarter, the Barrio de Santa Cruz, with its enchanting small squares, lamp lit and lined with jasmin and bougainvillea and bitter orange trees.

The April Fair lasts a week and each day begins (Spanish style, at noon) with a horse parade through the fairground on the edge of the city with flower decked carriages. A noisy, old fashioned fun fair with gravity-defying rides and stalls backs the equestrian elegance. Food is easily taken on the move when the city bar speciality of tapas, little snacks, miniature versions of full-scale dishes, moves out to the stalls. Olives, of course, which with oranges are one of the agricultural staples of the area; prawns cooked in oil; sustaining omelettes; fried squid; baby eels rather like thin whitebait; tiny kebabed meats, minute spiced meat balls; and, of course, plenty of local wine and the traditional copita of sherry from nearby Jerez to down. Chicken is barbecued in sherry with herbs.

Seville loves a display and with its tomb of Christopher Columbus in the cathedral is planning already for the five hundreth anniversary exhibition of the discovery of America to be held in 1992. Perhaps you had better book accommodation now or at least think about the Holy Week and *feria* well ahead. Reservations should be made a year or two ahead or you can pick a spot around the city for more peace and quiet. Details are available from the Seville Tourist Office, Avenida Queipo de Llano 9, Sevilla (tel. 954 221 1404).

Seville, of course, is not the only place in Spain in which to celebrate Holy Week. Others well worth taking in include those at Cuenca, Malaga, Valladolid, Cartagena and Lorca. In Cuenca, the penitents parade with their paso platforms of scenes from the Passion, borne in silence broken only by trumpet fanfares as they struggle through the high, rocky old city quarter. The Good Friday procession takes place at 6 am. At the same time, the city holds a religious music week (see March Arts section) with a new composition premiered each year. Concert tickets can be obtained from the provincial government building and the town hall.

In Malaga, the superb Virgin statues wearing silver and gold embroidered shawls are carried on baroque thrones. The standards of some of the 30 brotherhoods here have paintings by Moreno, Carbonero and Salaverria on them. On Friday morning the procession of Our Lady of Sorrows is lit only by the penitents' candles.

Valladolid boasts 18 brotherhoods for its Holy Week procession. At noon on Good Friday, an open air sermon is given in the Plaza Mayor before the procession begins. Cartagena's holy week began in the sixteenth century and still preserves much from that period; processions are led by two large brotherhoods, the Californios and the Marragos. Lorca's celebrations are original too, with a procession of over 100 historic or legendary figures on the Friday.

April activities are not over yet in Spain. Around the third week of the month come the Moors versus Christians festivals held in many places to commemorate the 800 years during which Christians and Moors fought to control the Iberian peninsula. The custom is particularly strong in the Valencia area with a show piece battle at Alcoy, Alicante on the Costa Brava. A mock battle between the two armies rages for three days with parleys, ambushes, castle seiges and street parades; the Christians triumph in the end, of course. Battles in other towns can be held through to September in the Alicante area.

The battles date from the seventeenth century and the opposing groups in the streets are accompanied by noisy bands. The Moors, blacked up like garishly dressed Al Jolsons, are eventually surrounded by the Christians. Military manoeuvres – musketeers' battles, the deployment of guerrillas, the sending out of embassies to talk – are performed against a background of fireworks and bell-ringing.

Customs: Foods, Easter and Eggs

April begins logically with the first. In countries like Britain 1 April, illogically, is a day for playing practical jokes, though these must end by the stroke of noon or the prankster becomes the fool. Don't believe all you read that day in the newspapers or see on TV. A TV film showing the gathering of spaghetti from trees in Italy was a classic media hoax.

European Easters   Easter is never earlier than 22 March or later than 25 April but whenever its moveable feast falls, some of the customs associated with it date back to pagan times and fertility cults. In Florence they burn a cart, the Scoppo del Carro, in Taranto a funeral supper is served on the quayside, while hooded penitents shuffle and sway as if in a trance and town bands play funeral marches. In Malta on Maundy Thursday special services and Last Supper displays are held in various churches open to the public between Wednesday evening and Friday morning. On Good Friday pageants are held in some 14 of the island's towns and villages starting at 1700. The Easter Vigil church service starts about 2000 on Saturday evening and early morning processions with the statue of the Risen Christ also take place. During the procession the *figolla*, a special sweet for Easter is blessed by the Risen Christ.

The Easter Sunday blessing of the crowds in Rome by the Pope is a highlight for many Christians. Throughout the year when the Pope is in residence in Rome he gives a mass papal audience every Wednesday morning (tickets available, about £9, from travel agents such as Appian Tours). Cardinals gather, the Swiss Guards muster in their uniforms (said to have been designed by Michaelangelo), and frock-coated Vatican dignatories assemble. The Pope arrives and tours the crowd before conducting a service of prayer, bible reading, homilies and hymns translated into about six languages. On Sunday mornings tours also take in St Peter's Square in time for a papal benediction.

In Austria in the Carinthia region Easter bonfires in the shape of cross symbols are lit the night before Easter Sunday, a reminder of the danger signals from the Turkish invasions of the sixteenth and seventeenth centuries. Also in Carinthia there is the Four Mountains run on the second Friday after Easter when 100–200 pilgrims start the run just before midnight Mass and cover about 50 km collecting magical leaves used in homes to avert thunderstorms. On top of the four mountains are little churches or inns where corn is exchanged for grain that has been blessed, to be mixed with other seed later to ensure a good harvest.

In Germany Easter bonfires are also lit and wheels or barrels of straw are lit and rolled down hills. In Germany, coloured eggs are prepared: in some places they are rolled down grassy slopes or the pointed ends knocked together; the child whose egg does not break gets the broken one too. Eggs are also hidden (by the Easter Bunny) for children to search out.

In Britain, coloured eggs are also traditionally given on Easter Sunday. On the three days of Easter holiday one of the biggest easter egg hunts takes place in the grounds of Leeds Castle in Kent. Over 9,000 children join the hunt, which also opens the castle's summer season of events. On the Saturday, Sunday and Monday of Easter over 5,000 mini chocolate eggs are hidden in the grounds as well as 50 silver-coloured eggs which win a small prize for finders and a gold-coloured egg which can be exchanged for an expensive toy. The castle gates open at 11 am and the egg hunt begins at 14.30 every day. Details from Leeds Castle Enterprises Ltd, Maidstone, Kent ME17 1PL (tel. 0622 65400).

Easter bonnet buyers can show off to their head's content at the annual parades in London or in Worthing, Sussex and Eastbourne at the latter's Congress Theatre. In London the first Easter Parade took place in 1962 in Battersea Park, though a forerunner had been held in Hyde Park in 1959. Since 1987 the event has been organised by the borough of Wandsworth. There are hat parades and Easter princess competitions with celebrity judges. Bands, London personalities, animals, flower floats, and jazz add to the appeal. The parade is on Easter Sunday around the outer ring of the park, beginning at 3.00 pm, and there are sideshows and entertainments in the park from noon.

A parade of a different kind of beauty takes place in Regent's Park in London on Easter Monday. This is the London Harness Horse Parade in which the working horses, surprisingly still large in number, compete for prizes. The day begins at 9.30 am with inspections and the main parade and then the judging of different classes for the horses ending with a Grand Parade of the winners at noon. Owners of private driving vehicles can now also join the parade. Information on 01–870 0141.

Also on Easter Monday there are extravagant events at Tunbridge Wells at the Calverley Grounds with egg rolling and also at Avenham Park, Preston, in Lancashire on the afternoon of Easter Monday when children roll coloured eggs down a slope. Easter buns, hot cross buns, are closely associated with Easter and the bun is used in the Easter Bun ceremony at the Widow's Son Inn, 75 Devon's Road, Bromley by Bow, London E3, at which a sailor adds a hot cross bun to the collection already hanging from the ceiling to commemorate the widow who baked a bun for her only son, who was lost at sea, although buns were believed to be a charm against ship wreck (information from 01–987 1865). At St Bartholomew the Great, London EC1 each Good Friday after the 11 am service, hot cross buns and coins are presented to the 'poor widows of the parish'. These gifts are placed on tombstones outside the west door. (Information from 01–606 1575.)

St George's Day, 23 April. St George is not only the patron saint of England but of Greece, Venice, Genoa, Portugal and Catalonia. In Greece the anniversary is celebrated at Kaliopi on Lesbos with horse races and at Arahova there is a non-stop three-day feast. At Aghios Gonia near Chanea on Crete the religious festival is followed by a sheep-shearing competition and a celebration of the old customs of the shepherds. The island of Cos has horse racing at the village of Pili which is followed by dancing and folk singing.

In Britain St George took over from Edward the Confessor as national saint during the thirteenth century. In the old days the day was for jousting events – today miming plays on a theme of the story of St George and the Dragon are still occasionally performed. At the New Inn Courtyard, Gloucester, morris dancers and mummers perform, but the day is probably better known as Shakespeare's birthday and in his birthplace Stratford on Avon in Warwickshire, there is an international procession around the town and flags of all nations are unfurled (information from tourist office, Judith Shakespeare's house, 1 High Street, Stratford upon Avon, Warwickshire CV37 6AU (tel. 0789 293127)).

Walpurgis Night, 30 April is when Sweden goes spring crazy, heralding the advent of spring with bonfires, songs and speeches in praise of spring. Students at the universities of Uppsala, Lund, Stockholm, Gothenburg and Umea indulge in lively celebrations.

Böögg is burnt on the third Sunday and Monday of the month in Zurich, in a festival dominated by Böögg – a giant snowman made of cotton wool and straw. On the Sunday the children parade in folk costume with a cart containing the Böögg. On the Monday, guildsmen of the city march with lanterns, banners and flags starting around 1800. The Böögg is finally burnt outside the opera house and in the evening dancing, singing and drinking celebrate the death of winter.

Food

Easter has its special foods: eggs and hot cross buns bearing the symbol of the cross originating from the sun that cut the world (and the bun) into four quarters. Hung from the ceiling, the buns contained special powers: a little ground into a powder would be added to medicine to cure the family and its animals. If the buns went mouldy, disaster was forecast.

At this time of year, elvers, baby eels, come up British rivers after migration from the Sargasso Sea. In Spain around Cadiz and Jerez and other areas, they are eaten a little earlier than in Britain (February on), cooked crisply in oil and flavoured with garlic. In Britain's Severn area the elvers are sold in Gloucester and often eaten for breakfast or as a snack cooked in egg batter, sometimes served with bacon. The elvers, borne on the Gulf Stream, are swept up river usually from March till May, and are often caught at night. At Epney on the Severn there is an elver collection depot from which exports are made by air to the Continent, especially to Poland and Germany, to restock rivers. Elvers are considered a local aphrodisiac and every year there is an elver eating competition on the huge 22-acre village green at Epney, Frampton on Severn (information from 0452 740118).

In Paris at Easter, they hold a gingerbread fair in the Avenue de Trone and a 700-year old ham fair in the Boulevard Richard

Lenoir. Details can be found in the weekly tourist paper *Une Semaine de Paris*.

Holland: from April until September every Friday morning there is a cheese market at Alkmaar in north west Holland which has been held for 300 years. Gouda and Edam cheese are brought in by barge and the cheese-bearers, members of the last active medieval guild, wearing white coats and different coloured hats according to the warehouse to which they belong, unload the cheeses on to wooden sledges and pull them to the market place. Gouda is made in about 1,000 farms in South Holland and Utrecht. Although it bears the name of a place, it is said to originate from Stolwijk, a place that still produces excellent cheeses. To make sure you are buying farmhouse as opposed to factory cheese, look for the 'Boeren Gouda' stamp. Edam lasts well; a sample which went with Scott to the Antarctic in 1912 was discovered in 1956 quite edible. Its characteristic shape has an enchanting history; the round moulds, called kaaskop (cheese head), made useful helmets in time of trouble, giving the Dutch the nickname of 'cheese heads'.

Lamb, the pascal lamb, is the meat associated with Easter. In England Welsh lamb is prized at this time of year, served with mint sauce; an unusual taste to others. It is said the habit started in the reign of Elizabeth I when sheep were valued more for their wool. To stop her subjects eating their golden goose, as it were, the queen issued an edict forbidding the eating of lamb except with a bitter herb sauce. The least bitter was mint – and so, they say, the tradition began. In Rome, the salt lamb from the marshes around the city is a delicacy at this time of year and the Italians use rosemary as their spicing.

Those who enjoy foods from the wild can start collecting this month in northern Europe with dandelions for tea and salad, seabeet leaves, caragean and hawthorn shoots.

Arts

Edinburgh (see March) and Wales have folk festivals. In Llantrisant at the Cross Keys Hotel in mid Glamorgan the festival covers international and British 'roots music' with concerts, workshops and events (information on 0443 226892). The Stratford on Avon theatre season opens at the beginning of the month (and runs to the end of August). Reductions on theatre seats are given subject to availability on Monday to Thursday performances in April and until 4 June. Day of performance and standby (immediately before curtain up any unsold tickets are sold to students, senior citizens and other qualifying groups) tickets are available. For £5 a year you can join the mailing list for all the Royal Shakespeare Company's performances with priority bookings, a newsletter and occasional discounts. Backstage tours are conducted on weekday afternoons and bookings should be made in writing to RSC Collection, Royal Shakespeare Theatre, Stratford on Avon, Warwickshire CV37 6BB or by phone (tel. 0789 296655 ext. 215). The Shakespeare stop-over package is available from Monday to Saturday, including a three-course pre-theatre meal and overnight stay in a choice of accommodation in five price categories. Details and stop-over leaflet from (for a sae) RST Restaurants, Royal Shakespeare Theatre, Stratford upon Avon, Warwickshire CV37 6BB (0789 295333 for round the clock information).

Salzburg has its Easter festival, founded by Herbert von Karajan over 20 years ago. The concerts and operas change each year and the audience tends to be one of knowledgeable music lovers who often book the same seats year after year. The faithful are allowed to attend one orchestral rehearsal so they can appreciate the intense concentration which goes into these particular performances. The works are chosen by von Karajan and he has put on the Ring in its original form; innovation is not part of the Salzburg Easter theme. Programmes are short, with the emphasis on quality rather than quantity, and concerts begin in the late afternoon leaving the evenings free to digest the experience along with dinner. Details from Osterspiele Salzburg, Festspielhaus, 5010 Salzburg (tel. 662 842541).

Madrid has a flamenco festival of song, dance and guitar. Details from Ministerio de Cultura, Oficina de Coordinacion Artistica, Plaza del Rey, 1, 28004, Madrid (tel. 91 429244).

At Denmark's Arhus's Musikhuset there is the Numus Contemporary Music Festival, the country's most important presentation of new classical music by international composers. Details from Musikhuset Arhus, Denmark (tel. 134344).

Sport

A month for moving fast to keep the circulation going. The Norwegians use reindeer power for racing at Kautokeino, the Belgians arm muscle in the rowing regatta at Bruges, the Spanish mechanised horse power for their Grand Prix and Londoners and visitors shanks' pony for the marathon in which 23,000 entrants start from Greenwich at 9.30 am hoping to finish some time later on Westminster Bridge. In Scotland the Highland Games at Easter are sensibly held indoors and at St

Andrews there is a golf week when Fife's famous course hosts competitors from all over the country.

The Badminton Horse Trials pit man and horse against obstacles and pitfalls and it is the month when racing brings out punters rich and poor. The Grand National held at the Aintree course near Liverpool is Britain's most exciting steeplechase, some say *too* exciting. Held at the beginning of the month, the race dates from 1839, and even then drew a 50,000 crowd. In that first race Captain Becher was dumped by his horse at the first brook, with the rest of the 16 runners passing over his head. The gallant captain's name is now remembered as that of the most hazardous of the jumps in the race. In 1847 the race got its present title, the Grand National Handicap Steeple Chase while the present-day course was shaped up by the Topham family in the 1890s. The race has only been run elsewhere three times, during the First World War, when the site of the present airport runway at Gatwick was used. The race is as much a sporting drama as a day out. Author Dick Francis, for example, led the field on the Queen Mother's horse Devon Loch, when the horse collapsed 50 yards from the finishing post. The British climate being what it is, though jockeys may drink a pre-race glass of champagne in the sauna, crowds dress warmly. In 1901 an owner packed his horses' hooves with butter to prevent the snow packing like ice in their shoes. Many horses having ditched their jockeys none the less carry on round the fences. Some have gone the course without a horse; in 1870 a Liverpudlian for a bet jumped the course on two legs. It's always an open race, great for the bookies. Outsiders romp home, but the king of the race is Red Rum, who won three times and came second once in five National races. He still returns each year, now in his twenties, to parade the course.

Many organisations now run day-at-the-races outings and British Rail often puts on special trains with buffets to get to leading meetings. Understanding what goes on at a race meeting is helped by information available from the Racing Information Bureau, Winkfield Road, Ascot, Berkshire SL5 7HX (tel. 0990 25912).

The Jockey Club, British racing's ruling body, was established in 1750 and today there are over 60 racecourses in the country, of which 20 race year round with two major types of racing: Flat and National Hunt. The Flat Racing season is from the beginning of April to the beginning of November and National Hunt racing over steeple chase fences and hurdles starts in early August through to the following June. Meetings are held somewhere on most days with the exception of Sundays or Good Friday.

Shopping

For antiques go to Edinburgh for the Scottish antiques fair, to Munich for the antique and flea market; for crafts to York or Llangollen. The latter is held at the town hall and features handmade crafts, in a retail outlet intended for people starting their own cottage industries (information on 0490 2803). In Barcelona, Spain in April there is the Bargain Book Fair and in Madrid the Old Book Fair. Spain's book day (dia del libro) is 23 April, when hundreds of stalls are set up in the streets of every town offering the latest literary works for sale. This event is especially popular in Catalonia with a festival of books, roses and flags. A rose and a book are bought by many people in Barcelona and other cities in the region.

Horticultural Happenings

In the UK, April is the month of Wordsworth's 'host of golden daffodils', seen to their advantage in his Lake District home, though Norwich holds a daffodil day during the month. To make sure the journey to the Lakes is worth while call the Cumbria Tourist Board, Holly Road, Ashleigh, Windermere, Cumbria LA23 2AQ (tel. 096 62 4444/7) and check the progress of the blooms. Leeming House Hotel, on Ullswater, Watermillock, Cumbria CA11 0JJ (tel. 08536 622) is a gracious converted Georgian house with extensive grounds stretching down to the lake shore. It is said to be the site where Wordsworth saw those hosts and over recent years the owners and guests have planted thousands of bulbs to ensure that each spring there are flowers to be admired.

The daffodil is the national flower of Wales and in 1986 25 tons (over £10,000 worth) of bulbs were planted along the A55 North Wales expressway, a new road linking north-west England and giving the 70-mile road the title 'the daffodil highway'. In south-west Wales, the southern part of the Pembrokeshire coast national park has had over three tons of daffodil bulbs planted in gardens and roadsides. These flower from late March to the beginning of May. A Festival of Daffodils is run to attract walkers and naturalists. Details from Festival of Daffodils, National Park Information Centre, The Croft, Tenby, Dyfed, Wales (tel. 0834 2402).

With an April walk along the daffodil coast from little coves to 300-foot cliff tops, the Pembrokeshire National Park is Britain's only coastal park. As well as daffodil areas, a 60-mile circular footpath round the east and west Cleddau rivers opens up a little explored area of woodland and estuary scenery. The average walker will take up to two weeks to complete the whole 180-mile coastal path, best in April with new green woodland and wild flowers as well as nesting sea birds from puffins to petrels to see. To the west are the cliff formations of the Stack Rocks which embrace a huge natural arch known as the Green Bridge of Wales, as each spring it is covered by a fresh carpet of grass. There is a National Park information centre at Tenby which organises a programme of walks and wild life talks and tours as well as human interest venues of potters, weavers and wood carvers to be visited. The Tenby male voice choir welcomes visitors to its weekly rehearsals.

The Netherlands boasts 2,000 varieties of tulips and the Keukenhof park near Amsterdam is the world's largest single flower garden (see March). At the end of April flower parades are held with flower smothered floats passing through the heart of the tulip country from Haarlem to Noordwijk passing fields neatly planted out with millions of bulbs to resemble checkered cloths of colour. During the flowering season the tension mounts in the auction rooms at Aalsmeer, the site of the world's biggest flower market.

Spring garden scene, Cornwall

Spring comes a little sooner in Cornwall, UK, where the land spears out into the Atlantic Gulf Stream. Each year a consortium of hotels in the Falmouth area get together to arrange a series of garden holidays in spring. The gardens, many in historic houses, house exotic plants made possible by the mild climate and of note are collections of magnolias, camellias and rhododendrons. Among the gardens which can be visited are Trengwainton, Trelissick, Caerhays, Cotehele and Trewidden. Details of the week-long holidays from Pamela Long, Cornwall House and Garden Holidays, PO Box 33, Falmouth TR11 3TY (tel. 0326 314744).

Nature Note

For bird-lovers an enchanting sight in April is the crane dancing on Lake Hornborgasjon in the Vastergotland area of Sweden. On their annual migration to their northern breeding grounds, thousands of cranes rest and 'dance' in the fields between Falkoping and Skara. The birds leave the lake at dawn for the fields and then fly back again at dusk.

Public Holidays

Good Friday, Easter Monday when in April.
In addition Denmark and Portugal take the Thursday before Easter off; and Italy and Portugal have a holiday on 25 April.

5

MAY

IS PARIS IN THE SPRING

HIS month is supposed to be merry, Maypole dancing in the past; plenty of nodding blossoms often dancing in the over exuberant breezes of a mercurial thermometer that underlines the old adage 'never cast a clout till May is out'. The 'season' such as it is still persists. It starts in many European countries with an outburst of music festivals and performances. There are the first of the year's fresh young vegetables and fruits. It is a month of 'premieres' for all the senses.

Chestnuts in the Champs Elysées

Paris is always a city for the young in heart and fits this youthful time of year. It is the month to sit on the Champs Elysées when the chestnuts are in bloom, take a picnic bought at a neighbourhood charcuterie and bakery of terrines, salads ready made, quiches, baton bread, cheeses and a bottle of wine and sit in the formality of the Maillol statues in the Tuileries gardens, amid nannies, their charges and dogs in the Palais du Luxembourg gardens, or go out to Fointainebleau and an area of woods and tumbled rocks in strange shapes formed by glacial erosion, known as Chaos, to picnic in a gothic setting.

Small tree-shaded squares soften the city's concrete and there are plenty of parks to see in spring. The Bois de Boulogne to the west, with 2,224 acres and two race tracks and accessible by metro has eight lakes, some of which in summer have small informal restaurants. To the east of the city is the Bois de Vincennes with four lakes. In the 16th arondissement in the west corner of the Bois de Boulogne is Bagatelle with its rose gardens, walled English garden and seasonal flower displays. The eighteenth-century Palais Royal gardens are stocked with lime and elm and arcade bordered. The Jardin des Plantes, 57 Rue Cuvier 5e, is a botanical garden with 10,000 species and Paris' oldest tree, a 300-year-old false acacia. The Tuileries gardens were designed by Le Notre and have not been modified since. They extend from the Louvre to the Place de la Concorde with the Maillol statues of bathers that initially shocked Parisiens. The Bois de Vincennes is a former hunting park now with France's largest zoo and the Floral Park with pine forest and four seasons garden.

Paris on a budget is very possible. Paris Travel Service (Bridge House, Ware, Herts SG19 9DF (tel. 0920 3922)) have year-round short or long packages with a choice of road, rail or air transport according to pocket. Choose a hotel a little off centre yet with TV, video, phone, bathroom and breakfast like the Brittany near the Gare St Lazare with views of Sacré Coeur. Using the metro (carnets of several tickets are cheaper and quicker; a single journey anywhere costs less than 50p), one pays less yet speedily covers the sights. In ten minutes from the Brittany one can be in the Place de la Concorde. VFB, 1 St Margaret's Terrace, Cheltenham, Gloucestershire GL50 4DT (tel. 0242 526338) offer two and three star inexpensive but central hotels on the left bank such as the two star Hotel de France in Rue Monge near the Rue Mouffetard and its market and the three star Hotel Verneuil St Germain in the Beaux Arts quartier. Before deciding on a Paris trip, check out with the French Government Tourist Office if there are any big fairs or exhibitions on as, at certain times, the city is booked out.

The top tours for first timers are the day and night bateaux mouches trips of illuminated Paris; Versailles (about three hours, with guided tour of the palace); the Louvre with the Mona Lisa and Venus de Milo and the new Musée d'Orsay (see below). Paris is a city to explore on foot, finding the section that suits one's personality and pocket, crossing some of the 30 plus bridges over the Seine, strolling the quais with their bouquinistes, stalls selling prints and second hand books, meandering the boulevards, especially St Germain and the student's Boulevard St Michel and just sitting in the little gardens to the south of Notre Dame viewing the grimacing gargoyles and flying buttresses – the haunt of the hunchback.

Paris is now a golden city, her stones cleaned and spiked with impudent new conceits like the 'plastic piped' Pompidou Centre and the redeveloped area of Les Halles, like London's Covent Garden filled with fashionable boutiques and cafes. But the newest and most stunning place to visit is the Musée d'Orsay, M'O, which opened in 1987 on the left back at the end of the Rue Bellechasse overlooking the Seine. The huge nineteenth-century railway station, Gare d'Orsay, was to be pulled down but was saved and turned into this superb setting for works of the nineteenth and twentieth centuries (the trains have gone underground). The impressionist works of Manet, Monet and Renoir have been moved across from the Jeu de Paume along with many more paintings, sculptures, architectural models, film, press and poster collections, furniture and decorative arts; even furniture by Charles Rennie Mackintosh and Frank Lloyd Wright.

But it is the concept and use of the building that makes such an impression. The vast curved glass and metal roof makes a lengthy hall with levels rising in galleries around. At one end is an immense gilded station clock and behind its shielding glass wall one can see the shadows of people crossing the walkways. With prancing bronzes of exotic animals on the broad stepped terrace outside, the museum is exciting from the moment of arrival. By the entrance are neat small maps language-coded by flags that are art forms in themselves. A rainy day can happily be spent here drifting the wide cool spaces, admiring paintings, tiny foot-square masterpieces or those that seem too big for any dwelling. One room is set off by chandeliers and gilded panelling, others have a station starkness about their display. There is plenty of seating, files of references to consult and of course refreshment is to hand. At mid level is a restaurant that is open every day for lunch and dinner (not Sundays or Mondays) or, right up in the roof behind yet another huge station clock (this one on the outside by the river) is a more casual cafe open during museum hours. (The museum is closed on Mondays.) General tours of the museum are organised every day and daily a single work of art is presented at 12.30. Activities are also organised for the 5–15 year olds in a special Young Visitors area and books, postcards and posters are on sale. An 'invitation to history' helps visitors understand French history from 1848– 1914. Concerts, films, lectures and art history courses are given in the museum auditorium.

On a bright spring day one can experience the wide open sky and light appeal of Paris even inside the M'O. Another big building where one can spend a showery day or more is the Galeries Lafayette. As in Britain, few retailers really do much to welcome the tourist spending market, but Galeries Lafayette has cornered the 'accueil' scene for Paris. It starts at airline desks like British Airways and Air France at Charles de Gaulle, where visitors can pick up an attractive free guide book to Paris with superb colour pictures while waiting for the baggage to arrive on the carousel. It gives plenty of practical sightseeing advice, addresses, markets, and maps and shopping clothing sizes.

The store has tied in with travel agents and hotels as well. Many hotels provide an excellent free map spotlighting the hotel and the Galeries Lafayette and backed by more practical information and metro details. The Paris equivalent of Harrods or Bloomingdales, Galeries Lafayette is from the outside like a street market of bargain stalls along the front, recalling the store as it started in the nineteenth century. After shrewd property buys, it now towers several blocks opposite the equally vast Opera House (see the architectural model in the M'O for an impression of this amazing building). Galeries Lafayette rises to the green roofline of the Opera which can be viewed from the non-smoking area of one of the top floor cafes.

Between the two buildings runs the Boulevard Haussmann, named for the man who created the wide avenues of Paris a century ago in the belief that street riots in such wide sweeps could easily be quelled by artillery fire. In the summer the visitor should seek the striped awning over the Porte Auber in the Boulevard Haussmann (there are dozens of doors, each with a name) where the welcome desk with hostesses assists foreign visitors. At the top of each section of escalator in the store are small desks with more hostesses, each with a language badge.

Galeries Lafayette gives the visitor the option of spending a whole day among the comprehensive departments of the store or using the Purchase Booklet scheme, for those with only a little time to spare. The booklet can be validated for a week, two or longer to cover the period of the visit. Each time a purchase is made, it is entered in the booklet, the shopper pays nothing and the goods are collected together in a central spot where at the end of the trip a single payment is made (credit cards are accepted), taxes and discounts arranged and all the purchases can be taken away in one go or delivered to your hotel.

Even if you hate shopping, a glance at the marvellous six-storey-high, deep blue ribbed glass and metal dome over the centre of the store with its lower golden and scarlet stained glass panels around the gilded arches of the supporting gallery (why did you think it has its name?) through which counters of merchandise peep out, is worth a visit. Under the central dome there is always a special perfume display on offer. Around this area are all the top French scent names on sale and GL is the world's largest perfumery. Here too are small designer boutiques for accessories. On two upper floors, fashion rules with the store having its own excellent collections offering chic styling at value for money prices.

Most of the top designers from Alaia to Yves are represented by their own small boutiques. If you don't want the time and trouble of getting a fashion show ticket from one of the leading houses (see February chapter) you can catch the collections any time of year on the videos showing in these boutiques. Pick your designer favourite from over 50 top names – Chanel, Dior, Montana, Dorothée Bis, Ungaro, Givenchy, Guy Laroche, Castelbajac, Lagerfeld, Kenzo, Lanvin, Louis Feraud, Ricci, Balmain – and just watch.

Every Wednesday (and on Thursday in summer) Galeries Lafayette gives a free fashion show which features models compered in English by the charming Madame Lapierre, head of the store's interpretation service. On Wednesdays, there is a breakfast with the show and on Thursdays a lunch; special shows can be arranged for groups. Travel agents in Paris and several hotels can arrange for tickets for the shows or one can ask at the shop's welcome desk.

Quite a lot of the tourists' needs can be solved in the store under a single very beautiful roof. On the first floor by the men's store there is a travel agency and theatre ticket agency (those on a budget should find the cut-price day-of-show ticket booth by the Madeleine); currency exchange is also by the men's store and for a hairdo (no appointment needed) there is a massive factory-like salon with 50 hairdressers and an Orlane beauty institute alongside for all kinds of treatments.

As well as a snack vending machine in this salon the store has plenty of reasonably priced (from 25 francs) eating places on the top floor where the self-service section even has a microwave oven so food can be heated. There is the grill for waitress service, the pub for grills and salads and Pavillon Lafayette for breakfast, light lunches and afternoon pastries.

Open from 9.30 to 18.30 the store has a kitchen basement and upper floor furniture and household linens area among its dazzling selection of goods. If you are scared, and most of us are, of committing yourself to fashion buys and making an expensive mistake, help is at hand. The Mode Plan International desk in the fashion department will help. Settled in a private room here with mirrors, soft chairs, clothes rail, coffee, desk and phone if you need to make business calls, counsellors will bring fashion items and if wished create a total look. A fashion file is opened and next time you are in Paris you can call in and they will build on ideas from there.

Toys and children's clothes are other good buys, but whatever you want to buy, you can leave your camera, umbrella, coat, scarf, bags, and other tourist paraphernalia at the cloakroom on the lower floor. There is also a 24-hour check room (79 Rue de Provence) where purchases can be left and picked up anytime – even on a Sunday or after the opera. The store has a Louvre museum shop selling reproductions of its treasures – as small as jewellery or as large as a life-size Venus de Milo, which will set you back about £2,700.

Napoleon may have called Britain a nation of shopkeepers but it now seems more true of Paris. Part of the fun of Paris is exploring the little neighbourhood shops around every hotel watching locals carry their baton bread, fresh cheeses and little bags of charcuterie home. Many close from 1300–1500 but are open in the early evening. The visitor may be nervous of buying charcuterie or cheeses or fresh pasta in a small, expert and non-English-speaking shop (it's an idea to take a cook bag for picnic buys and take-home goodies), but a culinary crutch is to hand in Paris. Robert Noah is a young, quiet American who came to France in 1971 to learn French and gastronomy. He worked in top kitchens, a charcuterie, wine cellar and cheese maitre and his 'Paris en Cuisine' service eliminates the wastage of finding out by trial and error. He will make reservations for restaurants, suggest budget bistros, *menus fixes* at glossier places, suggest good-value hotels and from April till October take visitors in small groups on regular foodie sightseeing. There are dawn trips to Rungis, the world's largest commercial food market (cost is about 325 francs up), demonstration classes in top Paris restaurants, and walking tours of restaurant kitchens from 200 francs. Other Paris day trips which can be booked ahead include bread, cheese and wine tours, visiting the bread shop of the Poilane family, sampling cheeses at La Ferme Saint Hubert, and seeing the ripening cellars; purchases at both these shops taken for lunch with wine to taste at the Academie du Vin. Pastry, spun sugar expertise, bread alone or wine are other day tour themes. The Paris food enthusiast can take out a subscription to Noah's informative gastronomic newsletter and he will also arrange day excursions with a food theme out of Paris to the Loire valley and Lyons and elsewhere in France with longer travelling time. Details from Robert Noah, Paris en Cuisine, 49 Rue de Richelieu, 75001 Paris (tel. 42 61 35 23).

Food markets are a Paris speciality to be enjoyed at any time of year and have been around since the fifth century. By 1860 there were 51 markets and now there are 57 moveable pavement markets that last the morning plus 13 covered markets. Inspired by the 'Dejeuner sur l'herbe' painting in the M'O, the markets are sources of sightseeing midday meals on the move (take your own shopping bag). Some to seek: Rue Montorgueil near Les Halles and the Pompidou Centre with Patisserie Stohrer, said to be Paris' oldest pastry shop founded in 1730 with lovely murals on glass, Marche des Enfants Rouges, 39 Rue de Bretagne the oldest; Rue Mouffetard the most touristy of the markets; Grenelle, Boulevard de Grenelle with the Poilane bakery on the corner and lots of farm produce on the stalls; and the Rue Poncelet and Rue Bayon off Avenue des Ternes at the back of the Etoile.

For non-food markets, there's the enduring Marche aux Puce (flea market) at weekends at Sainte Ouen, now with specialist sectors with its clothing sections. Flower markets are on the Ile de la Cité, Place Louise Lepine; on Sundays it becomes the bird market. Stamps are sold on the corner of the Avenue Gabriel and Avenue Marigny on Thursdays and weekends. If it rains there are the covered arcades which became fashionable in the early nineteenth century: most of those remaining are near the Boulevard des Italiens. In the Galerie Vero-Dodat, 19 Rue Jean-Jacques Rousseau there are painted ceilings and copper columns; the Galerie Vivienne, 4 Place des Petits Champs, has a restored staircase and circular hall, both in the Burlington Arcade style of up-market shops.

Window shop along the designer shops of Avenue Victor Hugo or go for the designer discount stores where clothes are usually about 30 to 50 per cent cheaper. Try the Annexe des Createurs, 14 rue de l'hotel Colbert 5e; Le Club des Dix, 51 Rue du Faubourg St Honoré 8e; Anna Lowe, 35 avenue Matignon 8e; and Sold'Dores, 6 rue de Constantinople 8e.

The first time I saw Paris, like so many people, I was a young and impecunious student. A girl friend and I had just the first course and a plate of bread – all we could afford – in a fairly classy restaurant. I've lost some of that nerve now as affluence has gained a little. It is pleasant to be comfortable and pampered in Paris and to have a good concierge to sort out visits.

An easy ethnic transition for the English speaker is the Club St James, sister to ones in London, Los Angeles and Antigua and the first club hotel concept in Paris. The club is set near the Avenue Foch in a nineteenth-century chateau built by the widow of the politician Thiers as a students' foundation. It was elegantly restored with interior decor by Andree Putnam and opened early in 1987. The ceilings were so high that duplex suites have been easy to create and there are two mini town houses complete with basement snooker rooms in the old gatehouse. The rooms are mostly suites and those on the top floor have a private patio and conservatory garden or thick green screening in front of each door. With the glass roofing, it is a perfect place to absorb spring sunshine along with a breakfast of fresh orange juice and croissants. There is a health club with gym and a library – filled with old leather bound books that can be borrowed – acts as the bar. Off this is the town house style dining room where an ex Taillevent chef creates superb nouvelle cuisine dishes.

It is a club but non members can stay as hotel guests paying a small extra daily fee. The reward is an intimate looked-after feeling, not that of the usual hotel battery hen. The English papers are available early in the morning and sent up to suites. There is 24-hour room service and maid service several times a day. The concierge, Jean-Paul Burot, will suggest and make sightseeing arrangements – anything from a sewer tour if the river is not too high to a couture show. With Karl Lagerfeld and Jean Paul Gaultier on the club committee, entrée is not difficult. In season, the Longchamps course is only a few minutes away in the Bois de Boulogne, which is a good exercise place, and the club can make arrangements for a day's racing outing.

To one side of the club is the Rue des Belles Feuilles that leads up past guarded embassies over the Avenue Victor Hugo to its market section, liveliest in the mornings with pricey, but excellent, fresh food. Regional cheeses, almost all made from raw milk in small production batches, can be found at Lillo in this street where seasonal selections will be packaged to carry home. At the end of Belles Feuilles one crosses Place de Mexico and views to the Tour Eiffel lead one a short walk to Trocadero and Palais de Chaillot. The Trocadero metro is a god hub with a direct line to Galeries Lafayette and it's fun to take the line to Pasteur, raised on bridges above ground. It offers river views, passes Les Invalides and gives glimpses into the streets of the Left Bank. Back in the 16e near the Club St James, crossing the Belles Feuilles, is Rue de la Pompe, a long thin street of tiny shops that ends in Rue de Passy with its covered Passy market and cut by the Rue d'Annonciation, a pedestrian-only street of food and antique shops. Supermarket signs here detail 'parking pour nos chiens': dogs and their traces are a hazard in this area. On the other side of the club is the elegant tree-lined Avenue Foch leading to the Arc de Triomphe and the delights of the Champs Elysées. Even though it is a smart quartier one can find a Prisunic and Gem supermarket for modest household buys in the Rue Belles Feuilles.

In May there are special events to lure the arts enthusiast. There is the 'extraordinary objects' five-day fair involving antique sellers from the Left Bank streets like du Bac, Beaune, de Lille, Saintes Pères, de l'universite, de Verneuil and quai Voltaire. In mid May the first part of the Saint Dénis music festival starts with promenade concerts in the chateaux, parks and historic monuments. At Versailles the festival of opera and concerts also starts in May and runs till towards the end of June.

Everyone has his or her own Paris, places they consider the best and piloting others must necessarily be subjective. The city scent of perfume, Gauloise cigarettes and a tinge of garlic in May is made headier with lilies of the valley – muguet de Mai – sold from street stalls. Time to sit outside, perhaps at La Palette cafe in the Beaux Artes gallery district or take an ice cream from Berthillon (who closes from July to September) or nibble an art-form bread from Rene-Gerard Saint-Ouen at 111 Boulevard Haussmann; bread rabbits, squirrels, dogs, cats, bikes, donkey carts and elephants are arrayed in the window of this zoolangerie.

A calming and thought-provoking spot to see is the Père la Chaise cemetery, a last resting place for a range of divergent characters from Abelard and Eloise to Colette and Oscar Wilde.

A!ternative Destinations

Greece for its flowers (see page 99) and warm sunny days.
Going north from mid month, the midnight sun shines over the
North Cape and the long days of light encourage potatoes,
barley and flowers to grow in North Norway and the glacier
buttercup starts to grow. On 20 May the sun rises at last over
Nuorgam, the most northerly city in Finnish Lapland near the
Norwegian border. It will set only in July. This is the time of
year to go far north to see the aurora borealis and the time when
one can fish, sail or bathe in the lakes and rivers long after
midnight as if in broad daylight; the only problem about
enjoying this extra plus of long, long days is the prevalence of
mosquitoes.

In Denmark, locals come out for fun with the opening of the
Tivoli Gardens (which stay open till mid September) and Lego-
land for children. The Tivoli Gardens cover 20 acres in the centre
of Copenhagen originally set up to take people's minds off
politics. It was opened in 1843 and now hosts around 50,000
visitors a day. It has walks of flowers, lights, fountains, fireworks, bandstands, dance halls, roller coaster, ferris wheel,
Chinese pagoda, Moorish palace, concert hall, with symphony
orchestra playing every evening, shooting and throwing galleries and 23 cafes.

Copenhagen also hots up this month with a 3-day carnival of
Caribbean-style music, blending Latin American and African
with streets full of musicians, jugglers, acrobats and dancers
from all over Europe as well as circus performers and food
vendors. Details from the Danish Tourist Board, Vesterbrogade
6, D, DK–1620 Copenhagen V (tel. 01 11 14 15).

Old Customs

There's a chance to take in Easter the second time around.
Greece celebrates its greatest festival roughly one month after
the Western Easter. Ceremonies start in the early hours of Good
Saturday when the church bells signal what is called the 'first
resurrection'. During this service the priest comes out of the
main door of the sanctuary saying 'God resurrects to judge the
people on earth' and scatters laurel leaves from a basket,
symbols of strength for those who can catch them before they fall
to the floor. The laurel tree has been sacred in Greece as the
symbol of the victory of the new god since the days of the
worship of Apollo. The resurrection service takes place in the
courtyards of the churches at midnight on Good Saturday night:

bells toll through the psalms sung by the clergy, fireworks are set off and candles flicker. The congregation kiss each other and after the Mass is over go home taking with them the 'sacred light' of resurrection in a white candle. At the entrance, the head of the family makes a cross with the candle smoke on the lintel of the door to bless the house and protect it. The family then eats the traditional Easter maghiritsa soup and other dishes; before the meal starts everyone bangs together red-dyed hard-boiled eggs. The white of the candles and red of the eggs symbolise the 'light' and the 'life'. The candle and egg are also sent to godchildren on Good Thursday. On this day Easter bread (tsoureki) and ring biscuits (koulourakia) are baked and offered as gifts to relatives on Easter day.

Roast lamb, spit-cooked in the courtyard, is another Easter custom. While the charcoal burns and the spit turns, the lamb is basted with a mixture of oil and lemon and oregano and passers-by may join in the feasts, helping themselves to pieces of the lamb and a glass of wine and toasting each other with the words 'Christos Anesti' (Christ is risen). In some towns such as Lamia, Levadia, Arachova and Amfissa, the roasting shops display their roasted lambs and passers-by can buy as much as they wish to celebrate in the traditional way. On Easter Sunday afternoon the church bells ring to summon worshippers to the 'second resurrection' or feast of love, originating from early Christian times when Christian groups met together in symposiums.

May Day

The month starts with Labour Day, a public holiday celebrated in most European countries since 1890 after the first World Labour Day was declared a holiday by the International Workers Congress held in Paris in 1889. Britain, a late follower of the holiday, has it on the Monday after 1 May though celebrations of May Day associated with maypole dancing go back to ancient times. In Greece, 1 May is also the feast of the flowers, when people go to the country for picnics.

Germany The 'Burschenschaften' groups of bachelor villagers traditionally organised May Day events and parties. The symbol of the 'Burschenschaften' was the maypole, for which a tall tree, usually a spruce, was felled and cropped of branches except for a tuft at the top. The bark was removed and the trunk of the tree, decorated with garlands and ribbons, set up in the village.

May Day in towns is now more usually observed with meetings, music and speeches and political rallies, as elsewhere.

Austria Maypoles are also erected on 1 May and at the end of the month cut down ritually. In Lower Austria, maypole climbing and ribbon dances are part of the ceremonies. Maypoles are additionally set up by innkeepers and others and special ones for girls are set up by young men.

Britain On May morning, go early to Oxford to hear choirs sing carols from the top of Magdalen tower by the river and

Raising the maypole, Germany

watch parades go past the colleges. In Padstow in Cornwall on May Day the 'obby 'oss (hobby horse) appears. Two 'osses and their supporters parade the streets of the town to commemorate the frightening away in the Middle Ages of the French army by a hobby horse stationed in the harbour. Another May Cornish custom that's exhilarating to take part in is the Helston Furry dance (around 8 May). It starts at 7 am with the adults' dance which continues to the well-known 'floral dance', scooping people in as it hops, skips and swirls around the town. At 10.15 am about 1,000 children perform their own dance and dancing continues all day led by the town band – which by the end of the day has covered about 15 miles. Morris dancing, with strange belled costumes, can also be seen in May originating from spring fertility rites. On the spring holiday at the end of May dances can be seen at Bampton in Oxfordshire and Thaxted in Essex.

May is a time for new mayors to be installed and various ceremonies are associated with this. At High Wycombe mayors are literally weighed in and out and their weight loss or gain announced publicly, an indication possibly of whether they have been slim and active or fat and idle. The mayor starts the cheese rolling at Randwick near Stroud in Gloucester which opens the Randwick Wap fair. After the church service on the previous Sunday, three cheeses garlanded with flowers are blessed. The first is eaten, while the other two are rolled down a slope to open the fair. Other events of the day are mayor ducking, morris dancing and the sale of local crafts (information on 04536 3942).

The Gloucestershire area is a rich source of traditional events in May. At the end of the month is the annual medieval festival of woolsack racing at Gumstool Hill, Tetbury, at 14.30. Teams of four aim to relay a 65-pound woolsack up and down the hill from the town centre in the quickest time. The course is happily set between two pubs, the Crown and the Royal Oak, and the custom is said to date from the sixteenth century (details from the Heart of England Tourist Office – see page 264).

Another old custom (dating from 1612) is an ancient olympic games called Robert Dover's Cotswold Olimpick Games held at Dover's Hill, Weston sub Edge near Chipping Campden. They were already known as Olympick by 1631 and were noted throughout England even then. Today a figure plays Robert Dover in period costume and supervises the athletics. A huge bonfire is lit at the end of the day and spectators march down the hill carrying burning torches to continue the day with dancing in the market square. *Annalia Dubrensia*, a collection of poems about the games, was published over 350 years ago. The

Scuttlebrook Wake, in the High Street at Chipping Campden, was the traditional finale to the games with the crowning of a queen, morris dancing and a procession around the town (information from the Hon. Secretary, 521 Ridge Road, Kingswinford, West Midlands DY6 9RE (tel. 021 476 1181, daytime number)).

In London, Samuel Pepys is remembered. Towards the end of May each year there is a commemorative service held at midday at St Olave's Church, Hart Street, London EC3. St Olave's was Pepys official church as senior administrator in the navy office. Pepys had a specially reserved pew and he is buried with his wife Elizabeth in the same vault here. At the service the Lord Mayor places a wreath in front of the vault; seventeenth-century music is played and the lesson given by a Pepys authority. The public are welcome to attend, but are warned to arrive early. Afterwards a buffet lunch and wine is available at a small charge but this should be booked a week or more ahead, by writing to the church.

The Mediterranean   Go to the Thessalonika area on 21–23 May for fire-walking performances dating from pagan times. Barefoot villagers at Agia Eleni near Thessalonika carry icons of Saint Constantine and Saint Helen and dance on live charcoal embers without burns. In Sicily a more comfortable spectacle is the festival of decorated donkey carts and costumes held in Taormina. Malta celebrates May with the Valletta carnival with brass bands, floats and dancing competitions in the Palace Square. Finland too has dancing in the streets on 1 May and in Whitsun week, the Ritvala Hellea festival, with processions and singing by costumed girls, takes place at Valkeakoski, Ritvala. Information from Valkeakosten Matkailu Oy, Valtakatu 20, 37600 Valkeakoski (tel. 9 37 46997).

Belgium   There are deeply religious and slightly bizarre ways of welcoming high spring. At the end of May in Bruges events centre round the relic of Holy Blood said to be collected from the wounds of Christ by Joseph of Arimathia, which the Count of Flanders brought back from a crusade. The Count built the chapel of the Holy Blood near his Bruges residence and feudal lords and burghers made oaths of loyalty around the relic. It developed into the practice of offering the relic for the veneration of the people of the town, which in turn grew into a procession. This still survives and the procession now depicts principal scenes from the Bible, mimed, spoken, acted and sung, in a sequence of colourful tableaux, groups and floats. The second part of the procession recalls the entry into Bruges of the

Count and his mounted retinue with the holy relic accompanied by chanting of the choirs of the Count's church. The procession takes about 1½ hours to pass, starting around 15.00; afterwards the town is blessed and the relic returned to its church, where it can be contemplated during May and on every Friday during the year. Reserved and numbered seats on the grandstands and benches can be bought and booked from 1 February through travel agencies or at the Tourist Office, Markt 7, B–8000 Bruges (tel. 050/33 07 11). Belgian Railways give a 50 per cent reduction to travellers going to Bruges for this occasion (obtainable at any Belgian station).

Ecaussines, a central Belgian town, originally had a bachelors' tree-planting ceremony in May, during which single men planted a birch in front of the house of the girl they wished to marry. To show her gratitude the girl organised a party at which sweets and coffee were served followed by an open-air dance. The custom lapsed until 1903, when posters were put up announcing that the young ladies of the town would give a 'mammoth tea party' on Whit Monday. Hundreds of people accepted the invitation and so the Matrimonial Tea Party was launched and the open-air ball revived. Now the ceremonies begin in the morning with a visit to the town hall by the Lady President followed by a tour of the main sights including the quarries, the 'tower' of 'madness hall' in the middle of a park, a twelfth-century castle and the Church of St Aldegonde. In the afternoon there is a parade of marriage candidates with hundreds of bachelors, young and old, marching in pairs through the decorated streets. At the tea party each person has a cup bearing the coat of arms of the town with appropriately added mottos. The Lady President makes a light hearted speech extolling marriage and happy homes, then follows a battle of flowers, dancing, and romantic walks to the 'Bridge of Sighs'. In the evening the castle is floodlit and the ball takes place by the light of lanterns (details from the Belgian Tourist Office).

Perhaps the oddest event is the Cats' Feast at Ypres, held on the second Sunday of May. Its origins would definitely not have been approved by the RSPCA, not to mention cat lovers. The ten-century old tradition, once practised in many parts of Europe, was to throw cats, then associated with the devil, from the top of the 230-foot-high belfry of the cloth hall, a building much admired by Victor Hugo. The sacrifice of the cat (some of which, the records show, landed and walked off unharmed) was a way of asking for the fields to be fertile. The ceremony was revived in 1938 and again after the war in 1946 and is now a happy and harmless event with toy cats being thrown down to the crowd who scramble to collect them; some of the cats have ribbons tied round their necks for which prizes are awarded. Since 1955 the ceremony had added a festive pageant of music and dance in which 2,000 costumed actors enact the cult of the cat through the centuries, in literature, language and folklore. Even witches on their broomsticks celebrate the sabbath with their cats – and of course there's always Puss in Boots. Seats for the event can be obtained from the Tourist Information Office, Stadhuis, Grote Markt, B–8900 Ypres (tel. 057/20 26 26). For a set charge the Tourist Office can supply a complete day with stand ticket, programme, a visit to the museum with a professional guide and lunch.

Spain   Corpus Christi is celebrated in Toledo with a morning procession bearing the Arfe monstrance and presided over by the Spanish primate. The medieval ways of life of this hill city, about an hour's drive from Madrid, are represented by nobles in red robes, Mozardine knights in blue, knights of the Holy Sepulchre in white and the knights of Corpus Christi in green.

But the most important pilgrimage spot in May (Whit Week, like Easter, being moveable, it could also be early June) is Almonte in Huelva province, 94 miles from Seville. For this event, carts are decorated with flowers and wax figures and accompanied by hundreds of riders with girls seated behind them Seville-style, dressed in flounced Andalucian clothes. People come from Huelva, Cadiz and Seville to the Sanctuary of Nuestra Senora del Rocio to take part in ceremonies such as the night rosary in which people come across the marshes with lighted candles and the Virgin figure is carried in procession on the shoulders of young men. Rocio style 'Sevillanas' and 'Seguidillas' are danced and sung continuously by the crowds. It is wise to book accommodation well ahead as the Spanish flock to this event. There are hotels in Seville, Cadiz or the parador Mazagon Cristobal Colon. The nearest accommodation is 15km from Rocio at Matalascanas.

More of Spain's horses can be seen at the Horse Fair at the beginning of the month held at Jerez de la Frontera, the home of sherry where one of the sherry family scions has established an indoor Arab riding school worth seeing at any time. The Horse Fair began in 1284 as a livestock and market fair and there is still a livestock exhibition with agricultural machinery on show. In the Gonzalez Hontoria park there are bullfights and songs and dances. Finally there is the Horse Fair itself with exhibition riding and competitions. Book hotels well ahead, as accommodation is limited; it's almost better to stay in the Marbella area and drive across through the little Moorish hilltop villages, above plains where bulls are bred. The spring Horse Fair is better than the autumn sherry wine festival (around 24 September), which has now become much more of a trade event and lacks the open celebrations and festival flamenco feel of the spring show.

Portugal   In the North of Portugal, at Barcelos, is the Festival of the Crosses, with dancing and firework displays. Barcelos is the place which gave Portugal its national symbol, the cockerel, said to have originated when a pilgrim on the way to Santiago de Compostela in Spain was accused of theft. He pointed to a cockerel the judge was about to eat and said it would stand up and crow – which it did. Barcelos is a place to visit any Thursday for the huge old-style craft market in the central square, where the brown and yellow flecked earthenware pottery of the area and the garishly decorated cockerel figures are worth considering. An exhibition and sale of crafts is housed in a nearby old tower. Around the tree-lined market place are little restaurants where one can eat local dishes cheaply and well, and drink the vinho verdes, young fresh wines of the area.

Food

Britain and the Channel Islands   The further off from England, the nearer is to France, said the Walrus to the Carpenter in the rhyme. The Channel Islands are a 'peculiar' of the British Crown. They were personally owned by the Duke of Normandy when he conquered England in 1066. Today they come under the Queen but not under the British Parliament at Westminster. They have their own tax laws, no VAT, and enjoy the lure of duty-free shopping. Being close to the French coast, the French love of food blends with English ideas and the public market. The Victorian Beresford Street market in St Helier on Jersey, is a May delight of new potatoes (Jersey Royals) – along with Cornwall and the Scilly Isles, Jersey is an early season producer. There are early tomatoes, cucumbers, cauliflowers, fresh lettuces, conger eels for soup, ormer (a local mollusc) for stews. The meat is marbled with fat as deep gold as the cream that comes thick from the Disney-eyed Jersey cows, which are the only breed allowed on the island; their cream is packed as souvenirs to take or send home. Fish and sea food also abound – sea bass, mullet, bream, plaice, lobster, crab, scallops, mussels, oysters and prawns. The old Second World War bunkers around the coast are now used as viviers for the lobsters. Little cafes and wine bars around the market serve at any time of day; in the market is a French bakery where one can also get old fashioned loaves baked in cabbage leaves and stalls sell yoghurt and ice cream made with the rich Jersey milk and cream.

In mid May, for a week, Jersey celebrates its love of food and abundance of good restaurants. The Jersey Food Festival, 25 years old and now with more public involvement, has competitions among the various grades of restaurants and pubs with menus judged by a team of visiting top French and British food experts. Visitors, residents and judges take part in the enjoyment of the special menus and tastings organised. The range is wide, from 'cuisine bourgeoise', brunch, tandoori . . . In addition during the week, there are special events. Typical festival offerings are free wine-tasting in Royal Square in the centre of St Helier with all-day Continental cuisine featured on fair stalls or a French creperie, charcuterie; fresh vegetable dips featured in the market, spaghetti-eating competitions and a special pub tour by the Mary Ann brewery. There's a vineyard tour to Jersey's only commercial vineyard, La Mare in St Mary, *fruits de mer* tasting in the fish market in St Helier, talks and films on wine at the Hotel L'Horizon, even a new potato Beaujolais Nouveau style race from Jersey to London's Covent Garden and back. In the last two days of the festival, the Salon Culinaire is held at the town hall for the presentation of prizes to island chefs each bringing his speciality dish to be judged; judgement includes helpful advice to restaurateurs to improve their table. Lists of award-winning restaurants are available from the Jersey Tourist Office, Weighbridge, St Helier (tel. 0534 78000).

Back in mainland Britain, on 27 May, Rogation Day is celebrated with the blessing of the nets and mackerel on the beach opposite the Old Ship Hotel, Brighton. There is a religious service at which the nets containing the mackerel are blessed, boats are brought up on to the beach and fishermen bring their catch ashore to be blessed (information from Tourist Office, Marlborough House, 54 Old Steine, East Sussex BN1 1EQ (tel. 0273 23755). In Ireland, at Bundoran, the lobster festival is held this month. Wild food: nettles, not the most lovable of plants, come into their culinary own this month in Britain and Ireland when they are young and tender and made into soup which is served in hotels and restaurants in certain areas.

Italy   The 800-year-old market by the Rialto bridge in Venice is the place to go to buy the first thin white asparagus of the year.

Various cures of Parma ham are also sold from several stalls. About an hour away from Venice is Bassano, the centre for the thick white asparagus and Bassano is also the place to buy grappa liqueur (marc).

Holland   May is the start of the herring season when green herrings are eaten raw. The Vlaggetkesdag festival marks the start of the herring fishing season from the main ports and the favourite place to celebrate is Scheveningen where the fishing boats are decked with bunting, there is a parade along the seafront with fish wives in traditional costume and the sand dunes around are full of people. In the Hague the trams and buses carry flags. The first fishing boat skipper back within 24 hours with his catch becomes a national hero and presents the first herring to the Queen. Gutted and boned herrings are then sold in the streets with just the head removed, and a bowl of onion on the stall to dip the herring in. It is then held by the tail and swallowed in one gulp, helped down by a shot of new gin.

France   In Cannes' charming covered market, to which farmers from the hills around bring their fresh produce, asparagus, wild strawberries and pungent Provencal herbs are good buys.

Germany   In Munich a garlanded maypole is set up for summer in the city's traditional food market, the open air Victualienmarkt. The maypole stands above the beer garden tables in the centre for drinking and snacking amid stalls selling herbs, sausages, cheeses, biscuits, meats, breads, vegetables and fruit. In season look out for the radi – huge white radish from which local chefs compete to form into the longest continuous curl.

Wine

Spain   In Cadiz province in the last week of May at Sanlucar de Barrameda, where they claim sherry originated, is the Manzanilla fair. Also in May (the very beginning) is what is considered the most important wine festival of the season, held in Ribadavia in Orense province and dedicated to the Ribeiro wines.

England   A festival of English wines is held at Leeds Castle in Kent over the three days of the spring bank holiday at which over 100 different wines from 22 vineyards are tasted at the four-year-old festival, mounted in enormous all-weather marquees in the grounds of the moated castle. The wines are displayed, and visitors get a sampling cup and free guide. Tasting samples are sold for a few pence and bottled wines are also on sale. Wineries taking part range from the well-established Lamberhurst in Kent down to the quarter-acre Conghurst vineyard in Hawkhurst in Kent and the oddly named Breaky Bottom in Lewes, Sussex. Open from 11.00 am to 5.00 pm each day, details from Leeds Castle Enterprises Ltd, Maidstone, Kent ME17 1PL (tel. 0622 65400).

Arts

France   Throughout the country many local arts and musical festivals are held. Among the May events are jazz under the apple trees at the end of the month at Coutances in Normandy (Office of Tourism, 50200 Coutances (tel. 33 45 17 19); 'Musical May' in Bordeaux Grand Theatre de Bordeaux, Place de la Comedie, 33074 Bordeaux (tel. 56 48 58 54) and 'Musical Spring' in Poitiers (Hall d'acceuil, Hotel de Ville, 86000 Poitiers (tel. 49 88 82 07). In Cannes the Film Festival runs for a week – the paraparazzis' open season and a chance for the movie fan to stand and stare at the stars and starlets. Everyone competes for publicity: in the past a starlet has stripped to reveal the name of her new film printed on her backside; British film promoters have hired camels or warships to boost wartime epics. About 600 films are shown, but for the visitor the real show is on the terrace of the Carlton Hotel. Best 'getting there' advice is to stay out of Cannes along the coast or up in the peaceful hills in the Val de Loup area and descend when one wishes upon Cannes. Wear flat shoes and jostling gear and park well away from the Croisette.

Denmark   Copenhagen has a ballet and opera festival producing twelve different shows, four different operas and seven ballets, plus a gala ballet evening. The programme at the Royal Theatre is international and includes the presentation (first made in 1988) of the Hans Christian Andersen ballet award for the world's best ballet achievement. For overseas visitors, tickets can be reserved in advance of the 7-day ordinary booking period and paid for by cheque or credit card and then collected up to an hour before the performance (unclaimed and unsold tickets are then sold at the entrance after this). Details from the Royal Theatre Box Office, Post Box 2185, Dk–1017 Copenhagen K (tel. 01 14 17 65, old stage; tel. 01 14 32 85 for new stage bookings).

Austria   Vienna has a spring music festival running from the end of May into June with opera and operetta. Details Wiener Festwochen, Lehargasse 11, A–1060 Wien (tel. 56 16 76).

Norway   At the end of the month, Bergen has its festival of theatre, opera, jazz, classical and modern music, ballet and folk dance, with Norwegian and international performers. Details from Bergen International Festival, Post Box 183, 5001, Bergen (tel. 05 32 04 00).

Glyndebourne picnic scene, Sussex

Britain   Here there is a surge of arts festivals around the country. Where else but in a country noted for its eccentricity would Glyndebourne open at the end of May, marked by the sight of couples and groups in full evening dress in mid afternoon at Victoria station lugging rugs, picnic hampers and equipment as they set off to Lewes station in Sussex and thence to this Sussex garden with its opera house to listen and, although there is a restaurant, to picnic between acts in the garden come rain or shine – though the Glyndebourne administration insists the area has little rain as it is protected by the Downs.

Those in the know stake out picnic sites before the performance begins at 17.30, which allows time for a 90-minute dinner break at which the picnickers, watched by sheep across the fields, outdo each other with clothes and cuisine, candles and chairs; even staff are brought by the non British Rail travellers. Before the third act there is time for another drink. There is a large Glyndebourne Festival Society (with a waiting list) whose membership gets priority on seats. These have to book by the end of January so returns are possible. Make early applications by post to Box Office Manager, Glyndebourne, Near Lewes, Sussex or call for information (tel. 0273 812321).

Bath is another beautiful venue for music and its international 17-day festival, offering around 90 events, is held at the end of May and beginning of June. Now nearly 40 years old, the festival has 1,000 performers, 70 concerts and 20 major exhibitions in its international programme. Around the city, the festival expands to cover dance, recitals, children's shows, puppets and jazz. Events are also hosted at Bristol. As well as music, including lunch-time concerts lasting just under the hour with unreserved seating, 30 galleries from all over Britain exhibit and sell art works. A Festival Club is run in the Four Seasons and Terrace Restaurant of the Old Pump Room, where morning coffee and Bath buns are still served to a palm court orchestra backing. The Terrace has superb views over the Roman baths and during festival time has a buffet lunch, and supper from 1800 with a special festival menu. Free jazz in the Four Seasons restaurant is played in the evenings and the club is open to all. Bookings and information from Bath Festival Box Office, Linley House, 1 Pierrepont Place, Bath BA1 1JY (tel. 0225 63362/66411).

Brighton: after six years this is now Britain's largest and most comprehensive mixed arts festival. About 100,000 people attend and over 1,000 take part in the town play project. Music, dance, opera, exhibitions and recitals are given and venues can include the Glyndebourne opera house and the Royal Pavilion music room. Street fairs, neighbourhood festivals, parades, fireworks children's events/workshops involve the community during the three weeks of the festival. Brighton Festival, 111 Church Street, Brighton, Sussex BN1 1UD (tel. 0273 676926/29801).

Exeter: held at the end of May/beginning of June, the festival mixes top professional performances and local and community based activities. The main setting is the cathedral for concerts; the Northcott Theatre in the university campus for drama and musicals; and the city's own arts theatre and churches for other events. Exeter Festival Office, Room 2.1, Civic Centre, Exeter, Devon EX1 1JN (tel. 0392 265200).

Sheffield: holds a chamber music festival in its modern Crucible studio theatre in May. It was established in 1984 by Peter Cropper of the Lindsay String Quartet and the quartet each year presents music by composers such as Beethoven, Schubert, Mozart and Haydn in an informal setting, wih musicians wearing sweatshirts and festival badges and introducing and playing fragments to convey little-known music to audiences. Sheffield Chamber Music Festival, 65 Rawcliffe Lane, York YO3 6SJ (tel. 0904 645738).

Wales: in mid May there is the Llangollen International Jazz Festival with three days of open air and indoor concerts. Details: Llangollen International Jazz Festival office, 366 Castle Street, Llangollen, Clwyd. In Llandudno in mid May the Annual Male Voice Celebrity Concert is held with international soloists performing at concerts held on the Saturday and Sunday nights at the Arcadia Theatre, Promenade Llandudno, Gwynedd. At the beginning of the month, Llandudno also goes Victorian; the period setting is already there. For the Victorian festival the streets are closed to traffic and thronged instead with theatre groups, fairground organs, buskers, carriage rides and attractions and individuals parading in Victorian costumes. Tourist Office, Chapel Street, Llandudno, Gwynedd LL30 2SY (tel. 0492 768413, ext. 264).

Sport

Cars: the Grands Prix are held in Monaco and in Belgium during the month; also at the very end of the month the 24-hour motor race is run at Le Mans in France organised by the Automobile Club de l'Ouest founded in 1905 which then set up a Grand Prix meeting for the French automobile club. Le Mans was the most easterly point on a 63½-mile course, twelve laps over two days. Le Mans was used by Wilbur and Orville Wright as a base for flight experiments and in 1908 from an airfield now in the centre of the Le Mans circuit, Wilbur Wright made his first flight in Europe, in which he was airborne for 1 minute 45 seconds. In 1922 a race based on endurance rather than speed was developed. The 1923 rule book has four pages; now it has over 40. Originally cars had to conform to makers' catalogue descriptions and the driver had to carry out all repairs himself during the race. After 1931 the overall lap distance was reduced to 8,383 metres, roughly what it is now; the lap record is 148.612 mph, established in 1985. The attraction of Le Mans rests partly on its slightly amateur feel, dating back to the days when racing was an adventurous hobby, and there is still a place for the lone hero to triumph with the entries divided into classes for different performance levels. The size of the event is compelling too; just as the marathon attracts even the most unathletic, so the endurance test of Le Mans makes for drama and attention. Each car has a two-man team. The eight-mile loop includes stretches of ordinary roadway and the race is as much a social event as a sporting one, watched by around 150,000 people.

The Historic Commercial Vehicle Run from London to Brighton has been held since 1962 on the first Sunday in May. The historic vehicles are all commercial – such as fire engines, delivery vans and military vehicles – and are not to be confused with the RAC Veteran Car Rally (see page 235). The vehicles leave Battersea Park at intervals from 06.30 and go along the A23 to Madeira Drive in Brighton. On the preceding Saturday entries are on display in the park as part of the Wheels of Yesterday rally; three days of vehicle parades, model steam railways and steam funfair, punch and judy shows and so on. Entry is free and visitors are welcome.

Horses: horse races and events this month include the Royal Windsor horse show, Hickstead show jumping, and Windsor horse trials and cross country in Windsor Great Park near London. In France there is the Longchamps 2,000 guineas race and the 1,000 guineas race. Staying in Paris, visitors can book a day out to the races here through Paris Travel Service, Bridge House, Ware, Herts SG12 9DF (tel. 0920 3922), which includes coach travel from the Paris Travel Service office in central Paris, entrance to the grandstands, lunch hamper and unlimited champagne at the course.

The polo season starts in Britain in the first week of May and runs until mid September. It is a place for 'royal-spotting' and all polo clubs have public admission. Membership of the three main clubs brings free entrance for the season for the member, his car and guests. The most popular club is the Guards Polo Club who play at Smith's Lawn, Windsor Great Park, information from Guards Polo Club, Englefield Green, Egham, Surrey (tel. 0784 34212). Other important clubs are the Cirencester Park Polo Club, Cirencester Park, Gloucester (tel. 0285 3225) and the Cowdray Park Polo Club, Cowdray Park, Midhurst, Sussex (tel. 0730 813257). The international day at Windsor draws a crowd of 24,000.

On two feet: The French open tennis championships run from May into June and are held in the Roland Garrof stadium in Paris for two weeks.

Britain: Milk Race. The 30-year-old road circuit cycle race

in England and Wales starts at the end of May and covers 1,150 miles over 13 days. Around 16 teams, 5 of which are professional, provide a field of nearly 100 riders; winning one of the 12 daily stages is worth around £1,000. Hills and mountains on all but one of the racing days make it no easy ride and 36 climbs count towards the Mountain Grand Prix. Where the route goes through towns and cities, the local communities are often involved with school projects and entertainment linked with the race. In 1988, Warwick Castle hosted the start of the final day with a knight on horseback to signal the final charge towards Birmingham where the race tied in with the Lord Mayor's parade. Details Milk Race, PO Box 119A, Thames Ditton, Surrey KT7 0EL (tel. 01–398 4101).

Shopping

Over the three bank holidays at the beginning of the month there is the Bank Holiday Country Craft Fayre held at Leeds Castle in Kent. Here over 100 craftsmen and women from all over the country show off their talents and sell their wares. Practical demonstrations are also given against a backdrop of maypole dancing, morris dancing and folk music. The crafts on show are as diverse as egg decorating, lace making, glove puppets, teddy bear making, silver smiths, and the Roses and Castles canal narrow boat art.

Horticultural

Britain A passion for plants can be indulged this month especially at London's Chelsea Flower Show, held in the third week of May in a marquee in the grounds of the Royal Hospital, Chelsea. It has been held since 1913 and is run by the Royal Horticultural Society. New flowers are introduced and trees, shrubs, planted gardens, books and equipment are displayed by over 360 exhibitors plus those from overseas in the 27-acre site, in the largest show of its kind in the world. There are specialists on hand to advise on problems as well as a scientific section and the 3½-acre marquee enables plants from all seasons to be shown, many of which are sold to the public on the last day. The royals attend the opening day and there is a RHS members' private view on the first two days, started in 1988 to try to ease the crush around the plants. Entrance is by ticket on sale in advance to a limited number and there are now only two public days. RHS members get two tickets each if they wish, and from

March onwards the rest are sold to the public. It is best to go early – about 0800 – or late – after 1600 – to avoid the worst of the crowds. No dogs or children under five are allowed. Details from Royal Horticultural Society, Vincent Square, London SW1P 2PE (tel. 01–834 4333).

May is a time to tour the apple orchards in Hereford, see the Spalding flower parade, the daffodil show in Banff, Scotland. Enjoy National Wild Flower Week with information, walks, workshops and other events organised by the Royal Society for Nature Conservation, 22 The Green, Nettlesham, Lincoln LN2 2NR. At Newborough School, Burton on Trent, Staffordshire and Endon in Staffordshire near Leek, wells are dressed with flowers and blessed after a procession to the wells led by clergy, choir, bands and the public. Maypole dancing and other events take place all day, in a ceremony dating from the plague days when it began as a thanksgiving for being spared. Details from Heart of England Tourist Board, PO Box 15, Worcester WR1 2JT (tel. 0905 29512).

Greece   Now is the time to head out to Greece to see the wild flowers, though if you miss this month, southern Greece is still lovely for flowers in June; Northern Greece is good in July.

Greece has more than 6,000 different species of wild flowers, in proportion to her size more than any other country in Europe. (France, for example, five times the size of Greece claims 3,400 species and Britain, twice the size of Greece, 2,500.) It is believed there are still many wild flowers undiscovered in Greece and in the past 30 years nearly 1,000 species of flowering plants have been found for the first time. The best chances a naturalist has of making new finds are in little explored areas like the Boz-Dagh mountains in Eastern Macedonia and the Vourinon mountains in Western Macedonia. In Crete, Mount Choreftres in the White Mountains has been little studied by botanists nor has Mount Simaitsikon in Western Macedonia. The rarest flowers are found in the higher mountains on cliffs and rocks inaccessible to grazing animals. Crete is especially rich in plants not found elsewhere and here violets and carnations grow as small shrubs with wooden stems. Greece is also rich in pharmaceutical plants. A special plant to seek out is Jankala Heldreichi, found only on Mount Olympus from 3,000 to 5,000 feet up, now fairly rare, with a silvery rosette of leaves from which grows a stem of flowers from pink to deep lilac in colour. Greece also has about 80 orchid species and 10 tulip species.

Holland   Cherry, apple, pear and plum orchards are in full bloom till about the middle of this month. The best areas to see the blossom are De Betuwe in Gelderland province, the south of Limburg and South Beveland in the province of Zeeland. In the river area of Gelderland four blossom routes have been set out, marked out with a fruit symbol. The 140 km apple route is the longest, and about half the route leads over the dykes of the Rhine and Waal rivers. The 125 km cherry route follows the rive de Linge, while the 100 km pear route leads through the Land of Maas and Waal. The strawberry route is through the Bommelerwaard and is 65 km long. In the Zeeland area of Zuid-Beveland one can map a route of 100 km through the area but the local tourist offices also sell a comprehensive brochure naming the sights along the way (in Dutch only). South Limburg is hilly country and the tourist office issues a booklet detailing various orchard routes, varying in length from 35 to 100 kms. Again only in Dutch, the booklet is on sale in the flower season.

In the second half of May, the rape seed fields are in bloom creating swathes of yellow in the North of Groningen, Friesland, the north-east Polder and south and east Flevoland. A route has been planned for drivers starting at Grijpskerk where short route descriptions in English are available from tourist offices during May. The 100 km route is changed slightly each year and follows quiet country roads where possible and includes sights such as a corn flour mill and a fourteenth-century castle which can be visited. In Flevoland the rape fields form an annual attraction with some 5,000 hectares planted and has a signed route in May (all month) with free leaflets in English.

From the beginning of May till the middle of June the blossoming Japanese garden can be visited at the Clingrndael park in the Hague and from the 1 May the Helloo botanical garden has an exhibition of flowering historical plants (bulbs); the Keukenhof displays flowering lillies at Lisse.

Exhibitions

The Royal Academy summer exhibition of paintings opens at the end of May. At London's Olympia there is a fine art and antiques fair with all items for sale.

Public Holidays

1 May, Labour Day, most European countries except Switzerland, Netherlands. Uk holds this on the Monday nearest to 1 May.

Whit Monday celebrated as a holiday by Belgium, Denmark, France, Germany, Luxembourg, Netherlands, Norway, Spain, Sweden and Switzerland.

Ascension Day, Belgium, Denmark, Finland, France, Germany, Netherlands, Norway, Spain, Sweden, Switzerland.

8 May, France, Victory Day 1945.

5 May, Netherlands, Liberation Day.

17 May, Norway, National Day.

Last Monday of month, late May bank holiday in UK.

JUNE

THE SEASON FOR
THE SEASONED

J UNE is bursting out all over, in the words of the song. With the trees and flowers in full bloom, humans put on their finest finery and head out to the social events of the 'season', which this month are decidedly outdoor in spite of the possible chill or wet weather in northern Europe. The days grow longer up to 21 June, the summer solstice and longest day, and an endless summer seems to lie ahead.

The English 'Season'

According to actor Cyril Fletcher, London taxi drivers say the 'season' begins after the Chelsea Flower Show (see page 98). Though the word 'season' once implied exclusivity and the freedom to indulge in social events, the events persist today and those with a special interest take time off and make sure they get tickets.

The season originally stretched from Derby Day to the Glorious Twelfth (12 August) and grouse shooting. In the nineteenth century, during this period marriageable noble girls were presented at court, then chaperoned round balls, concerts and dinners in search of a suitable husband; a girl was considered a failure if she was not engaged or married in her first season. The American heiresses rocked the boat when British nobles got them into events for money and through the world wars, the fossilised formality continued till the mid 1950s when the Queen stopped the presentations. Then Queen Charlotte's Ball was invented in which the 'debs' curtseyed to a cake instead of the Crown to keep up the illusion of society's season.

Everyone beams on tradition and now the season is supported and in many cases kept alive by commercial firms who sponsor sports and spectators with lavish entertaining and the opening up of events to everyone even if barriers are put up for royals and members of organising societies so they have an exclusive bolt hole club at each event. Several companies specialise in providing the hospitality, offering tickets, transport, and food and drink at packaged prices. One of the largest organisations setting up packages for the season's events is Keith Prowse, Banda House, Cambridge Grove, London W6 OLE (01–741–7441).

Apart from private occasions like the Fourth of June celebrations at Eton, held to celebrate the birthday of George III, and the May Balls (held in June) at term end at the Oxford and Cambridge colleges, most events are sporting in nature. An exception is the Royal Academy summer exhibition at the academy's headquarters in Piccadilly (see also page 100). This has adopted a rather less traditional approach in recent years. It's a place to buy paintings, some at modest prices. Before the exhibition opens, 1,200 paintings are selected from about 15,000 sent in annually. In Edwardian times the RA gave its selectors beef tea to sustain them in their efforts, now it's Bovril. The private view now runs to three days and is not necessarily simply a fashionable gathering. Apart from Friends of the Academy (£22.50 a year, country £15) one pays at the door for a ticket from around 6 June running to the third week of August.

Viewing rather than doing is also the scene at test cricket at Lords, the Badminton horse trials, the Derby, Royal Ascot, Henley and Wimbledon, the English June season. Covering it all demands not only stamina but stoicism. The British after all take their pleasures damply. Cricket and croquet (more about the latter in the July chapter) are their inventions for often sodden summer days. They pack a lot into June, supposedly a drier month than July or August. Admission to Lords' cricket matches for non-members is from about £10 a ticket for a unique glimpse of England, in a game taking days to complete watched from hard, unforgiving benches.

Horse racing is still the sport of kings in Britain – or Queens – with the Queen and Queen Mother leading owners and spectators. In June the two great races are the Derby, held at the beginning of the month at Epsom Downs just south of London, and Royal Ascot near Windsor, which the royal family open by driving down the course in open carriages, Canute-like defying the rain to ruin their elegant racing silks.

Epsom's Derby Day, run since 1780, is more of a cockney fun event and includes a funfair. Open-topped double decker buses are at a premium, the bottom deck handy as a buffet bar, the top providing a mobile grandstand view of the racing. Companies and corporations increasingly hire them to entertain clients for the day. The catering heads of British Airways complain they cannot get enough salmon and strawberries to serve in their economy class flights until after Derby Day, when every caterer in London is preparing the traditional cold salmon and strawberry fare for the race. Derby Day is the race when the crowds, from millionaires to miners and in particular the bookies, are fun to watch. No fancy fashion but comfortable clothes and the windmill arms of the bookies as a cabaret. The race is usually open and a real gamblers' occasion. The Derby was the first race I attended. I eyed the field bouncing round the ring in high spirits; only one horse stood still, head lowered, pondering. This was Parthia, the oldest horse in the race. I reckoned she knew a thing or two and was sensibly conserving her energy. She did and was and came in first after coming from behind to the mighty roar of the crowd. I celebrated winning the equivalent of my then week's wages with the Queen's police guard who had also backed the horse. My first race, my first winner. I never looked back, and vowed never to chance my luck or my money again. But win or lose, the Derby is a wonderful day out. Get your fortune told in one of the neatly arranged caravans, though you won't be told the winners. A tour of the fairground, time just for a picnic on the Epsom Downs; the pearly kings and queens are there and, of course, somewhere in this huge mob, are the horses. Getting there and back is not fun; the traffic jams are horrendous unless you can afford a helicopter from Battersea, Cobham and Elstree (about £100 return including champagne and rail connections from London). But rail services take only 16 minutes from central London to Epsom Town, Tattenham Corner and Epsom Downs stations, all within a mile of the course. Special race day bus services also run. Tickets can be obtained from 1 January on from the Secretary, Racecourse Paddock, Epsom, Surrey (03727–26311).

In mid June for four days, Royal Ascot attracts top horses, owners and prize money but the four legged fillies take second place to the finery displayed by the two legged variety. It is a mad hatter's tea party, with men in grey morning coats and grey toppers and the women in the frilliest, silliest, silkiest outfits and hats they can get away with, given it will probably rain as high heels sink steadily deeper into the Berkshire ground. The women aim to attract photo coverage in the media and many go for outrageous hats to do just that. For years, Mrs Gertrude Shilling led the headway with amazing creations by her son David, who is now a leading milliner creating styles for half the race course in more discreet but very glossy toppings (see p. 125).

The most exclusive place to enter perhaps in the whole of the London season is the Royal Enclosure at Ascot, strictly ruled by etiquette and dress codes – no trousers for women. In the past if you had been involved in a divorce case you were relegated to the Iron Stand overlooking the bookies. Now there is a new grandstand with elegant boxes.

Dramatic dressing up is a way of saying 'I'm here' and being locatable in the dense, non-moving 200,000 strong crowds over the four days. It is not a place to take the racing too seriously unless you are an owner eager to receive the Gold Cup for a 2½-mile stamina race. But it is a place to people watch and picnic in the car park around the elegant cars. With the crowd pressure, organisers suggest first timers come on the Friday. Thursday (Gold Cup Day), however, is the famous Ladies Day when all the fashions are out, OTT or not. The true horse fancier is dismayed at the fashion parade, but the sartorial excesses are nothing new. A report of the 1829 Ascot meeting noted 'Lords with white trousers and black whiskers; ladies with small faces, but very large hats.' And, of course, the lovely black and white Ascot scene in *My Fair Lady* did no harm to the popularity of this race event. This sombre shading was perhaps inspired by the 'black Ascots' held after the death of Queen Victoria and then of Edward VII. Well dressed or not, you do not get in without a tie, but these are on sale at the gate with 50 per cent of the money going to the Jockeys' Fund.

Even the grass is well groomed at Ascot. It is cut, trimmed, brushed and fed by the course's own full-time staff of fifty people. Though one hears less about it, racing takes place here every month except March and August. The staff numbers rise to 480 for the Royal Week with 120 car park attendants and with the catering organisations (leading ones have recently noted trends towards pink in food and settings and of course in the champagne, similar to Wimbledon and more brunch style food) there are around 6,000 workers on the course. They reckon Royal Ascot is the biggest outside catering event in Britain. The horses, 400 of them a day, get fed in the 150 course stables.

The course was founded by Queen Anne in 1711 and the present Queen is personally involved, being consulted before changes and improvements take place. She leads the royal carriage parade along the course at the beginning of racing each day of the meeting, starting at 1400; the first race starts at 1430.

Ascot is handy for the Queen staying at Windsor, but for others there are frustration-beating trains from Waterloo, Guildford or Reading to Ascot. At Ascot the station is about a ten-mintue walk from the course. By car, get a reserved car parking ticket in advance and fill the boot with comforts for the day. Anyone can be admitted to the grandstand, Silver Ring, and Heath for a ticket price. The Heath is the cheapest area. The Royal Enclosure is quite another pearly gate to storm. Early in the year, one must write to the Ascot Office, St James's Palace, London SW1A 1BP, fill out a form which must be signed by a sponsor who has been allowed into the Royal Enclosure on at least four previous occasions. If you get permission, the cost is around £50 (compared with about £1 to go on the Heath). For other course areas, tickets and information are from the Secretary, Grandstand, Ascot, Berkshire (0990–22211).

Henley Royal Regatta nudges into July and overlaps with Wimbledon's second week. Wimbledon, where the crowds go for the tennis and a chance to see their idols in action, is covered in the sports section of this month's chapter. Henley is another social occasion when champagne, catering and chatting take priority over the rowing. I recall the dazed expression on an American boat crew when they defeated a popular British boat yet were received with deafening cheers. What they did not know was that it had just been announced on the radios and portable TVs to which many of the regatta crowd were glued that Virginia Wade had won the Wimbledon singles title.

But Henley, whether you know a scull from a skiff, is a lovely summer's day out on the river. Strangely the weather is usually sunny (as is the second week of Wimbledon compared to the first, when it usually pours down and there are often thunderstorms). The atmosphere of Henley has a timeless comforting Edwardian atmosphere, reminiscent of nannies and old-fashioned puddings. As at other events, the car park picnic is a high spot with friends reserving the same spaces each year to meet up. Though the women dress up (trousers are frowned upon) in Ascot-style finery, and at least wear hats, straw boaters with ribbons the most favoured, it is the time of the peacocks. Men's blazers live up to their name in strident stripes, bright tickets dangling from the lapel. The obligatory tie is flamboyant too and the whole ensemble is topped by a straw boater or a panama. It is a crowd of all ages; older men reminiscing over the rowing victories of a distant youth; the young showing off along the sparkling wide expanse of the Thames.

One arrives in good time to avoid queues in the loo at the club house and to allow a drink before lunch. This is the event where Pimms (with their own tent) really come into their own. Then one meets up with friends for pre-booked lunches at various spots. Or the day can be spent messing about in boats. One can hire a rowing boat for the best views of the races. The Berkshire Station on the opposite bank is now tented too, with a whole village of eateries for corporate entertaining, a ferry to the stewards enclosure and TVs in the marquees on which to watch Wimbledon.

After lunch many sit on over coffee and champagne or more Pimms. Others stroll the river bank greeting friends, watching a race or two, taking tea. It is unhurried, unforced and, away from the oars, gently uncompetitive. A modest payment gains one entrance to the Regatta Enclosure. Members only are admitted to the Stewards Enclosure and only they can purchase guest badges. Henley is in Oxfordshire, 36 miles from London by car on the M4 and A423; slow at the end of the journey. From Paddington there are trains to Henley, or coaches from Victoria. Car park tickets can be ordered in advance from Regatta Office or bought on the day. The Wednesday is the cheapest rising on Friday and at weekends. Tickets and information from The

Secretary, Regatta Head Quarters, Henley on Thames, Oxford-shire RG9 2LY (0491 572153).

For all the seasonal events described above, one can put an advertisement for tickets in *The Times* or be a very good customer of a large company with their own entertainment marquee. After all, underlying the whole English 'season' is still snobbery, the lure of being somewhere privileged.

The Place to Be

Apart from London one can make the most of the 24 hours of daylight this month and go north to Scandinavia and Iceland. June is the best month for the latter though I have been there in June and sunbathed in the morning and snowballed in the afternoon. In Scandinavia the midnight sun gives longer days for sport and sightseeing. The Swedes say midsummer eve (June 20) is the 'true climax of the year'. Maypoles or mid-summer poles are erected in city parks, on village greens and in private gardens. Maypole derives from a Swedish word maja, 'to make green', and leafy branches of birch are twined round the pole and two circlets of flowers hang from the cross bar. Games and dancing to fiddle and accordion accompaniment are part of the celebrations. The most traditional events take place in Dalarna province, at Naas manor house in Vastergotland, and at Gammelgarden Bengtsfors, Dalslan, at Hogbobruk Sandviken in Gastrikland and Fatmomakk in Lapland. At midsummer the Lapps hold a festival and market fair, the Ankaredemassan at Ankarede in Jamtland.

In Norway the midnight sun curves tantalisingly along the horizon north of the Arctic Circle at Bodo. One can fish at midnight in the fjords, take photos of the catch and then grill it over a fire, eating it with melted butter and flotbrod, thin crispbreads and beer and aquavit. The whole of Scandinavia parties on midsummer night. In Norway bonfires are lit and the parties continue with fireworks and in Sweden birch twigs decorate buses and even weapons in military camps; business-men go to the forests to drink fresh spring water to give them strength. Young girls put seven different flowers under their pillows to dream (if they get to bed at all that night) of their future husband.

Or go south for quiet, escapist uncrowded sun. South from Naples in Italy, 3½ hours down the autostrada del sol and on south into Calabria with 500 miles of little developed coastline separating the Ionian and Tyrenian seas. In the east are flat long strands; in the west the mountains tumble down to the sea.

These beaches and resorts become crowded in July and August, when the inhabitants of Naples and other Italian towns move in, but in June and again at the end of the season, Calabria remains the almost forgotten part of Italy. In the past its remote hill villages became refuges for persecuted groups of Europeans as well as a place of political exile for Italians. In the Albanese villages of Spezzano Albanese, San Demetrio Corona and Vaccanizzo Lungro one can still see remnants of the customs of Albania and occasional reminders that the area was once a Greek colony.

The publicity slogan 'four months extra sunshine' has been used by Calabria and swimming and sunning is possible in mid May at temperatures that compare with the Channel in August. The nearest accessible resort from Naples is Maratea, where hotels and pensions are scattered along spurs that branch seawards from high mountains. Aquafredda nearby is a massive humped cliff full of caves and coves where one can often go fishing with hotel proprietors for tuna, clams or swordfish. Along the coast at Scilla and Palmi they still shark fish in the way Homer described, harpooning from the high prow of the boat.

The Santa Venere hotel at Maratea is set on a hill, cool and cloistered below the brooding mountain of San Biaggio with its Rio style statue of Christ. The Santa Venere has plenty of flowers, arched cool terraces and extensive gardens with steep paths down to the beach.

Even near more developed areas one can find unspoilt sites like the hill top village of Cirella near Scalea. Cirella was destroyed first by Hannibal and later by Napoleon but its proudly defensive walls and crumbling houses provide an afternoon's clamber among wild flowers with a sea vista far below and the air scented by ginesta (broom).

One should venture into the interior curling up from Cosenza, a pasta and tomato-paste producing town. In nearby Luzzi the women wear traditional black and white costumes on special occasions, and Calabrian folklore is displayed at Palmi's museum. Giovanni in Fiore on this route is a village where they produce fine weaving, ceramics and terracotta figures. If you come across a hill funeral you may hear the 'repitu' chants accompanied by tearing of the hair and dramatic gestures, reminiscent of a Greek tragedy chorus. Camiglistello is north-east of Cosenza, a small ski resort in winter and in summer a cool base for exploring the Sila Grande forest and lake area of high central plateau rising to 6,000 feet.

Old Customs

Britain Military manoeuvres for public view are part of traditional June in London. Beating the Retreat, marking the retreat of sunlight not withdrawal in battle, is a short late-night performance held in the barracks of regiments in London; in June friends and families are often invited to witness this. Beating the Retreat by the Household Division, with display marching, drilling, mounted bands and trumpeters, pipes and drums is performed on Horseguards Parade, Whitehall, at the beginning of the month (sometimes in late May). Some performances are given in the evening by floodlight and tiers of seats for spectators are erected around Horseguards Parade. Tickets are available at the end of February from The Ticket Centre, 16 Bridge Street, London SW1 (01–839 6815/836–4114).

Trooping of the Colour is the Queen's official birthday parade in Whitehall before stands of spectators. The drums roll, the cymbals clash and pipes skirl and the skin prickles as the tall guardsmen stamp their feet till the bearskins shiver on their heads. The Queen herself no longer rides since her steady side-saddle trained mount Burma was retired, but she arrives to take the salute in a carriage leaving Buckingham Palace at 10.40 driving down the Mall and arriving for the 11.00 start of the Trooping. The Queen's official birthday is usually around the second Saturday in June and the ceremony dates from 1805 in its present form. Originally trooping the colour had the practical purpose of displaying the colour (flag) of the regiment, so that it would be familiar as a rallying point in battle. The Queen wears the uniform of the foot guards whose colour is being trooped. The occasion starts with a gun salute in Hyde Park, the Queen then inspects the parade and each regiment passes in front of her. At the end she returns to the Palace at 12.30 for the Royal Air Force fly past at 1300 and a Tower of London gun salute. Tickets are limited to two per application and rehearsal tickets on the two preceding Saturdays can also be applied for – this should be noted on the application before 1 March. Apply to the Brigade Major (Trooping of the colour), Headquarters Household Division, Horse Guards, Whitehall, London SW1A 2AX.

Belgium This month the sea inspires the Sea Nymphs pageant at Bredene. The pageant is broken up into three parts covering the world in which the Nereids, sea nymphs, live with fishes: sea gods, sculpted in traditional forms, usually backed by beautifully costumed groups swaying and dancing; the life of fishermen at sea, the dangers threatening them and the help they get from the nymphs; and finally the attractions of the sea

Rabelos boat race, Oporto

nymphs and portrayal of the various areas of Bredene's seaside resort. The pageant takes place on the last Saturday in June, usually at 1600. Information from Tourist Office, Bredene, Driftweg 6, 8401–Bredene, Belgium (050/32 09 98).

France The sea also inspires a festival on Whit Sunday held in Honfleur south of Le Havre when fishermen decorate their boats with brightly coloured paper flowers and flags and bring them into the harbour to be blessed by the local priest.

In the south of France, around Saint Martin de Londres, the sheep are sheared leaving three thick ridges along the back. These are later dyed in bright shades and then decorated with home-made woollen bobbles; bell-hung patterned collars are put round the animals' necks. This startling adornment cele-brates the sheeps' trek to summer pastures in the mountains past Cevennes. The decorations are steeped in superstition to ward off various evils. In June the large flocks are led through the streets by their shepherds and off to pastures new. The procession uses roads used for centuries. If a shepherd has died, the flock may be left undecorated as a mark of respect. The custom and indeed the raising of sheep is gradually dying out, but during the summer visitors to the area may come across the brightly woolled animals grazing in the hills.

Portugal Boats that never see the sea or fish are featured in races at Oporto in June, when the *rabelos* revive. The rabelo is a fragile looking boat with high bridge and huge square sail, guided by a vast rear oar. These once brought the port wine down river from the estates. The Douro River is a fierce gorge with white water rapids and rock strewn passages that are always dangerous to navigate. For the past six or so years, the races have been organised by the Confraria do Vinho do Porto from the sand bar at the mouth of the Douro (over which every barrel of port wine must still be shipped to earn its name) up to the cast iron bridge designed by Eiffel of Paris tower fame in the city centre. About a dozen preserved and restored rabelo boats owned by the port wine companies are crewed for the races by port company employees dressed in burgundy coloured capes and Henry the Navigator style hats. A recent winner was an unnamed boat owned by a local historical society and crewed by expert sailors. A good spot to watch the races is by the market stall area along the north river bank below the piled up old town and old river arches. In one of these arches quite near the bridge is a tiny restaurant, Bebelos, offering good local style food and at any time a charming spot to dine and look out across the river to the port wine houses with their rabelos moored below.

Linger in Lisbon on a late June night to hear the traditional fado songs sung on street corners of the steep stepped alley area of Alfama, once the Moorish quarter. The sky deepens to turquoise as the anguished wails tell of heartbreak and sadness. Fado is fate, and fate is Portugal, as the saying goes. The word 'saudade', sadness, is much used in the lyrics. Fado has none of the theatrical flamboyance of flamenco from neighbouring Spain, but it can become compulsive. Traditionally on these hot still June nights, the fadistas stand still under lamps on the corners of tiny squares with a black shawl over black clothes and sing plaintively. In earlier days, the songs were associated with prostitutes and Severa, an early populariser, became the mistress of the Marques de Marialua in the eighteenth century. Fado was once explained to me as similar in sentiment to 'my Bonnie Lies Over the Ocean', the Scottish song. It is a sailor's leaving home, the parting from loved ones. Fado is popular with Portuguese sailors and special programmes of fado requests are played on the radio. Top singers include Amalia Rodrigues, who started life as a market fruit seller, and Maria Teresa de Noronha, married to a count – fado covers both ends of society, much inspired by the Moors and blended with Portuguese sailors' songs. In June the fado moves outdoors during the Lisbon festival when there are also stalls in the streets selling freshly grilled sardines and the light petillant vinho verde that heralds summer in Portugal.

Luxembourg On Whitsun Tuesday at Echternach in Luxembourg, there is a dancing procession in honour of St Willibrord (an early English visitor). This is a medieval custom with participants dancing to a tune played over and over by the bands. The procession goes through the narrow cobblestone streets of the town before entering the Basilica with the shrine to the saint.

Cyprus The festival of Cataclysmos, the Flood, is marked with the blessing of the sea for the coming year. In towns on the coast such as Larnaca, a procession goes to the sea after Mass. A cross is thrown into the water and the waters blessed, to be followed by various competitive water sports, boat races, slippery-pole climbing and fairs and food stalls, all making the day more festive.

Spain Fire is the theme at San Pedro Manrique, 48 kms from Soria (where there is accommodation). On 23 June in the evening the local men take one another on their shoulders and walk barefoot across a bed of coals. The women, known as 'mondidas' for this festival, are dressed in white to represent, it is said, ancient priestesses. They process and make presentations to the priests.

On 21 June in Alicante bonfires are created which are more artistic monuments of woods, cardboard and fabric with figures satirising the bad habits of the people. Three days later on 24 June the bonfires are burnt in a ceremony known as the 'crema'. There are processions through the city; the Cabalgata del Foc, representing the cult of fire at different periods in time; the Coso Infantil, with costumed children; and the Coso, multi-coloured in costumes and including a flower battle, confetti-throwing and a parade of bands hired by different parts of the city. Regional folklore, a firework competition, bullfights and religious ceremonies, including a floral offering to the Virgin of the Remedio, complete the festivities.

Malta   On 29 June the feast of St Peter and St Paul is marked with a public holiday. The day is known as Mnarja, traditionally a harvest festival held at the Buskett Gardens, a wooded park near the town of Mdina. On the evening before 29 June there is an open air folk song and music competition in the gardens, with an all night picnic. On the morning of the 29th there is an agricultural show with horse and donkey races to Rabat. The name Mnarja means 'illuminations' because the Mdina battlements were once lit with bonfires on that day. During June and until September, Malta has what is called the Festi season as each town and village parish church celebrates the feast of its patron saint. There are church services, band marches and firework displays. The feast day is normally on a Sunday and marked by carrying a life-size statue of the saint along the village streets.

Food

June is the month of strawberries. They say the English mark the beginning of summer from the date when they can buy their own native-grown berries, mainly from the Hampshire area around Southampton. Before that, the approach of the world's summer can be charted in strawberries as they arrive from New Zealand, California, North Africa, Spain, Italy. Strawberries are served at the events of the 'season', particularly for pricey strawberry teas at Wimbledon. In Spain even as early as March, one can buy strawberries at Aranjuez just south of Madrid and eat them by the stalls and little restaurants or in the park by the old royal summer palace with its cooling river running through, a perfect place to nibble in June under fresh leaves of tall trees, many originally brought from England by Philip II.

In Italy there is a strawberry festival at Nervi. On June 28 at Samer, a town near Boulogne in France, there is a three-day strawberry festival that offers baskets of the fruit, concerts, evening dances and a traditional fair. Another berry, the gooseberry, appears in England at the beginning of the month, traditionally made into tarts or purées and tanged with elderflower sprigs drawn through it.

The marsh samphire (salicornia), emerges in June and July when the young shoots are eaten as salad or cooked with lamb especially lean and salty meat. It also goes well with oysters and poultry, and with salmon. Clams in a cream and butter sauce with samphire is another June delight. Later in the season it is served particularly in Norfolk hotels like asparagus. The real asparagus from the Vale of Evesham has its last cutting in England on 21 June.

Salmon is the June fish in Britain, and fish features in Continental menus too. In Scandinavia Gravadlax is salmon marinated under pressure in salt, brown sugar and dill till tender and served with a mustard dill sauce. From June until August Sweden has the Notdragning seine sweep, an old fishing method especially common in the north of the country. This is combined with rural festivals at which prepared dishes based on the catch are for sale. Seine sweepings are usually arranged on summer Sundays.

In the Algarve in southern Portugal, around June, the tuna is fished mainly off Vila Real de Santo Antonio near the Spanish border. The sea, as the huge fish are brought in, purples with their blood. In restaurants the Algarve way of serving tuna is in steaks with fried onions and bacon with white wine. It is also served cold in a salad with slivered almonds, olives, hard-boiled eggs, celery and mayonnaise.

Shrimps and sweets are palate pleasures in Belgium this month. Around the third weekend of June at Oostduinkerke, a fishing village on an unspoiled part of the west coast, the Shrimp Feast is held. The port was at one time a stronghold of Icelandic fishermen who fished along the shore on horseback. This tradition has survived and every year a shrimp feast takes place: since 1950 it has been held on the next to last weekend. The celebrations start with a big dance that culminates with the election of a master of ceremonies, the Mieke Garnaal. On the Saturday the fishermen compete for the best catch. On the Sunday the town is filled with the scent of fresh shrimps and hotels and restaurants put on special shrimp dishes. There is a procession with the master of ceremonies and his retinue preceded by the fishermen on horseback who are given their prizes by Mieke Garnaal. Information from Tourist Office Koksijde-Oostduinkerke, Section Oostduinkerke, Town Hall, B-8458 Oostduinkerke (058/ 51 11 89).

On Whit Monday a sweet market is held at Kemmel, always the centre of a festivity which attracted people from villages around and from Ypres and Poperinge. Many young men came to the event to find a sweetheart and from sweethearts to sweets is a short step. Now the sweet market has been organised in Kemmel for nearly ten years, at which bakers and members of the baking trade come to exhibit and sell sweetmeats and sweet specialities. Among the temptations are many local flans: Geitetaart, Mattetaart, Kalletaart, Eierkoeken, Limburgse vlaaien (another traditional flan), Daiselse Pompeschitters, Izegense schoentjes, Beauvoorde waffles and pancakes. There is also a stall which sells home baked items made by the women of Kemmel. A sweet-maker works at the market and there is a 'sweet chemist's shop'. As the tourist office says, 'the dentists are rubbing their hands in anticipation.' The market place becomes the centre for various entertainments with fanfare, drawings for and by children, an exhibition of sweets, a sugar walk (with games for sweets). The market begins at 1400. Information from 'Werkgroep Zoetemarkt', c/o E. Breemeersch, Molenstraat 1, B-8948, Kemmel, Belgium (057/44 51 21).

Wine

Germany hints at glories to come with a grape blossom festival at Heilbronn and wine and roses festivals. In Greece, starting in June and running till September, there is the wine festival at Dafni (11 km from Athens). This is organised by the Greek National Tourist Office and local information is obtainable on 01 322 1459.

In Spain, the Battle of Wine at Haro in the Rioja district is held at the end of the month. This is a unique occasion with 50,000 litres of wine used, not to drink, but thrown from wineskins, buckets and bottles over anyone and everyone. The ground gets so saturated with wine that it forms puddles – fine for the local dogs. The city corporation issues groups and teams with the wine to be flung and it is traditional to wear white clothes with a red neckerchief to make the maximum messy impact. At the lunch the wine is happily of a superior quality than that allowed to be used for the 'battle'.

Belgium is Europe's great beer-drinking country and on the third weekend of June there is the Belgian Beer Weekend at the seaside at Middelkerke. Over the weekend local beers are available on 40 decorated terraces and there is street entertainment, shrimp-catchers to watch and music. In Belgium, they distinguish between eight important types of beer: (1) trappist beers brewed by trappist monks; (2) abbey beers brewed to old recipes in the abbeys; (3) gueuzes, including cherry and raspberry beers; (4) the various types of ale; (5) old brown beers; (6) white beers; (7) local beers, usually made in small local breweries and a number of beers brewed for special promotions on the orders of different municipalities; and (8) the pilsen type, which as far as possible is excluded during this beer weekend. The weekend, however, enjoys the participation of a third of the existing Belgian brewers. Along the 2 km of seafront, with the wide beach on one side and shops and hotels on the other, are the 40 terraces, decorated and promoting different breweries, where the visitor can sample beers. Cheeses, sausages, fish and snacks are also on sale. Some restaurants adapt their menus and serve meals cooked in beer. On the Friday evening some 2,000 sportsmen work up a thirst by running the 100 km night run, the Night of Flanders, an official Belgian championship run which draws top runners. During the three-day event the local tourist office lays on marching bands and music and shrimp-catchers' competitions after which the shrimp boats come into the seafront. The Nieuwpoort fish-fryers are there and hand out free fish. Information from VZW Zeeschuim, c/o Mr B. Van Troosten-berghe, Zeedijk 83, B-8430 Middelkerke (059/ 30 08 85).

Luxembourg starts wine festivals early with events held during the month at Grevenmachera wine festival with concerts and dance and a wine fair at Wormeldange with sampling, concert and dance; there is a sampling day of Luxembourg Moselle wines at Wellenstein and Ehnen holds a wine fete in a large marquee. Towards the end of the month Grevenmacher holds a sampling day in the cooperative wine cellars.

Arts

This is another great month for music lovers. The festivals begin to move out of doors and by August have reached full musical pitch. In Rome, concerts are held in the Basilica of Maxentius starting in June and continuing through to August. Shakespeare starts in the park in London with the Regent's Park open air theatre staging of *A Midsummer Night's Dream*; details from Regent's Park, London NW1 (01–486 2431) with the box office open from 1 May. Britain's National Trust properties have many musical entertainments during the summer season: most of the 500 public events take place out of doors and a third involve music in some form. Open air theatres are found at Polesden Lacey near Dorking, Cliveden near Maidenhead, Fenton House in Hampstead and Hidcote Manor garden near Chipping Campden. Details from The National Trust, 36 Queen Anne's Gate, London SW1H 9AS (01–222 9251).

Austria The Haydn festival is held at Eisenstadt in the Burgen-land wine area (which introduced a special Haydn wine for the 1988 festival). This is a three-part festival held in the second half of mid-March, June and in late September, with works per-formed by the 45-strong Austro-Hungarian Haydn orchestra formed specially for the festival and featuring the best Austrian and Hungarian musicians under the direction of Adam Fischer.

The performances of Haydn's works are given in their original settings such as the Esterhazy Palace, Haydn house and Haydn church. In the palace, the concerts are given in the music salon, the Haydn room adorned with frescoes by Carpoforo Tencalla; the excellent acoustics have remained unchanged since Joseph Haydn was music director of the Esterhazy court. Originally built in 1371 as a moated building, the castle was later elaborated in baroque style. There is a museum in the house where Haydn lived from 1761–90. The composer now decomposes in the Haydn church. Performances are also given in the Esterhazy castle in Fertod in Hungary, where Haydn spent the summer months in his capacity as musical director. Information and ticket sales: office of Bld. Haydnfestspiele A-7000 Eisenstadt, Schloss Esterhazy (0043 02682/61866).

France This month has an eclectic choice with international chamber music festival at Divonne in the Rhône Valley (Bureau de Festival, 01200 Divonne les Bains (50 21 06 63); a dance festival in Montpelier; a sacred music festival at Nice (Hotel de Ville, 06000 Nice); a festival of international young solists at Bordeaux (les Hesperides, 4 rue Beaubadat 33000 Bordeaux (56 79 03 14)) and an international festival of experimental music at Bourges in the Loire valley with free entrance to 32 concerts and performances by musicians from 30 countries.

Greece The Athens festival, organised by the Greek National Tourist Office (local information on 322 1459), has performances from June to September in the Herod Atticus Odeon at the foot of the Acropolis, built in 161 AD in memory of Herod Atticus' wife. Spectacles include ancient drama, opera, music and ballet by national and international groups. Some events are also held in the Lycabettus theatre. From mid June to the beginning of September there is also the Epidaurus festival started in 1954. It is held in a third century BC theatre that seats 14,000 and is renowned for its acoustics. Visits to the theatre to see ancient and modern plays can be combined with sightseeing at Epidaurus and Argolis on excursions from travel agencies. In the third week of June (till the end of August) Heraklion offers concerts, theatre, opera, ballet and exhibitions. Patras has its summer festival from mid June in the ancient Odeon with ancient and modern theatre, ballet and concerts. Information from the Artistic and Cultural Office (061 279866/276592). For the Athens and Epidaurus festivals, details from the Athens Festival Box Office, 4 Stadiou Street (322 1459) and on days of performances at the Odeon of Herod Atticus (323 2771).

Athens Festival and fireworks

Germany Munich is a good place for many kinds of summer music. An especial delight are the candlelit concerts given in the Nymphenburg Palace with interval strolls while still light to sip sparkling sekt wine among the formal gardens.

Italy Venice holds her Biennale at the end of June through to the end of September. It is a festival of mostly contemporary art and ranges the world from South America, Middle East, Scandinavia and the United States, all set out in national pavilions in the Giardini di Castello. Each year a central pavilion exhibit theme is set. Details from La Biennale de Venezia, Settore Arti Visive, San Marco Ca' Giustinian 30124, Venezia.

119

Finland   There is a fairytale theatre festival in June and July of plays performed by children in the castle ruins at Hameenlinna. Details from Hameen Matkailu, Palokunnankatu 11, 13100 Hameenlinna (9 17 202649). In Vaasa in June there is the international puppet theatre festival with Finnish and international performers with concerts, exhibitions, dancing and puppet theatre. Details: Vaasa Festival, PB 3, 65101 Vaasa 9 61 253755). In Kuopio there is the dance and music festival with different themes set each year and a programme of classical ballet and modern dance performances. Details: Kuopio Dance and Music Festival, Tulliportinkatu 27, 70100 Kuopio (9 71 221844/118103).

Norway   The Bergen International Festival features concerts, plays, ballets, open air shows, folk dance and song; for Grieg's birthday, on 15 June, there are concerts in his honour at Troldhangen and Lofthus.

Holland   In June and July, the Holland Festival has music, opera, ballet, dance events in Amsterdam, Haarlem, Rotterdam, the Hague and other centres.

Yugoslavia   The Ljubliana Festival takes place in early June with folklore, opera, drama, ballet and music events.

Belgium   At Knokke-Heist there is the nearly 30-year-old international cartoon festival, with exhibits from over 50 countries and an exhibition of some 600 cartoons from which an international jury selects and awards prizes of gold, silver and bronze hats. From mid June in the Humorhall, Laguna Beach at Duinbergen. Information from Dienst Toerisme Knokke-Heist, Stadhuis, B-8300 Knokke-Heist (050/60 61 85).

Ireland   The festival of music in Great Irish Houses is a series of concerts arranged in stately Irish houses which are usually closed to the public. Venues in past festivals have included medieval castles, palladian palaces and neo-classical houses. Serenissima, 21 Dorset Square, London, NW1 (tel. 01 730 9841) and Heritage Tours, can arrange packages to this event.

UK   Britain has plenty of festivals again this month. In London there are the Kenwood concerts from mid June to the end of August, mainly on Saturdays, given by leading orchestras and including a couple of jazz evenings. They start at 20.00 in a concert bowl in the gardens of Kenwood House in north London. The orchestra is seen across a lake from the audience.

Individual concert tickets and season tickets are available in advance from early May from Box Office, Royal Festival Hall, South Bank, London SE1 8XX. One can reserve numbered deck chairs or sit more cheaply on the grass.

The Lufthansa Festival of Baroque Music takes place every June when the airline sponsors a series of baroque concerts at St James's Church in Piccadilly, an eighteenth-century building. In addition to evening concerts there are lunchtime recitals and other events such as a harpsichord master class and early music Network Young Artists competition. The Wren restaurant in the church is open through the day for refreshments and wine. A silver collection is made at the lunchtime recitals for which no tickets are required. Advance booking for evening concerts begins on 1 June and box office booking from 8 June in the church. Details from the Lufthansa Festival of Baroque Music, St James's Church, 197 Piccadilly, London WIV 9LE (01–434 4003).

The Aldeburgh Festival of music and the arts was founded over 40 years ago by Benjamin Britten and Sir Peter Pears. The festival is international but with an essentially English atmosphere. The performances take place in the restored Maltings at Snape as well as in the village of Aldeburgh, which is decked with flags for the occasion, and in some of the older and famed Suffolk churches. Films are shown in Aldeburgh's mock Tudor cinema and late night events in the Jubilee Hall near the sea. The Wentworth Hotel overlooking the sea at Aldeburgh is a good place to stay if you book well in advance. Transport from London can be by train and festival buses meet the 1530 from London's Liverpool Street on weekdays; travellers are returned to London just after midnight. An alternative and much more leisurely way of getting to Aldeburgh is a Thames barge trip. 'Aldeburgh at Ease' offers a series of packages, including accommodation and tickets, which are available from the Aldeburgh Foundation, High Street, Aldeburgh, Suffolk, IP15 5AX (box office 072 885 3542); bookings from March.

Castleward Opera, Northern Ireland's answer to Glyndebourne, gives five performances of a Mozart opera at the end of the month in the National Trust property of Castleward near Belfast. On the last Friday there is a gala evening with the performance preceding a gourmet meal. Opera goers can take their picnics to other events and enjoy the estate's surroundings. A place to stay is Glassdrumman House, Annalong, County Down B7 4QN (03967 68585), an extremely comfortable high standard small country house hotel run on house party lines. The butler, a descendant of Charles Darwin and Josiah Wedgwood, will arrange a superb picnic with silver candelabra, freshly made hot coffee, cold buffet and champagne set out on bone china with wines served in Tyrone crystal glass. As well as at Castleward such a picnic can make a superb fête champêtre during a walk in the mountains and forests around the hotel estate. Castleward guests are asked to wear evening dress. Details and tickets are available from Mrs Hilda Logan, 61 Marlborough Park North, Belfast BT9 6HL (0232 661090).

Ludlow Festival; established over three decades ago, this festival includes a full open-air Shakespeare production, orchestral concerts, opera, mini drama, light entertainment and children's events over two weeks in south Shropshire. The centrepiece is the Shakespeare play set against the backdrop of the 900-year-old castle; other events include jazz, gardening talks and sport lectures. Details from Ludlow Festival, Castle Square, Ludlow, Shropshire SY8 1AY (0584 2150).

York: Festival and Mystery Play. Once every four years (it was held in 1988) for four weeks from mid June the centrepiece of a cycle of medieval mystery plays are run for the first three weeks every night in the open air in the grounds of the ruined St Mary's Abbey. Hundreds of local York citizens make up the cast, along with a professional actor who portrays Christ. Other events take place around the city's historical buildings including York Minster. On the music side, British composers from classical to jazz, rock, pop and folk take part and develop musical projects. Regular British Rail trains take 2¼ hours to York from London. Details from 1 Newgate, York YO1 2LA (0984 610266). Box office from February (0904 6110890).

Sport

Tennis: Wimbledon at the end of the month is the highlight, whether watched on TV or as one of the 15,000-strong partisan and vociferous crowd. Spectators are casually dressed (except in the royal box); one needs sneakers to get round the courts, fold up rainwear, particularly for the first week, and a cardigan for the matches that go on till the light fades.

The charm of Wimbledon, apart from the gathering of all the tennis greats, is its mixture of tradition and at the same time its casualness. One can wander the grounds, see tennis stars walking to their games, get good close ups of them on outer courts if you haven't got tickets for the Centre or Number 1 courts. Take a strawberry tea, buy tennis-decorated souvenirs and see the museum that charts the history of the century-old All England Lawn Tennis Championships, the official title.

The club was originally called the All England Croquet Club and was founded in 1869. In 1876 lawn tennis was added after a garden game invented by Major Wingfield, whose scoring rules are little changed and which, though some think they are illogical, can keep the game in the balance till the last point, an essential part of the high drama at Wimbledon. The 15–30–40 terminology comes from the progress of rallies once recorded on the quadrant of a clock at the edge of the court. As the player won a point, he moved the hand on a quarter. 'Love' is from the French l'oeuf (zero). Deuce, 40 all from deux à deux, two all equal; terms derived from the older court game of real tennis.

In 1871 it was decided to organise a tournament at Wimbledon to pay for a roller for the lawns. In 1887 the women's singles were started and in 1907 King George V accepted the presidency of the club. In the 1920s Susanne Lenglen won three titles in the same championship. In 1922 the event was broadcast for the first time and spectators were outraged when a woman player appeared without stockings. Later it was Gussie Moran who caused attention with her frilly knickers and in the 1980s another woman player in a skintight white body stocking riveted more than the media's focus. Wimbledon insists its players wear white.

As in other London season events, company entertainment has become important at Wimbledon. The smart marquee spot is on the old hard courts at the southern end; second best site is the old rugger pitch in Aorangi Park at the other end, and the later joiners are on the golf course. There are over 40 splendid commerical marquees, but at Wimbledon the lunches are shorter and entertainment less grand to allow guests to finish in time to watch the tennis. A leading British bank, for example, flies in clients from France and Germany in charter planes. Fleets of cars rush them from the airport to lunch at Wimbledon; seats are taken sharply at 13.55 on the Centre Court and the day ends when the tennis does. A tent costs about £70,000 for two weeks including catering for 30 to 35 people with 16 centre and 10 Number 1 court tickets each day. Steadily growing profits go to the Lawn Tennis Association to develop the sport.

For the individual fan, you can get in by queueing, paying £4 for entrance and wandering round outside courts and using standing room for the show courts. After 1700 the admission is £2. Black market tickets can cost £200–£400 for the finals matches. The way most (non-members) get a Centre or Number 1 court ticket is by public ballot. Apply with a sae to the Secretary, All England Lawn Tennis Club, Church Road, London W19 to get an application form. By hanging around during the tournament you may get a £1 ticket from those who leave early and put their ticket for that day's play in special boxes to be re-sold. Car park queues and costs, about equal to an ordinary day ticket, deter drivers. It is best to take a train from Waterloo or Blackfriars or the District Line underground to Southfields.

Horses: The Badminton Horse Trials are set in parkland around a stately home with hundreds of tents selling country goods as well as food. Lucinda Green, six times winner of the event, calls it the Mecca of horse jumping. Entrance doubles for the popular cross country day. The event takes four days and you also need a grandstand seat to watch dressage or jumping. Get there by train from London's Paddington, Swindon is the nearest station, with a bus onwards.

Plenty of Derby choice: the English (see page 144), the Irish at the Curragh, a convivial event with packages organised by Keith Prowse Travel including return Dublin flight, two nights accommodation and one-day admission badge to the race-course; the German Derby and the French, the latter run at Chantilly. At London's Wembley there is the Royal Horse Show.

Golf: the Irish Open, British Amateur championship and midnight golf matches in Northern Scandinavia.

Boats: Germany, the Kiel Regatta. One of the loveliest events since at this regatta, unlike Cowes (see page 171) you can see it all in comfort freely from the sides of the canal. One can examine the many and varied boats moored alongide the quays, beyond them watch the races and on a budget, stay in camping sites on sand dune beaches nearby. In Denmark there is the Round Zealand yacht race and 1,000 yachts go in for the round the Isle of Wight race; details from Island Sailing Club, High Street, Cowes, Isle of Wight (0983 296621). In Sweden there are mid June balloon festival with an international rally at the the world's longest of its kind starting from Leksand in July with other races held from midsummer's day onward. The rowing recalls the days when villagers from communities around Sweden's lakes travelled to church by rowing boat.

Ballooning: Switzerland, the Dolder international alpine ballooning race at Murren. Leeds Castle, Kent, in England has a mid June balloon festival with an international rally in the moated Tudor castle. Cross country races are organised with the Vintage Bentley Drivers Club pursuing the racing balloonists in their cars and bringing them back to the castle. Details, Leeds Castle Enterprises, Maidstone, Kent ME17 1PL (tel. 0622 65400).

Fishing: the coarse fishing season opens in England and there are 24-hour fishing contests held in Sweden.

Walking: Henningsvag in North Norway in the middle of June hosts the North Cape March. This is one of the world's toughest marching tours covering a distance of 70 km from Henningsvag to the North Cape and back which attracts around

1,000 participants from all over the world. In Wales around Llanwrtyd Wells, there are drovers' walks following the footsteps of the old sheep and cattle drovers on their way to market; the walkers cover hills and valleys and an old pub, the Spite Inn, stays open for the day (details 05913 236). A more gruelling Welsh run is the Three Peaks Race, from the Quay at Barmouth, to Caernarfon and to Ravenglass and Scotland's Fort William, and including running to ascend the peaks of Snowdon, Scar Fell Pike and Ben Nevis; details from the Secretary, Tregarn, Barmouth, Gwynedd LI42 1DY.

Others: Belgium, Vise has annual competitions for cross-bowmen and arquebusiers; skiiers can still get their thrills with summer races on the glacier in Klosters, Switzerland, and St Moritz holds an international clay pigeon shooting contest.

Shopping

A time to find old things at London's antiquarian book fair, and Grosvenor House antiques fair; bric-a-brac from Belgium's toy market. In Luxembourg city there is a meeting of European collectors of football badges for exchange and sale; and at Vammala in Finland they hold the 'days of old literature' with book evaluation, sales, auctions, exhibitions and seminars. And if you want to get that hat to get ahead with in the 'season', go to David Shilling's small shop at 44 Chiltern Street, London W1 (01–935 8473/487 3179).

Horticultural

Everything's coming up roses this month with Hanover's baroque gardens filled with dancing, singing and music on a June evening, ending with a baroque firework display to the music of Handel. The fountains are illuminated three nights a week all through the summer. The Queen Mary garden in London's Regent's Park is full of roses, Geneva holds its festival of roses with 100,000 rose trees in bloom, and in Vienna the scent of roses from the Hofburg gardens drifts into the operetta house. In Luxembourg at Wiltz on Whit Monday they hold the 'genzefest' broom flower festival. At this time of year the Ardennes slopes are covered with golden gorse blossom and a parade is held with folklore groups, bands and floats decorated with broom. A dance follows in the evening.

Public Holidays

2 June, Anniversary of the Republic, Italy.
5 June, Constitution Day, Denmark.
6 June, Public Holiday, Ireland.
7 June, Republic Day, Italy.
10 June, National Day, Portugal.
17 June, Day of Unity, Germany.
Mid June, Corpus Christi, Spain.
20 June, Midsummer Day, Sweden, St John's Day, Finland.
23 June, National Day, Luxembourg, with traditional festivities, parades, services, concerts, dancing with torchlit procession and fireworks in Luxembourg city the evening before and city illuminations at night.
24 June, King's Day, Spain.
20 June, St Peter and St Paul, Spain.

JULY

HAS A RING TO IT

J ULY is something of a change-over month. The 'season's' events are dying down in favour of a national exodus to the coast. From 14 July, Paris becomes a deserted city with burglar alarms ringing unattended in the emptied streets and the restaurants displaying their 'fermiture annuelle' signs. The movement out gains impetus as the schools close and summer courses move into the buildings and university colleges. In Iceland and parts of Scandinavia, schools double as summer accommodation, especially where few hotels exist. Climatically Britons button up their cardies in anticipation of summer at home. On 15 July an extra careful note is made of the weather, for this is St Swithin's Day. If it rains on this day it will then rain for 40 days. St Swithin was a ninth-century bishop of Winchester, a modest man who when his body was moved to its shrine from a humbler burial spot, wept for 40 days. On the other hand, it was believed if it rained on this day, the apple harvest would be good.

Ring in the View

An antidote to the lemming-like beachward rush is the plethora of summer music festivals that abound, almost outdoing the formal city seasons of the winter. *The* one to go to is the Bayreuth Wagner Festival in Germany which begins at the end of July and runs through August.

Set amid the rolling vineyard country of Franconia and accessible by car from Nurnberg, the aerial gateway, Wagner's ambitious theatrical dream was realised in Bayreuth through the earlier ambitions of Wilhelmina, Margravine of Bayreuth. This lady would have been queen of England had not her fiancé, Frederick Prince of Wales, son of George I, died an untimely death. The lady, instead, left her historical mark in chateaux round the city, including the fanciful Hermitage summer palace where Hitler buried much of his archives in the war – still a charming summer day's venue to stroll in the formal gardens.

In 1745–8, Wilhelmina created the elegant theatre of the Margraves in Bayreuth as a show case for her own operas and plays. It is now Europe's only baroque opera house; locals staunchly say the Swedish Drottingholm (see below) is a re-construction. The Bayreuth Theatre, its baroque ornamentation updated only by the addition of electricity in the chandeliers and heating, retains its herald's box by the stage and the white masks of ballet girls surround the gallery. It is still in use. Every year in late May and June festivals of ballet and opera are produced here by the Cuvillees company from Munich. The original eighteenth-century backdrop, which was never changed whatever the setting of the piece, is still there and the stage is 2½ times the depth of the auditorium, which seats 520. Nowadays, it takes two days of preheating before each usage.

In nineteenth-century Germany, this stage was the country's largest and it was the lure of this that brought Richard Wagner to Bayreuth. He decided it was too small for his mammoth production ideas and the city therefore gave him ground on the Green Hill on which to build his own opera house. Cynically termed the 'Bayreuth barn' by locals, the red brick nineteenth-century industrial architecture with huge windows is not the most soothing of sights. Wagner designed it for nearly 2,000 people, a capacity still not big enough to satisfy current ticket hunger during the annual festival.

Wagner wanted to try out his theory of having a recessed understage shell for the orchestra which would bounce sound back to the stage and out again to the audience. He declared that if this worked he would pull down the red brick edifice and rebuild it in the form of a Greek temple. But by 1876, after the first performance of the *Ring*, Wagner's money had run out and he had to sell scenery and curtains to pay the singers. His widow Cosima kept the theatre going and now their grandson Wolfgang is the theatre's working director.

Though some conductors object to being in effect hidden under the stage, the festival, presenting an average of 30 operas, fills the city. Tour operators like Heritage Travel arrange packages and tickets. Otherwise tickets have to be applied for nine months in advance and the German National Tourist Offices have helpful information sheets about the festival with details of dates, operas and ticket prices. Tickets must be obtained from Kartenburo, Bayreuther Festspiele, Postfach 2320, D-8580 Bayreuth 2, Germany (from UK 01049 921 20221).

For most performances the 'barn' opens at 1600 with the assembly of elegantly dressed ticket holders to see the start of *The Ring* which continues until 2200 with two intervals of one hour each. During the break, the audience flows out into the park that surrounds the opera house on its hill set with the busts of Wagner and Cosima. There are theatre restaurants in the park complex. Trumpets summon the audience back to their seats from the balcony over the entrance by playing the opera's theme three times.

It is not wise to book a hotel in Bayreuth till sure of opera tickets. When you have tickets contact the Gastedienst des Fremdenverkehrsvereins, Luitpoldplatz D-8580, Bayreuth, who will book rooms in or near Bayreuth. There are hotels in the surrounding countryside that offer quiet relaxation, comfort and good food and that are within reach of the opera. The romantic Hotel Post, Marketplatz 11, Wirzberg is 20 km from Bayreuth and the English-speaking owner sends guests to the opera in his London taxi. His country inn in a geranium clad village is by a maypole-like post depicting village crafts. As well as stube style dining rooms the Post has a Roman style indoor swimming pool and attached sauna. Rooms are well furnished and have opulent bathrooms.

The ticketless Wagner fan can console himself with a homage trip to the composer's home and theatre in Bayreuth and stay at the Pflaums Post hotel D-8580, Pegnitz. Here one can have a surfeit of Wagner music in this Michelin starred inn south of Bayreuth. The Pflaum family (the name means 'plum') have run this inn since 1707. Napoleon stayed there and did not pay his bill. Now, top conductors and performers at the Wagner Festival stay here and the hotel provides a car service to Bayreuth and an after opera dinner. The hotel is run by three Pflaums: one is the chef; another is the manager and wine buyer; a third brother runs the local butchery.

A highlight of the year, and an event which could be much more fun and certainly less crowded than the actual Bayreuth festival, is the Pflaum's annual pre-festival week in the third week of July. Special dinners and recordings of Wagner opera are then put on. These evenings begin around 2200 and end around 0200. A set price includes listening to an opera with a different part of a six course nouvelle cuisine meal accompanied by Krug champagne, fine French wines and Napoleon brandy interspersed by a different act of the opera listened to in a different part of the hotel from the sauna or swimming pool to the dining room, which is decorated with modern paintings. The dinner menus are linked to the operas. Manager Andreas Pflaum thinks Parsifal calls for light red foods, for example a dessert of swan shaped meringue on a fresh raspberry puree. In the intervals clothes can be changed or more champagne sipped. The hotel also runs an evening Wagner concert and dinner at which unknown pieces by the composer are played.

At any time of year, day or night, one can listen to Wagner at Pflaums. The 80 rooms are spacious, restful with huge lushly appointed bathrooms, some with roomy jacuzzi and many mirrors to practise bathroom opera. The bedrooms have chiffon swathed four posters, chintz covered day beds and views of hills behind the hotel and mini bars with elegant long stemmed Rosenthal glasses specially designed for the hotel. A splendid meal can be ordered on room service and reclining on the day bed, one can settle down before the TV having first requested the transmission of a favourite Wagner opera, which is relayed on closed circuit channels. The hotel has all the operas on tape and the afficianado can lock him or herself in for several indulgent days. The more active, according to season, can walk or cycle on marked trails, fish, ride, take a picnic or in winter ski cross country.

Time Warp on the Water

Sweden's Drottingholm Slottsteater (court theatre) was built in 1776 about ten miles from the centre of Stockholm in the grounds of the Royal Palace beside the Malaren lake. The approach is part of the charm of events here. One takes a 50-minute ride on a small snub-nosed ferry through the Stockholm islands seeing wild birds such as osprey, crested glebe, goosanders and terns among the reeds. The ferry stops by the lawns of the palace where the Swedish royals now live. The theatre itself, designed by Carl Fredrik Adelkrantz, stands to one side. It has not changed since it was built. It was the scene of the assassination of King Gustav II at a masquerade ball in 1792, an incident which inspired the story for Verdi's *Un Ballo in Maskera*, but which also closed the Slottsteater.

The theatre was shuttered and sealed for the following 130 years. Like a sleeping princess, it was awakened in 1921 when a royal library assistant, searching for a painting, found a fossilised eighteenth-century opera house complete with its complex stage machinery system of wheels, lifts and counterweights by which the *deus ex machina* opera scenes were contrived – gods and goddesses lifted to or lowered from heaven on their 'gloire' cloud chariots. Demons went down to hell through trapdoors and thunder effects were created by throwing lumps of granite around in a box. Ropes and windlasses, more like a clipper ship, change the scenery and wings smoothly while a 25-piece band plays – still dressed in eighteenth-century costume and playing original instruments. But as critics report, if, as in *Don Giovanni*, changes take place during a recitative, the stage creaks and groans like a clipper in a gale.

Contrast indeed with the century-younger 'Bayreuth barn' of Wagner, but Drottingholm's delight is stepping back as a spectator 200 years into the exact environment of that time down to the huge *trompe d'oeil* vistas depicting the parkland scenery around the theatre with eighteenth-century stock stage scenes. In reality the stage is only about 20 yards deep and to keep the illusion of space, the chorus range themselves with the smallest at the back; tallest in front. The only concession to the twentieth century is that the candles have been replaced by electricity but – that is of a low and flickering power wattage to preserve the illusion of the past.

Drottingholm's opera season is only in summer from mid May to early September but, because of the age of the theatre, performances are held only two to four times a week and are of mainly eighteenth-century operas. Visitors usually stay in central Stockholm and take the ferry out and the bus service back after the performance. There is a restaurant near the theatre and packages can be arranged to the theatre, including a backstage tour. In the past, the theatre acted as a hotel for the 150 singers, musicians, actors and stage hands who sailed to the summer palace in barges along with their costumes and instruments from Stockholm's Bolhus and lived the summer in the rooms at the back of the theatre. Expenses were originally paid for by the king in accordance with strictly laid down guide lines: the conductor, for example, got two bottles of wine at dinner; the leading singers only one. The rooms have also remained unchanged – right down to the fading wallpaper.

Today things have certainly been more rationalised. The theatre has only five full-time staff swelling to 250 in summer. These have the daunting task of running the theatre as it was. If something wears out, it just stops and is not replaced. But the artistic side can develop, experimenting with ways of presenting eighteenth-century works, especially those by Mozart where, as in *Idomeneo*, the composer wrote special passages to cover the kind of scenic change that only happens with this type of stage machinery.

As well as exploring the parkland around the theatre by day and riding the ferries, the area also offers a soothing summer setting for water exploration. The royal waterway to Uppsala can be taken and steam boats cross Lake Malaren. Stockholm itself is walkable. The opera there may be empty in summer but its Bake ficken (back pocket) food shop and restaurant is a good place for a cold table meal or the Opera Cafe at the back with its chandeliers and frescoed ceilings.

The Place to Be

Certainly not the big cities, unless you like the feeling that the plague or holocaust has struck and everyone has fled, offering fine times for walkers and loners. Paris dies from 15 July but is fun for Bastille day on the 14 July (see below). In Vienna even the horses of the Spanish riding school go on holiday in the country; the boys' choir vacations too. Lisbonites go south to the Algarve or north for summer festivals. Madrid is far too hot to stay in, so go north for city vitality. Copenhagen, Stockholm, Oslo and Amsterdam are all cooled by water a plenty and London too keeps busy with hotels full and plenty of things to do.

Looking early in the month for less spoilt parts of Europe to see, Italy's Gargano area still retains its character. South of Pescara, the wide flat lands round Foggia are its entry point. The Gargano peninsula becomes mountainous and rugged with ancient olive groves, stony soil, a chopped and fingered coast line of narrow inlets and coves. At San Mennaio and Vieste the inlets become broad sandy beaches with shallow, safe bathing. Villages like Peschici and Rodi Garganica are perched on cliffs. Peschici's houses are no more than hollowed out little hillside rock dwellings or piled white cubes. In the south east roads burst up into olive, lemon and orange groves to a thick, dark, lush forest, unexpected in the arid area. This is the Umbrian forest, one of Italy's ancient woods, a cool, calm picnic place. Above the tree level, rocks and hills emerge and an evening drive across the centre of Gargano's high hump is impressive as the sun sets behind the hill pilgrimage town of Monte San Angelo dedicated in its heights to the archangel Michael; a place for a drink in the bar-lined squares with terraces looking out across the valley.

A seaside resort that retains elegance and a sense of space on its sands in high season is La Baule on the Cote d'Amour of France's Atlantic coast. One can stay at top hotels like the Hotel Hermitage (40 60 33 06) 44504, La Baule. Hotel Royal (40 60 33 06) 44504, La Baule and Castel Marie Louise (40 60 20 60). In the Lucien Barriere group, the Hermitage is right on the beach with garden paths to the sands, open April–October on the Esplandade François Andre BP; 73, 44504 La Baule. It has its own fitness centre, and golf, tennis, wind-surfing and riding can be arranged. Le Castel Marie Louise is set in a large park, an Edwardian manor styled chateaux building while the neo-romantic architecture of the Royal leads to the casino terrace. The beach casino is open from June to mid September and the resort boasts 30 tennis courts in its club and an 18-hole golf course.

La Baule has an extensive July list of activities including bridge, international dance, tennis competitions, European roller skating cup, afternoon and evening racing, international horse competitions, concerts, a public ball in the Place Leclerc on 14 July, fireworks on the beach and a festival of international folklore ballet in its theatre.

Old Customs

Spain Horses and bulls wild and running are themes for Spain's top traditions in July. The San Fermin festivals in Pamplona are the better known with men from all walks of life running in the narrow streets with the released bulls, often with nasty results. This festival, begun in 1591, won't seem to go away and begins with a rocket fired from the balcony of the town hall on 6 July. It continues day and night until 15 July, as groups roam the streets singing, dancing and drinking backed by fireworks, markets and a gathering of over 100 'txistularis' – Basque flute players who march through the town with bands of bagpipes at the beginning of the festival, playing songs that announce the bull running of that afternoon, when men dressed in white costumes with red sashes run before the bulls towards the bullring where fights are held.

The 'A Rapa das Bestas' festival, when young men round up the wild horses of Galicia, takes place at San Lorenzo de Sabucedo, a quiet and simple village that is galvanised into life on the first weekend in July. Cars are parked in hundreds, tents are erected and food stalls serve *pulpo a la gallega* (octopus stew) and enormous round thick loaves.

The festival title means 'the shearing of the beasts' and on the first Saturday of July each year the young men set off to search for herds of wild horses in the surrounding hills. The horses, mostly mares and foals, are rounded up on foot and brought to Sabucedo. The dust cloud as they approach through the bush is dramatic, punctuated by the neighing and shouting as the men run alongside to prevent escapes. The horses are then divided into groups and moved along the single village street to the river where they graze until evening while the village celebrates with a feast, and a siesta if time permits. Visitors eat and rest at long rustic tables under the trees off cheap and plentiful Galician fare. There is impromptu dancing to bagpipes before the horses are moved back through the village to a corral beside the church. Tickets are sold for admission to the main festival event, the curro, or cutting of the manes; the children first separate the foals from the rearing, kicking protesting mass, then the men vault on the horses' backs, gripping by the mane; four more men wrestle the horse to the ground and the mane and tail are cut off, to the cheers of the crowd. After the clipping (the hair is later collected and sold) the owners count their horses and brand the foals. This continues through Sunday and Monday till the process is complete and the horses are then led back to the hills and freed until the next July. The tradition is believed to go back to the fifteenth century, when the plague decimated the area. Two sisters left the village and built a hut in the hills swearing to San Lorenzo the local saint that, if they were saved, they would donate their two horses. They were, and did, giving the horses to the priest, who let them loose in the hills – the ancestors of the present herds. But since the ritual is also held in a number of Galician villages, it could be that the custom dates from the Viking visitations when free roaming horses were a less lootable spoil. The nearest accommodation to San Lorenzo is at Pontevedra, 37 km away.

Belgium   This is a country particularly rich in folk customs and July is no exception. At the end of the month is the Witches Pageant at Beselare, a village between Menen and Ypres. At the beginning of the century a writer, Warden Oom, wrote stories about witches set here. On the last Sunday of July these witch characters get together in a pageant beginning at 1530 which combines witches with local history and 1,000 costumed actors take part with many floats. At 2130 the judgement of the witches takes place followed at 2200 by the burning of the witches. Information from Tourist Office, Zonnebeke, Ieperstraat 5, B-8688, Zonnebeke (051/77 04 41).

Also on the last Sunday of July there is the procession of the penitents at Veurne, known as the most 'Spanish' town in Flanders. The procession itself is a relic of the Spanish period, an event organised for the first time in 1644; since 1646 a religious brotherhood, the Sodality, has supervised the arrangement of the procession. The procession, unchanged since the end of the seventeenth century, portrays the Old and New Testaments with a central theme of the Passion, represented by old sculpture groups hauled or carried by penitents in robes. A group of brown dressed penitents carrying crosses follow the footsteps of Christ. Information from Tourist Office Veurne Market Square 29, B-8480 Veurne (058/31 21 54).

At the beginning of the month, heralding a week of fair events, there is the Marian procession in Poperinge. The procession commemorates a curious story of a still-borne child born on 11 March 1479; buried in the garden, exhumed by a neighbour on 14 March and found to be alive, the child was baptised, lived only another half hour, and was buried in front of the altar of St John's Church. A papal bull of 1481 confirmed the miracle and stipulated that an annual procession should be arranged to thank the Virgin for her blessings. Now 1,200 costumed actors and ten decorated floats set out through the town at 1530, with the three parts of the procession depicting scenes from the life of the Virgin, the history of Poperinge and the miraculous event. To be a true 'Poperingenaar' you must have taken part in the procession as a warrior, monk or plague victim. Information from Tourist Information Office, Stadhuis, Markt 1, B-8970 Poperinge (057/33 40 81).

The Sunday around 12 July is the procession at St Godelieve devoted to the wife of the Lord of Gistel who was strangled in 1070, and beatified in 1084. It is recorded that the procession through the streets of Gistel dates from 1458 and today 1,300 actors in costumes re-enact the history of the saint's times and death, portraying medieval Flanders in great detail with historical costumes. Information from Tourist Office Gistel, Hoogstraat 1, B-8240 Gistel (059/27 81 95).

Held only once every five years (the most recent in 1987), the Pageant of Flanders commemorates the Battle of Kortrijk in 1302 when Flemish foot soldiers defeated mounted French knights. The date of this battle of the Golden Spurs, 11 July, was chosen for the official festival day of the Flemish community. The pageant illustrates the highlights of Flemish history. Information from Tourist Office Kortrijk, Grote Markt 54, B-8500 Kortrijk (056/22 00 33).

Germany The marksmen's festival (5,000 of them with 130 bands and 5,500 musicians) is held in Hanover with ten days of parading in traditional costumes, with masques, stalls, beer tents and fair grounds. The festival is 450 years old and starts with a huge firework display. The organisers claim one million pints of beer are consumed, along with the local schnapps. There are also hot air balloon displays, waterskiing, competitions, canoe, yacht and cycle races, and hovercraft racing. DER Travel Services, 18 Conduit Street, London W1R 9TB (01–408 0111) will arrange tours).

Italy At the festival of the Redeemer in Venice, gondoliers make a bridge of boats across the Fondamente S. Giacomo. In Rome there is the *festa de Noantri* which takes place in the Trastevere area with a procession for the Vergine del Carmine, folk dances, songs in the squares, carnival floats and fireworks.

Finland At Naantali and Hanko sleepyheads' day is 27 July. Those who sleep late and longest are thrown into the sea and there are fun events all day long. Information from Naantali City Tourist Office, Tullikatu 12, 21100 Naantali (9 21 755 388) or Hanko Tourist Office, Bulevardi 15, PO 10 109101, Hanko (9 11 82 239).

France 14 July is Bastille Day. The fourteenth-century Bastille prison in Paris housed political prisoners and became a symbol of royal oppression in the eighteenth century. On 14 July 1789 it was stormed by the mob, the prisoners released and the fort pulled down, marking the start of the French Revolution. Now the date is celebrated all over France as a major holiday with varied celebrations starting on 13 July with balls lasting through the night. In Paris, there are military parades in the Étoile and Place de la Concorde areas on 14 July, often based on a theme. Hundreds of foot soldiers and mounted riders take part and planes and helicopters circle over head.

Brittany has a folklore Festival de Cournouaille in the third week of July, based in Quimper since 1923, developing from a parade of costumes, dances and songs to a range of past and present art forms, shows, concerts, entertainments and exhibitions. Local Bretons wear their traditional costumes.

Younger visitors to the French resort of Deauville in Normandy can take part in the regional sand castle building competition at the end of the month.

Luxembourg   At Ettelbruck at the beginning of the month a Remembrance Day is held in honour of General George Patton, the liberator of the duchy in 1944. He is buried in the American army cemetery in Hamm and on Remembrance Day there are military parades, an exhibition of military equipment and concerts.

UK   Swan Upping: The swans on the Thames are owned by the Queen and the city trade companies of dyers and vintners. Each year for the past 300 years the birds have been sorted out and their beaks clipped at 'swan upping'. It starts in the third week of July at Sunbury on Thames with boats pulling up river to Whitchurch, catching the birds and recording the numbers. Nicks are made on the beaks to distinguish the birds belonging to the dyers and to the vintners but the Queen's birds remain unmarked. The swan marking is carried out by Swan Masters in bright costumes. Each day the boats start at different points: call 01 236 1863 for details.

On the third Saturday of July at Stroud, Gloucestershire, there is a Brick and Rolling Pin throwing competition – men throw the bricks, women the pins. The competition is between teams from the four Strouds in England, Canada, USA and Australia. The results are exchanged by cable and the winning town takes the trophy for a year.

Food

Italy   A peach festival takes place at Castel Gandolfo on the hill rim of a lake in the Alban hills south of Rome. The little squares on which the papal summer palace looks out are filled with stalls selling peaches.

Greece   In Corfu priests bless bread and hand it out at meals of suckling pig and lamb prepared on the feast day of Saint Marina.

Finland   At Sulva there is the Kalas pa Stundars, an old fashioned feast in a genuine craftsmen's village at which traditional Finnish food is served and there is folk dancing. Information from Stundars, 65450, Sulva (9 61440 282).

England   The oyster festival is held in Whitstable. In the Heart of England in the Vale of Evesham and round Broadway in the Cotswolds, apples, plums and soft fruits are sold from roadside stalls and the tourist office, PO Box 15, Worcester WR1 2PW (0905 29512) has leaflets and maps guiding visitors to pick it yourself farms and other ways of enjoying the local fruits.

France   Tours holds a garlic and basil fair on St Anne's day 26 July for no known historical reason. On that date the pavements of the Place du Grand Marché and adjacent streets carry a pungent scent from the produce sold. The bushes of basil in pots form a city garden sold from the square's centre. On one side garlic is pyramided up, coming from places like Poitou, the Charente and Gers, the country's biggest producing area. The garlic savant can pick white to keep well through winter, or violet shaded to use at once. Garlic is sold in all forms from bulbs, bunches, garlands and plaits to sacksful. Onions and melons also jostle for the buyer's attention. It is a time for growers to socialise and to sip wine at the cafes. Each knowing housewife has her favourite garlic seller.

Cancale, Brittany, near St Malo, sells oysters and lemons from baskets in the street. The tinier and cheaper oysters are usually delicious and one can watch tractors pulling in loads of oysters.

Wine

Greece   Dafni Wine Fair, with free tastings of a variety of Greek wines, is held near Athens from the beginning of July to September. There are self service tavernas with Greek specialities, dance floors and singing competitions open to visitors. There is a regular bus service from Athens and the event is organised by the Greek National Tourist Office.

Spain The *Fiesta de Verana* (summer festival) is held at Borio near La Corunna on the first Sunday in July and features competitions among the wine producers. In San Leonardo de Yague in Soria, there is the *Fiesta de la Magdelena* on 22 July.

Luxembourg During the month wine festivals are held at Mertert, Ehnen and Schengen, the latter with concerts and dances during the 'festival du Pinot'. At Diekirch there is also a beer festival on the third weekend in July.

UK The World Wine Fair is held in Bristol in mid July with exhibitions featuring wines from countries as diverse as Wales and Japan. A decade old, the first day of the ten-day event is for the trade and press only. The fair lives up to its title with fireworks, talks, live music and water events on the quayside in the restored warehouse area where the fair is held. Bristol has long been the UK's leading wine importing town and companies like Harveys have their sherry cellars here, along with a superb wine museum and restaurant. Direct fast trains link London and Bristol as does the M4 motorway. Information from Bristol Tourist Office, Colston House, Colston Street, Bristol, Avon BS1 5AQ (0272 293891).

Arts

UK As in the next month, the offerings are plentiful and varied in location and styles. Britain in particular has an impressive number of arts festivals. In London: The Promenade concerts, founded in 1895, are held annually at the Albert Hall. The Henry Wood Promenade Concerts, shortened to the Proms, last eight weeks starting in mid July and end with the famous 'last night', at which streamers, balloons, flags and hats decorate the floor on which the Promenaders, those who queue, stand and crush near the orchestra and are led by the conductor in singing 'Land of Hope and Glory', join in hornpipe stamping and insist on yet another encore. Each year themes draw together a wide range of music; all 66 performances are broadcast by BBC's Radio 3 and the major ones are also televised. Like any institution, tales, dramas and legends persist: the showmanship of Sir Malcolm Sargent, the baritone fainting during a performance of *Carmina Burana* and a student coming from the Promenaders to carry on the role. They say when you graduate from the queues and the standing area to seats and boxes, some of the fascination goes. The music is not all strictly 'classical'; there are jazz and brass bands, Viennese waltzes, dancers and folk music all blended into the programme. Season and individual tickets are obtainable from the Promenade Concert Box Office, Royal Albert Hall, London SW7 2HR. Tickets for the last night are allocated to those who apply at the same time for at least four other concerts.

City of London Festival: a series of classical concerts including lunchtime concerts in city churches and Bishopsgate Hall. There is also a popular festival programme with lunchtime jazz in the foyer of the Barbican Centre and in the evening at the Sir Christopher Wren pub; street theatre, evening events in Central Square, lunchtime prose and poetry readings in the church of St Mary Woolnoth are among the offerings. Information from Festival Office, City Arts Trust, Bishopsgate Hall, 230 Bishopsgate, London EC2M 4QH (01–377 0540).

Summerscope, the South Bank Festival, takes place from the third week in July to mid September with events for every taste: medieval and renaissance music, themed composers, electronic music, dance, opera, jazz, folk and cabaret take place in the Royal Festival Hall, Queen Elizabeth Hall and the Purcell Room with many free events in the foyers and on the South Bank itself. Details from The South Bank Centre, Royal Festival Hall, London SW1 (01–921 0631).

Cheltenham Festival runs for two weeks in a centre that makes a good base for touring the Cotswolds, staying in some of the manor house hotels like the Greenway, close to the town. The festival has been running for over 40 years with international music, ballet, opera, street theatre, morris dancers and jazz bands building up the atmosphere. About 60 concerts are given over 16 days with fringe events as well. Box office opens early May, Town Hall, Imperial Square, Cheltenham, Gloucs. (0242 523690).

Chichester has its festival at the beginning of the month in this south coast town in Sussex sheltered by the Sussex Downs. The festival is centred round the 900-year-old cathedral, with concerts, exhibitions, fireworks, al fresco jazz and recitals at nearby Goodwood House. The Chichester theatre season attracts many top stars and runs from May to September. Details from Canongate House, South Street, Chichester, W. Sussex (0243 785718).

Cambridge: in the second half of July there are concerts in college chapels like King's, jazz in the Corn Exchange and exhibitions in the Fitzwilliam Museum. Details from Mandela House, 4 Regent Street, Cambridge CB2 1BY (0223 358977).

Henley Regatta

Henley as soon as the regatta (see page 106) is over, a festival is staged in the Stewards Enclosure by the river. The regatta marquees become concert halls, theatres, art galleries and restaurants. On the river there is a floating stage which will take a full orchestra for nightly symphony concerts. There is a puppet theatre, a barge and madrigal singers in punts. A sculpture lawn leads to an open air public dance floor. Dress code calls for regatta white trousers and blazer or dinner jacket. The crowd is young and lively as are the performing artists; the festival ends with a gala firework concert. Tickets from Henley Festival Box Office, 27 Hart Street, Henley on Thames, Oxon. RG9 2AR (0491 575751).

At Llangollen in Wales, the International Musical Eisteddfod lasts for six days in July. Established for over 40 years, competitors, singers, dancers and musicians come from over 30 countries to join the 3,000 local population in this North Wales town. There is an audience of about 150,000. In 1987 a new event, the Choir of the World competition, was added. The event is organised entirely by local people who after the war decided to promote international understanding through music. There are also informal street performances. Competitions (musical) are held in a pavilion which will hold 10,000 people, and are judged by an international board of adjudicators. 'Eistedd' in Welsh means 'to sit' and this is the traditional 'sitting together' of the bards (poets). Information from Executive Secretary, International Eisteddfod, Llangollen, Clwyd, North Wales (0978 860236).

Spain San Sebastian holds a 25-year-old jazz festival in the third week of July at the city's sports stadium. Tickets can be bought in Spain from Viajes Ecuador offices or Reina Regente s/n San Sebastian (943 421002).

Italy The Macerata Opera Festival is one of the lesser known. First held in 1967, and sponsored by Martini and Rossi, it takes place in an elliptical outdoor stadium, the Arena Sferisterio, which has superb acoustics and tiered and balconied seating, giving a theatre feeling though in the open air. The opera festival runs through July and August but other music options are also covered, such as symphony, ballet, chamber and modern music, the latter two in concert halls round the town. But Italian opera is given the emphasis, though interpretation can cause problems. The festival was sued by Puccini's granddaughter after the 1984 *La Boheme* directed by Ken Russell. Visits can be arranged by Lerica Travel, 9 Burgess Road, Sutton, Surrey SM1 1RW (01–643 9077).

Norway Molde holds a nearly 30-year-old festival at the end of the month, which is the oldest and largest jazz festival in Norway. Molde is set on the Romsdal fjord and attracts international artists. Poetry readings, folk music, and art exhibitions are included, but jazz rules supreme. The festival is non-profit-making and volunteers organise the festival without payment while the board is concerned with encouraging new and emerging groups as well as stars. Various jazz styles are presented. Information on tickets, accommodation, etc. from Molde International Jazz Festival, Box 261, Molde, Norway (072 53779). It is possible to fly to Molde from Oslo or go by coastal steamer from Bergen.

At Lervik there are midnight sun rock programmes for three days with international performers and also an outdoor midnight sun rock festival at Lakselv, set near the fjord.

Sweden Midnight concerts of renaissance and baroque music, dances and the annual Jenny Lind scholarship are held in July in the ruins of Alvastra monastery.

Finland At the end of the month there is the Lieksa brass week near the eastern border of Finland in North Karelia, with a series of concerts running simultaneously with courses for brass instruments. The concerts are held in the Lieksa Church, which seats 1,000, and in the new culture hall seating 400. Brass chamber music forms the basis of the concerts which include songs, wind and light music, church music and strings. Information and tickets from Lieksa Brass Week, Koski-Jaakonkatu 4, SF-81700 Lieksa, Finland (9 75 23 133).

France Has her Mediterranean festival along the south coast running through July and 1 August, details BP4, 13129 Sain de Giraud (42 86 86 86). A festival of music takes place at Locronan in Brittany through July; details from Syndicat d'initiative, 29000 Locronan (98 91 70 14) and at Nice, you can enjoy a modern art festival with exhibitions of photographs, furniture, books, art objects, printing, video, synthesis images and holograms; details: Palais des Congres, Esplanade de Lattre de Tassigny, 06300 Nice (93 87 37 34).

Hungary In Budapest's Hilton Hotel complex there is a thirteenth-century Dominican church which now forms an open air courtyard at which for the last ten years a summer festival of baroque concerts, opera, folklore, jazz and ballet has been given, recalling the atmosphere of musical salons, called 'amusements', which were held in Esterhazy when Haydn led the orchestra. Hilton arrange two-day packages including concert ticket. The Budapest Hilton is in the Buda Castle district with the remains of the thirteenth-century monastery within its walls and its design also merges in to a sixteenth-century Jesuit façade which blends with the contemporary architecture. Bookings can be made through any Hilton International Hotel or direct to H 1014, Budapest, Hess Andras ter.1–3 (751 000).

Yugoslavia The Pula Film Festival is held in the Roman amphitheatre. At Ohrid there is the Balkan folklore festival until late August with classical music and drama as well as folk dance. The Dubrovnik summer festival runs from mid July till mid August and puts on over 100 performances of concerts, opera, drama and dance with international artists performing in old buildings and squares. Details from Dubrovnik festival, Od Sigurate 1, 50 000 Dubrovnik, Yugoslavia (27 995/6). Split has a summer arts festival from mid July to mid August, using part of the forecourt of the place of Diocletian. At the end of July Zagreb has an international review of original folklore with costumed performers from all over the world.

Belgium For over a decade a rock festival has been held at Torhout, attended by about 50,000 people. International groups take part on a ground at the Hillestraat/Hogestraat, a natural amphitheatre with good stage views. Information from Rock Torhout (051 /58 10 20).

Greece   For the past few years an Englishman who owns a house on Paxos in the Ionian islands has organised a Paxoi Music Festival with the Mistry string quartet and additional student string quartets. Concerts are presented in each of the fishing villages on the island including outdoor recitals under the olive groves in which Paxos abounds. The festival takes place in the second half of July over two weeks and information can be supplied (along with details of accommodation) by Greek Islands Club, 66 High Street, Walton on Thames, Surrey KT12 1BU (0932 220477).

Sport

Boats: Malta has a number of yacht races organised by the Valletta Yacht Club with the Malta–Syracuse boat race in the second week in July. Sweden has the Gotland Runt sail race from Sandhavn to Gotland and round Gotland island – an annual event which attracts many expensive boats with big dinners and parties given during the race. In July also there are the sail races and regattas at Marstrand, little islands north of Goteborg, where there are lots of restaurants, cafes, and night clubs where yachtspeople go to see and be seen and to entertain. In July on the lakes of the Sijan area there are the church rowing competitions (practised for in June, see page 124). Finland has an Arctic canoe race for canoes and kayaks, one of the hardest in Europe covering 334 miles. Details from City Tourist Office, Lukiokatu 10, 95400 Tornio (9 80 40 048). Sporting Travel Services, 9 Teasdale Close, Royston, Herts. SG8 5TD (0763 42867) will arrange entry to this race and accommodation in log cabins or hotels. As part of the Summer Festival in Southampton, UK, there is an international power boat and multi-hull yacht race in Southampton Water. Ocean Village, a £100-million waterside housing marina and shopping complex, is the base for the Southampton Power Boat Grand Prix and Southampton Formula 40 Multi-Hull Grand Prix. In addition, an international balloon festival is held with races each morning and afternoon as well as a mass fly-in in which all the balloons have to land as close as possible to a predetermined site on Southampton Common, the base for the festival. Tethered flights for visitors will also be offered. Details from Southampton City Council, Southampton SO9 4XR (0703 832000/ 832001).

Horses: Goodwood race meeting at the end of the month takes place on the South Downs near Goodwood House, 60 miles south of London and 30 miles from Brighton, with a regular train service from Victoria to Chichester and connecting coach service to Goodwood on race days. The course, in addition to good children's play facilities, has its own aero- drome two miles away and there are helicopter landing facilities before and after racing at the course. With races held between mid May and the end of September, the 'glorious Good- wood' main meeting is at the end of July and beginning of August, when the Goodwood Cup takes place. The Richmond enclosure is for members only and has lovely views of the downs. Others choose between grandstand and paddock, public enclosure or Trundle enclosure. Goodwood is included in the Venice Simplon Orient Express 'train days at the races'. Information from Goodwood Race Course Limited, Chichester, W. Sussex PO18 OPX (0243 774107).

In Ireland racing is more of a way of life for 250 days of the year at least. In July there are the Killarney Races in mid month and Galway has meetings at the end of July. In mid July there is the Gilltown stud Irish Oaks, one of the classic Irish races held at the headquarters, the Curragh. A 6,000-acre plain around the course holds many of the top studs and training stables includ- ing the Irish National Stud. Entrance and car parking are much more relaxed and free and easy than in England. The *Irish Field*, published weekly on Saturdays, provides form details for the Saturday meetings. The Irish Tourist Board publishes a compre- hensive leaflet covering the necessary information about racing in Ireland, ranging from who the leading jockeys are to how to bet on them. A special feature of Irish racing are the 'bumpers', two mile or more flat races for amateurs which are usually the last race of the day. Keith Prowse tours arranges accommoda- tion in Dublin and flights for the Irish Derby held at the end of July at the Curragh.

Combining turf and surf – not an American steak and lobster dish – the Laytown Races are an unusual and very Irish day out. Fully entitled Laytown Strand Races, the course is on the beach between tides roughed out by a tractor and edged with aluminium running rail or red flags on poles. The beach is backed by a three-acre field which forms the racecourse enclo- sure with marquees with orange boxes for the bookies. Laytown is a resort on Ireland's east coast, about 27 miles north of Dublin. The races, the only beach course in Europe's official racing calendar, have been run since the end of the nineteenth century. Prize money is small but it attracts plenty of entries. The races can easily end in chaos in spite of red-coated huntsmen patrolling the course and trying to contain the crowds; if the tide time table has been misread, the race may well end up in the surf.

In Belgium The Wellington Racecourse at Ostend, inaugurated in 1883, is the meeting place for French, English, Irish, German and Belgian stables to compete. The trotting and galloping races here are a traditional feature of the Ostend summer programme from the end of May till the beginning of September. The galloping races are run on Monday, Thursday, Saturday and Sunday in July and August. The races begin at 1412 and attract thousands of spectators. On 21 July there is the Grand Prix Prince Rose race with high stakes. The race is named for a notable horse which helped create the fame of this racecourse. Information from Tourist Office Ostend, Wapenplein, B-8400 Oostende (059/70 11 99).

Golf: one can play at midnight in competitions this month in Finland; compete in the Engadine Golf Cup at St Moritz; or watch the British Open in mid July, a recent addition to the country's sporting 'season' already attracting corporate entertaining in tents where the event is usually watched on TV.

Croquet: taken very seriously by its followers and considered part of the season's events in the UK. The top events are the Open Championship in mid July (and in mid September, the President's Cup). These events take place at Hurlingham Club in West London. Tickets and details from the Croquet Association, Hurlingham Club, Ranelagh Gardens, London SW6 3PR (01–736 3148) which is five minutes from Putney Bridge tube station. It's a game linked in most imaginations with vicarage lawns, afternoon tea and Lewis Carroll's Alice where Alice has to hit a hedgehog 'ball' with a flamingo 'mallet'. A short croquet version on a tennis-court-sized course through six, not twelve, hoops speeds up the game and could do for it what TV has done for snooker. Australia, New Zealand and Britain are the world's major players; the USA has different rules; and the Japanese play gateball as well as British-rule croquet. The aim in Britain is to develop it as a national sport, run by a Sports Council grant, in which men compete alongside women. In the nineteenth century, tennis allowed even more unchaperoned playing and squeezed out croquet as the social garden sport.

Wheels: in France the exhausting 3½ week 5,000 km Tour de France cycle race continues round the country; in Britain at Silverstone there is the British Grand Prix on the fastest circuit in Europe, run over three days in mid month. Keith Prowse tours can arrange accommodation in London or Birmingham and return coach transfer and entrance ticket.

Feet: In Wales, the Snowdon Race takes place, an international running race from Llanberis in Gwynedd to the 3,560-

foot summit of Mount Snowdon and back. Information on 0286 870721. Big flat feet may be an advantage in the World Flounder Tramping Championships held in Scotland at Palnackie near Dalbeattie in Dumfries. After a preliminary meeting at the Glen Isle Inn, competitors splash through crab filled mud to the Urr estuary with homemade tridents and spears, feel for the flatfish with the toes and strike, with luck catching fish not toes.

Fishing: The more orthodox pursuit of sea edibles begins in July with the opening of the sea trout fishing season in Loch Harray in the Orkney Islands, a mecca for the fly fisherman. Drifting by boat, the casts are made in the teeth of fierce winds, though there are plenty of birds to watch as compensation. On a good day up to 100 wild trout can be taken by guests at the Merkister Hotel from where Prince Charles has fished. Fishing package details of the Orkney trout fishing holiday from American Express Travel Service, 115 Hope Street, Glasgow G2 6LX (041 221 4366).

Shopping

For the July sales in London go to Harrods and stock up on Christmas puddings made the previous year; they will mature nicely in time for the next Christmas. In Germany there are sales at the end of July till mid August with bargain prices. In the first fortnight of the month Luxembourg city holds summer sales in its shops, and at Nospelt towards the end of the month there is a pottery and handicrafts day with a sale of pottery. In Finland at Outokummun there is a mineral fair with sales and barter of semi-precious stones; details: Outokummun, Matkailu Oy, Sepankatu 6, 83500 Outokumpu (9 73 54 793).

Horticultural

The baroque royal gardens of Herenhausen in Hanover, Germany, are claimed to be the best in Europe. In July and August there is a festival of music and theatre in the gardens with ballet, concerts, plays and other events. Weekend packages are available through DER Travel Services.

Holland holds its international rose show at the Hague and in Britain the British Rose Festival is held at the end of the month at St Albans organised by the Royal National Rose Society and rose growers. It lasts two days; details from The Gardens of the Rose,

Chiswell Green, St Albans (0727 50461). More roses are on show at the Royal Windsor Rose Show, also for two days this month, and at the Kendal Rose Show, England's second largest.

The gardens of England's stately homes, their temples, follies, parkland and lawns, come into their own for the fêtes champêtres, with eighteenth-century costumed guests picnicking under parasols to a background of music and dancing. At Stourhead, the evening climaxes with fireworks above the lake, in the third week of July, 100 miles south-west of London. Similar occasions are organised every other year at Claremont landscape gardens at Esher near London in mid July. Visitors are encouraged to wear eighteenth-century dress for a programme of light opera, theatre and fireworks. Details from Claremont Fete, Box Office, National Trust, Polesdon Lacey, Dorking RH5 6BD (0372 57223). Summer is also the time for other stately home garden events such as medieval jousting, flower shows, theatres, hot air ballooning (at Holker Hall near the Lake District). Hever Castle in Kent has roses and statuary on show, Balmoral opens in July, showing the Queen's Highland retreat with its wooded grounds. Roses are at their best in July, and Castle Howard in Yorkshire, the background for the TV series *Brideshead Revisited*, has thousands of them. A map folder listing the 150 most beautiful British gardens is available from the British Tourist Authority offices. Jersey holds a floral island week in mid month with special events such as flower shows, walks and talks and an island floral competition.

Exhibitions: Royal International Show, Stoneleigh: Britain's most important agricultural show is held during the first week of July covering several hundred acres with prize livestock and the latest farming technology on show. In London, the Royal Tournament has been held since 1880. For 2½ hours the armed forces put on a show for service charities over 2½ weeks at the end of July. The musical drive of the Kings Troop, Royal Horse Artillery and the Royal Navy Field Gun race are highlights. The Royal family attends and take the salute. Tickets from mid March, from the Royal Tournament Box Office, Earls Court Exhibition Centre, Warwick Road, London SW5 9TA (01–373 8141).

Public Holidays

14 July, Bastille Day, France.
21 July, Independence Day, Belgium.

AUGUST

HIGH NOONS AND NIGHTS

A WICKED month, so they say. August is the mass holiday month of the year, when hell on earth is an airport anywhere, though perhaps Europe's worst is Corfu where it is standing room only in the departure lounges amid picnicking and drinking debris. All airports are overwhelmed; an oasis of peace during a long delay can be the chapel, where you might contemplate why you are travelling at all. One medical theory is that holidays should not take place in high summer, when the body is at its best, but in winter, when we have more need of such a break.

But some people love the sardining on the beach; others, like an American gynaecologist, will do anything to escape everyday life; he opted for Greece's Mount Athos monastery, where no women are allowed. Monasteries and religious orders do provide the opportunity for the sort of retreat our ancestors found so soothing. My idea of the perfect setting for one that admits guests is San Francisco del Deserto in the Venetian lagoon, with lovely water-lapped gardens in which to think about life cut off from the crowds that struggle in St Mark's square.

Spas began the summer social habit of getting to a place to people watch, see and enjoy eating and sports. Health farms are taking over from both monasteries and older-style spas as holiday retreats for those who want to emerge back into the real world of their work feeling and looking a lot better. A health resort or hotel with large grounds is a fine bolt hole in August. People escapers can also look for places without much road or airport access, or water shortages as in Greek islands like Paxos which effectively limit the people press – but beware the boat people who invade the most isolated of beaches.

Going Hot and Cold All Over

August is a pursuit around Europe of the four 's' s: sun, sea, sand and sex, in roughly that order. In spite of what the medical profession might say about the dangerous effects of sun, a tan is essential to a successful holiday for most. A beach to tan upon wearing as little or nothing at all is a year-round dream. Many beaches tend to be overcrowded, dirty, pricey and hazardous with main roads or railways cutting them off. An early warning on how dreams can crumble in holiday resorts was given by travel-writer Robert Byron in 1937, writing about the Venetian lido waters in *The Road to Oxiana*: 'the bathing on a calm day must be the worst in Europe; water like hot saliva, cigar ends floating into one's mouth and shoals of jelly fish.' On visits to

Greek islands like Ithaca, Homer's birthplace, one can find deserted strips of shingle for the day, but the idyll of naked tanning is diminished by the need to wear shoes as protection against the jagged tin cans and broken glass that litter the shores. The beaches are used as local rubbish dumps to which is added the debris thrown overboard by yacht flotillas and overnight backpackers.

The water too may be polluted. As a British Member of Parliament once remarked, swimming off the UK was really only 'just going through the motions'. The Adriatic and Mediterranean are also considered none too healthy. There are guides to clean beaches and efforts have been made since 1976, when the EEC asked its members to clean up their coastal acts. A Golden List of British Beaches is available from The Marine Conservation Society, 4 Gloucester Road, Ross on Wye, HR9 5BU costing £2.50 including postage and packing.

But one can be well beached even in August. It helps a lot to get a boat of any size. Even a portable canoe or fold-up dinghy can be rowed out from the packed cliff terrace sun traps of the Sorrento coast in Italy to uncover mini strands on cliff hem coves. On Greek islands like Paxos, Ithaca and Zakynthos, it is cheaper and easier to hire a boat than a car, and less dangerous to the body than a motor scooter on the pot-holed roads. Greek Island Holidays, 66 High Street, Walton on Thames, Surrey KT12 1BU (0932 220477) have sailing schools on these islands and with experience one can hire a villa through them and have a rented boat moored nearby.

A chain of perfect boating and beach islands not over-developed even now is the archipelago of over 1,000 islands off Zadar, straggling down the Yugoslav coast. They have names like fierce Indian gods, Zut, Pag, Uglian, Krk, Iz, Cres and Kali. Seen from the coastal cliffs, to the west the islands snooze in a gelatinous sea like humps of whales. The tourist office proudly boasts that the islands have a similar climate to Andalucia in Spain and the summer average air temperature is 24–25°C; in winter the air temperature does not fall below 10°C.

Some 66 of these islands are inhabited; the largest is Krk, from which wine comes. Life is simple in the islands, though hospitality is often warm. Grilled fish and sardines, local wine and figs are staples served on terraces under rusty red tiled roofs. Perhaps the most enchanting of these islands are the Kornati, forming a national park. Local legends say these islands were created from the tears of the stars and the breath of the sea on the last day of creation. They stretch from off Zadar down to Sibe ik and are used as summer grazing for farmers who row out their sheep from the mainland and larger islands.

Among the larger islands here are Uglian, Pasman and Dugi Otok, all with small hotels mostly used by Yugoslavs.

Three other national parks can be found in the Yugoslav islands. Lokrum, facing Dubrovnik, is the most southerly of the Elaphite Islands (the islands of deer). The islands have islets of their own, and some have freshwater lakes or underground sea-formed caves lit by sun through the water. There are also many uninhabited islets without water called the 'islands of love'.

Beaches are indeed prized benizons. There has even been a case in the Canaries when a beach was reported stolen. Gales can remove or endow and many beaches can be manmade. I once attended the inauguration of a so-entitled beach hotel in Cyprus. Over the sea wall, there was sea but no beach. I enquired. 'The beach will arrive on Thursday', said the manager. And it did. Thirteen lorry-loads of sand from another part of the island. One of Europe's biggest beaches, seven miles long, is little known and under used. This is on Porto Santo Madeira's sister island from which sand is exported to Madeira – an island that lacks more than a few lava ledges. (On volcanic islands like Ithaca there are little more than fringes below steep sea-plunging mountains: black lava sand can be scaldingly hot to step on.) Vulcano's beach in the Lipari islands off north Sicily (boats leave from Cefalu) has a beach that literally boils with volcanic activity.

Pure, white, untrammelled sand, on the other hand, often equates with a climate too cold for much usage – though on a good day, and these do happen, they are exhilarating. Examples are found near Cape Wrath in Scotland (especially Balnakeil Bay), Sandend near Elgin (huge cliff-sheltered sands), and Nevlunghavn on Norway's southern coast; clean wide and soft backed with sheltering dunes. Pembrokeshire in south-west Wales has some superb beaches like Broadhaven, Whitesands and Newgale and secluded coves and river estuaries for sunning and paddling. A windsurfers' paradise with good beaches is found around Tarifa in southern Spain, west of Algeciras.

Beachcombing adds to the pleasure of sand between the toes. Beady Beach on St Agnes in the Scilly Islands may reveal Venetian glass beads from old galleon shipwrecks. Chesil Beach near Lyme Regis is a good hunting area for agates, semi-precious stones and fossils. Alum Bay on the Isle of Wight has coloured sands sold in small bottles and the Harvesters Hotel in East Linton in Scotland will provide guests with information on local beachcombing possibilities. Shell Beach on Herm Island, a 20-minute boat trip from Guernsey, is scattered with tiny cowries, a lovely strip backed with wild flowers in the dunes descending from cow pastures and stretching out to a sandy tip;

it has inlets and pools and views of rocky islets and a well designed terrace cafe tucked under a dune's lee.

Cold Comforts

It may be better to cut one's financial losses rather than one's feet and head to skiing resorts which have plenty of sports facilities for summer usage. Gstaad is a very chic ski resort called The Green Highland in summer for its tranquil valley and alpine slopes around. In summer, tennis is the resort's parallel sport to winter skiing and the Swiss open championships are held there shortly after Wimbledon. Tennis courses are available year round and in summer tennis can be coupled with summer skiing on the Les Diablerets glacier. Next to the courts is a building with an olympic-sized swimming pool, together with sun beds, sauna and massage to iron out any muscular cramps.

Scandinavia, Iceland and even Greenland are places for out-door holidays where the air is pure and one can enjoy natural solitude. If the sun shines it gets quickly through the unpolluted air – and sun bounced off glaciers is doubly tanning.

Space places are Sweden and Finland. Sweden is Europe's largest country after Spain and France but only has the popula-tion of Greater London. Finland is larger than the UK but has only 4½ million inhabitants. Go north in August and it's the only place in Europe where there are low season discounts (even more so in early September). The Viking area takes its holidays earlier and July is the peak month.

The Lofotens are unique and lovely islands, perfect for bird watchers, fishermen and walking. In winter the cod fishermen, some 15,000 of them, are there stocking up on supplies and drying the fish. In summer, the visitor season is from June to mid August, when the cod fishermen's simple wooden chalets, rorbu, offer accommodation, often with a row boat moored in the water below included.

Norway's Lofotens are reached on coastal steamers that connect via Bergen (book well ahead) with ferries to the UK. They travel from Bergen up the coast to Bodo (or one can fly) and then the boats travel out to the Lofotens – a 100-mile horizon scribble of seemingly continuous mountain pinnacles. In the misty approach people have seen in this mountain mass shapes of men lying down, trolls, saints, castles. The peaks are more prosaically used as net markers by the cod fishermen. Up close, each of the islands is dominated by a wrath of God mountain, below which villages cower on narrow ledges of land. Around each island are a myriad of satellites, scattered rocks, stopovers for gulls and a place for the visitor to enjoy picnics and Arctic sunshine afternoons.

Horizontal land is hard to come by. Stamsund, the steamers' first port of call, was literally blasted out of rock at the beginning of the century, its square wooden houses worming into glacier-worn rock crannies and painted yellow, green, pink or russet against the overriding grey of sea, sky and mountain. Summer gardens snuggle round rocks blooming yellow and scarlet and on the spongey moorland rises, bright berries cling low to the ground.

Though 100 miles north of the Arctic Circle, the climate is mild enough for cows to graze outdoors year round. Building land in the villages is extended by going out over the water with shanties on water-sucked piles nuzzled by boats. Kabelvag's museum shows the rorbu of 200 years ago, little changed today, together with such curiosities as an albatross foot like a monster pincushion with claws, unborn whales in jars and a rabbit fish with wings.

Cabins for rent are listed by the tourist board and there are small 'hospits' or inns. Svolvaer, the 'capital', has good hotels. The midnight sun (even in August there is daylight till around 2300) gives plenty of time for exploration. There is a 100-mile road linking the island chain and there are ferry links to the west, from the mountains above which the Moskenes mael-strom famed by Jules Verne and Edgar Allan Poe can be watched. Reine, six hours by bus from Svolvaer, provides some of the sheerest drop vertical mountains and the puffin colonies on the bird islands of Rost and Vaeroy can be reached by ferry. One can fish, row round the nearby islands, or mountain climb. Rock hounds can leap the five foot gap between the 'goat's horns', a freak formation on Svolvoergeita above the town (information on the Lofotens from the Norwegian Tourist Board).

From some of the North's smallest scraps of land to the world's largest island – Greenland – means travelling further north from Scandinavia, though visits can be coupled with Iceland. SAS have flights from Copenhagen to Narssarssaq in the south-east. The airport comes under the control of Canada's Gander it is so near, and is a land-if-you-can-see-it airport. Often you cannot and the flight shuttles back and forth to Sondre Stromfjord on the west coast, an American base. The best way to see a lot of the 840,000-square-mile land, of which over 780,000 square miles is snow capped to a depth of 1½ miles, is by cruise ship up Greenland's west coast 400 miles north of the Arctic Circle as far as Umanak – the furthest a ship of this type can go in the pack ice. Others use Greenland for walking and backpacking. Accommodation is in simple hotels; a few Greenland farmers in the south-east also offer rooms.

In Narssarssaq the locals tell stories of the tourists who come with their car hire vouchers and the man who brought his bicycle. The roads stop at the fringes of house clusters. From then on it's a track or just out over bogland rock and up the hills among the springy bilberry bushes, no trees, nothing except for ravens and gulls and pure snow-fed streams for refreshment – you take anything you may need with you.

The tourist offices, housed in something the size of a superior garden shed, are welcoming and helpful. Greenland is still a country where locals take photos of the visitors. For land holidays or touring by coastal boat, the most extensive programme is offered by Arctic Experience Limited, 29 Nork Way, Banstead, Surrey SM7 1PB (07373 62321). They also have tours in Iceland and visits to the Faroe Islands with old sailing ship trips round the islands. In winter the company arranges adventures such as husky sledge expeditions in Greenland and Arctic Norway.

Greenland's icy mountains, of hymnal fame, produce the icebergs that doomed the Titanic – eerie, fascinating objects seen at their most spellbinding in August as they drift away from Greenland out into the Atlantic. One can take small boats along the Qoroqfjord near Narssaq (helicopter rides too) along the glacier face to watch the bergs calve (break off) or turn turtle in a sinister hiss of water. This ice, so the guide books say, was formed 'from snow that fell when Moses was in the Wilderness'. Chipped into a glass of Scotch it effervesces with the compressed air of centuries. It is exported to Tokyo, Copenhagen and London's Selfridge store, where it can be bought at a price for that special cocktail party conversation piece.

The ice castles (most of them concealed beneath the waters) are nature sculptures in their own right. Some are as big as houses or double-decker buses, some a simple scoop of ice that bears along a single seal. Some are frozen fountains, others smooth caverns; the oldest are the deepest blue in colour. Others resemble a slip off the white cliffs of Dover.

After the ice cap of Greenland, Iceland, in spite of the name, seems almost tropical. Well, there are plenty of tropical plants around; bananas grow and pepper vines curl. The snow may top the dark rock mountains in August but campers, particularly on the first long holiday weekend of August, crowd the roads and camp sites mostly wearing shorts and sun tops even though it is not *that* warm. Iceland has a true inner warmth from the volcanic hot springs which give householders their central heating and warm the greenhouses, especially near the capital

Reykjavik at Hveragerdi, where flowers, fruit and vegetables and the tropical plants are grown in naturally heated greenhouses and visitors can shop and eat in one of the greenhouses.

On a cold day one can ease aching muscles with a swim in one of the hot pools (or the natural hot tubs inside mountains) at spots like Geysir on the King's Path or Hveravelin in the wilderness between the Hofsjokull and Langjokull glaciers. Lava beds and even sandy deserts can be part of the amazing and varied scenery offered on 'safari' holidays here; no wonder Jules Verne set the place where his characters went down into the centre of the earth in Iceland and astronaut Armstrong trained for his walk on the moon in northern Iceland. Some 13 per cent of Iceland's surface is covered by glacier, the rest a heaping of brown lava rocks, a swirling of rivers and thundering falls cutting deep into rock gullies and cracks. Mountains like Hekla, which blew its top in 1970, are active: Surtsey, in the Westman Islands, appeared out of the sea in the 1960s and at Geysir there are regular explosions of boiling water shooting into the air, occasionally encouraged to blast further by adding slithers of soap. The mighty power of water is seen nearby at Gullfoss (golden fall) where it thunders down a narrow canyon throwing up mist curtains into camera lenses. The lake scenery around Thingvellir, the site of the ancient parliament, is more peaceful. The lake, with good trout fishing, is set in the shelter of a rift valley like walls of dark lava. In the long pink evenings of August, horse-riding round the lake is an excellent way to relax after a buffeting on the hard roads. One can walk around the lake area from the base of an excellent lake-side hotel.

One can fly across to Akureyri on the north of the dividing mountain chain from Reykjavik which, although almost on the Arctic Circle, has an impressive botanical garden made by local women who carried rocks and earth in their aprons to create it. Up and over the southern fjord walls of Akureyri, some of the most spectacular scenery in Iceland can be seen on a day's drive going round Lake Myvatn backed by tumbled rocks and heather banks below the mountains. Fishing and bird-watching are popular in the area. Here, dunes of sand-coloured earth roll away near a hotel at the head of the lake. In the midst of the dunes are bright yellow pools and in the silence a harsh hissing of sulphur gases escaping. The air is foetid with the dank, heavy smell and there is an uncanny feeling that intense upheaval is going on under one's feet.

Norway offers one mountain for every two members of its population – and there is gold in some of them there hills. I have panned for gold in August right up on the Arctic Circle near the North Cape where mosquitoes rather than frost are more likely to bite. In Finland at the beginning of August at Tankavaara they hold a gold-panning competition (details from Tankavaaran Kultakyla, 99695 Tankavaara (9 693 46 158), and at the Lemmenjoki National Park tourists can also pan in an area where some claims are still professionally worked. At Tanka-vaara south of Inari one can get advice on how to wash gold: the village has the only gold-prospecting museum in Europe.

In Norway's North Cape area I have sat atop the world shaking my pan hopefully. The few flecks I collected were not the fastest way to my first million but in Finnmark, the lust for gold has been harnessed to encourage visitors off the beaten tracks into the wild tundra and hills. From Oslo one can town hop on SAS flights up the length of the country, as far north as one would fly south to Rome. Lakselv is the nearest airport to the gold camp. From Alte, the previous stop, the plane hardly bothered to raise itself above the rolling hills. In mid August the reindeer were returning from summer grazing on the coast and islands. A line of grey rounded bodies backstopped by a rear flash of white plodded across the faintly purpling heather of the plateau. From Lakselv one drives for an hour to Karasjok, past an occasional house, numerous small lakes – Finnmark has 30,000 lakes – calm and still with sometimes a weekend chalet tucked among trees and accessible only by boat.

Karasjok is the Lapp centre from which the gold tours are run. It is a cluster of wooden painted buildings on both banks of the wide Karasjok River with good guest houses among pine trees, a Lapp crafts centre where they sell 'skaller' – furry reindeer skin boots with braid and felt decorations. The curled toes are padded with dried grass which the Lapps use to keep feet warm in winter. Here the Lapps still wear their traditional costume of blue and scarlet belted tunics, baggy pants and a three-pointed hat for the men, full skirts and braided bodice for the women.

The Lapps operate long canoe-like boats up river to the gold camp which, when the river dries up in summer, is often cut off. Two hours boating away, the camp is set on banks lined with birch trees. It was abandoned in the 1930s but in the late 1960s a geology surveyor thought it could be used to encourage tourists to enjoy the empty countryside. A small fee gets the loan of shovel, pan and test tube of spirit in which to store the gold. The gold is there all right, but getting it is exhausting – squatting, digging, shaking, washing. In two to three days of such steady work, nine hours a day, you might get enough gold for a thin ring or a lump that could be mounted in a setting. Occasionally, small rubies are also found. The camp is just five or six tents in fields run by an ex gold miner Lapp.

The trip to the camp can be arranged from the Karasjok guest house, but the area is also superb for trout and salmon fishing and walking. The energetic can walk the Lapp way. In the days before cars, and in winter, before snowmobiles became popular, walking or skiing were the only means of communication between Lapp settlements. The government set up small chalet-type inns within a day or half a day's walk of each other. These are being turned into simple accommodation for visitors and can be found on specially marked trails. This is an area for the crowd dodger whether fishing or walking in the almost continuous day light; even in August the fjord has a pallid glow throughout the night round Alte.

Sweden's 96,000 lakes make ideal holiday areas with plenty of self-catering chalet accommodation or more isolated cabins for rent. The resort of Are in Jamtland has an imaginative tourist office that tailors sports facilities to suit. Cycling on dirt roads, by the lake, canoeing, fishing, even 'pimpling' or fishing through the ice in high summer on altitude lakes, helicopter rides to see the reindeer, summer skiing, walking on coded tracks, into the long summer evenings. Here the Hotel Tott looks down the lake length and accommodation in the resort includes a hotel designed especially for the disabled and their families. Jamtland is a couple of day's drive from the DFDS ferry terminal at Gothenburg (DFDS Scandinavia House, Parkeston Quay, Harwich Essex CO12 4QG (0255 508122)).

Varmland alone, by the Swedish/Norwegian border, has 2,500 lakes for canoeing, fishing for trout and salmon (permits are obtainable from tourist offices) and walking. Open access to the countryside is a right Swedes prize. 'Everyman's right' is being able to collect wood, light fires and pick wild berries. A good base from which to experience this open air life on a daily outing (or tourist offices locally will arrange tours and itineraries back packing) is the Ransatter chalet village, 200 miles north of Gothenburg in pine, birch and spruce woods on the banks of the Klaralven River. The chalets are built in the old country style of log cabins with turf roofs. In the centre is the Wardhuset where traditional meals are prepared by local people for guests; in August crayfish evenings (see below) are arranged here with music and folk dancing. The chalets are pine log traditional outside and inside have modern equipment and heating.

On the River Klaralven Canadian-style canoes are used for touring and trips. The regional tourist offices and canoe centres in Varmland offer independent canoe packages including life jacket, paddle and an optional package of provisions, spirit stove, tent, etc. Weekly coach trips are also organised into the wilderness to see elk, beaver, ptarmigan, hares and other animals.

One of the most exciting and unusual ways of exploring Sweden from its waters has been set up by Anders Wiss. Bookings are made directly with him at Sundbergsv 13, S–68500 Torsby, Sweden. He pioneered the programme in 1979 and it is still unique. A weekly charge is made for river rafting, which begins with the visitor helping to haul logs into the Klaralven River at Branas and constructing a raft in three tiers weighing 1½ tons. This only takes an hour. The raft will accommodate up to twelve people in comfort and provisions, tent and portable toilet are provided. The river, already filled with logs flowing from Norway to the paper mills at Karlstad in the south of Sweden, meanders gently through pine, spruce and birch-clad hillsides at a steady 2 km per hour. Anders provides life vests and all the equipment needed for the week with paddles, stove for cooking and instructions before rafters leave. He collects his clients some 70 km south at Bergsand. Rafters can either sleep overnight on the raft or on shore in tents. While drifting along, it is possible to hear beavers thwacking their tails on the water, and see ducks, geese and sand martins. Food can be eked out with wild berries and mushrooms collected from the banks.

Beach buffs may try Denmark's peninsula of Djursland, good for family holidays in central Jutland. It has large, safe, sandy beaches and is warmer on the east coast. Driving is on straight roads with light traffic through rolling country that is popular for cycling. The port of Grenaa has four miles of beach facilities for fishing, riding and tennis and a museum with prehistoric relics, summer demonstrations of cottage crafts and cycle hire. Ferries from Grenaa link with Zeeland and so to Copenhagen, or to the sandy isle of Anholt or to Sweden. To the south of Grenaa is Ebeltoft with behind it the Mols hills, a good beach with free golf for visitors, tennis, boating and fishing. Inland, Silkeborg is a lakeside town with Himmelbjerget behind it, at 600 feet Denmark's highest point. Steamer excursions can be made on the lake and at Randers a country town there is Hamlet's supposed grave.

In southern Finland, hiking, bird-watching and canoe safaris can be arranged. The canoe safari on the River Vaarajoki is for groups of 4–16 people and is suitable for beginners but not for children. The two days of trip along the river and lakes include rapids, and a base at Ikaalinen spa. Details of various tours from Ikaalisten Kylpylakaupunki Oy, Valtakatu 7, 39500 Ikaalinen (358 33 801 221).

August

The Place to Be or Not to Be

The coolest spot in the European August is probably the
Jungfrau ice palace. In the 11,330-foot-high glacier pass in the
Swiss Oberland there is an illuminated skating rink carved out
of ice in the ridge reached by the Jungfraujoch railway and then
by sledges drawn by husky dogs to the glacier. The views at
sunrise and sunset are sensational and the area is also a summer
skiing centre.

Going up and inland one can find the quietest holidays; old-
style spas like Baden Baden in Germany's Black Forest or Italy's
Montecatini, a superb hill base for touring, and charmingly kept
in nineteenth-century period with gardens and parks for sunny
relaxation with band or fountain background. In Britain, the
season's followers decamp to Scotland by 12 August and the
opening of grouse shooting. There are house parties and shooting lodges hired by groups; more house owners now rent out
their private houses to the public. Fishing, shooting and walking are the pursuits. The royal family move up to Balmoral on
Deeside and appear at the Highland games and gatherings in
the area such as the Braemar Highland Gathering (see following
chapter). Exclusive invitation-only dances are held in Skye and
Oban, the latter called the Northern Meeting.

Some seasonal traditions die hard. Biarritz was *the* royal resort
when Europe had plenty – in the late nineteenth and early
twentieth centuries. Napoleon III and the Empress Eugenie built
a puce and white summer palace there in 1854 on a low cliff
overlooking the town beach curve. Queen Victoria and her
family came as Napoleon's guests. In 1904 the palace became a
hotel, still the Palais Hotel. Edward VII held summer court there
from 1906–10 and the hotel was later visited by the Duke of
Windsor, billed on the gold and marble plaque in the lobby as
Edward VIII. Biarritz is linked with Paris by fast overnight train.
It is almost impossible to get rooms in August. One sees and is
seen on the beach or golf course by day, in the casino and top
restaurants or at the August events such as the international
horse show, mid month gala evening and fireworks, Côte
Basque musical events and such notions as an imperial night.
There are important golf matches at the century-old (British
founded) golf club, playable year round, and from here several
other golf courses in the area can be booked.

The Palais Hotel, with 200 rooms, accommodation for 100
chauffeurs and staff and two casinos is the heart of fashionable
Biarritz with its marble floors and walls, velvet and silk hang-
ings, gilt furniture, pendulous chandeliers and the bedrooms'
marble bathrooms almost as vast as the period-style rooms. The

opening and closing dates of the Palais define the extent of the Biarritz season: May till the end of September. The season's gala dinners and balls, including one for the city festival in mid August, are held in the hotel. The smartest day spot is a couch beside the Californian style terrace pool of the Palais (there is a day entrance fee for non-residents). The poolside cabanas have shower unit and day lounges with dining tables to which friends can be invited to share the lunch served from the pool bar.

There is of course plenty of alternative accommodation at all price levels in and around Biarritz. The sporting life offers everything from baccarat to bull-fighting, chess to karting, surfing to skating. Wide sandy beaches are separated from each other by rocky headlands. These Atlantic rollers provide France's premier surfing area – best on the Chambre d'Amour and Cote des Basques beaches, one each side of town. The Chambre d'Amour at Angelet, Biarritz's northerly point, has a grimly square cliff-set swimming pool with cabanas and bar/restaurant, the second most fashionable sunning spot with a younger and more athletic clientele. The beach gets its name from a legend about a rock grotto which became a 'room for love' for a courting couple, so engrossed in each other that they did not notice the rising tide and drowned in each other's arms. The town's buildings embrace the main beach; the Grande Plage sweeping majestically from the Palais to rocks below the Bellevue Casino where occasionally there are free *son et lumière* shows on the floodlit waves and rocks. The beach is backed by a small formal garden with a monument to Edward VII and Queen Victoria. Round the headland are two small enchanting coves, the Petit Port de Pecheurs, with old fishermen's cottages and boats, and Port Vieux for wave-free sheltered swimming.

Sister city is Bayonne with a festival held in mid August with bull races in the streets. Pelota, a fast game played by slamming a ball against a walled court from a cane basket strapped to the wrist, can be watched here. Day-by-day details of sports and social events in the area are contained in a booklet issued by the town tourist office opposite the Plaza Hotel. Basque culture wafts into sophisticated Biarritz at the beginning of August with the folklore festival; men dress as women, and wear huge dolls with long skirts over their shoulders or stiffened skirts to represent horse riding. They dance and sing to the martial accompaniment of the txistu flute and drum. Buy Basque souvenirs like the Malika cane walking stick which unscrews to show a savage stiletto, or more gentle table linen banded in red or green. Details about Biarritz from French Government Tourist offices or Comité du Tourisme et des Fêtes, Square Javalquinto, F-64200 Biarritz (59 24 20 24).

Old Customs

Italy Twice each summer Sienna stages the Palio, when galloping horsemen in costumes compete for the black and gold pennant (palio means banner). The Palio dates back to the twelfth century and its jousting background draws in locals who support the different horsemen. The second celebration takes place on the second Saturday in mid August in honour of the city's patron saint. It is held in the Piazza del Campo where the narrow track permits only ten riders: three places from the seventeen districts of the city are drawn by lot. The banner, horse and amateur rider are blessed in the cathedral or local church before the race. If a horse relieves itself during the blessing it is considered lucky. A costumed procession with mace bearers, knights, trumpeters, pages and drummers takes place before the race with city elders dressed *à la* Renaissance times. The Palio is paraded in an ox cart; after the race everyone goes to the church of the winner where the winners are blessed and the horse also attends the victory banquet. In the Ascoli Piceno area of Italy at Sant 'Elpictio a Mare, the bucket contest is held, a fifteenth-century re-enactment of the quarrels which took place among women of various towns in the neighbourhood over rights to draw water from the well.

At Piazza Armerina in Enna province the Norman Palio, another ancient piece of gamesmanship takes place for two days in mid month. A 300-strong historical procession in medieval costume takes place on the first day, followed on the next day by the palio or jousting match. Twenty knights divided into four groups try to hit a Saracen-shaped target with their lances. Next they try to throw a javelin through an iron ring held by the Saracen figure's arm. A jury decides at the end which team has won.

Spain Eliche, 22 km from Alicante, has a mystery play dating from the thirteenth century, the performance of which has been declared a 'national artistic monument' since 1931. It is the only example of living primitive lyrical theatre performed inside a Roman Catholic church, the basilica of Santa Maria, under papal dispensation. The two acts represent the death of the Virgin and her Assumption into heaven. The play has a musical backing. Tickets are needed for the first three days available from the city tourist office. Entrance is free for the following three days.

Portugal Viana do Castelo in the north celebrates the feast of Our Lady of the Agony with a week-long *romaria* (pilgrimage) with parades, processions, folk dancing, bullfights, fairs and fireworks. Regional costumes are worn and special sweetmeats and dishes are cooked, including bread baked in the form of couples making love, based on old fertility rituals.

Yugoslavia   At Planica and Zezersko in Slovenia there is a shepherds' fair to celebrate the return of the flocks from the mountains.

Luxembourg   In the last week of August and the first week of September there is the Schuberfouer, an ancient shepherds' market founded by John the Blind, Count of Luxembourg in 1340. It has now become the capital's amusement fair and on the last Sunday of August sheep decorated with ribbons parade through the city accompanied by shepherds dressed in folklore costumes and a band playing an old tune, the sheeps' march (*hammelsmarsch*).

Ireland   A billy goat, not a sheep, is the important animal at Puck Fair, a three-day event at Killorglin. A beribboned goat is 'enthroned' on a platform and watches the fair at which sheep, horses and cattle are sold.

Sweden   Visby in Gotland in early August has a medieval week complete with period music, Hanseatic merchants, craftsmen and monks dressed in medieval clothes and there are dances, games, walks and church services. In the ruins of St Nicola's church, concerts and pageants are held, the music drifting out to Visby lanes on the August night air. In the illuminated open-air chancel of the church one can see *Petrus de Daaia*, a musical pageant; concerts of folk music are given in the museum courtyard.

In the middle of the month there is the Lapp holiday, celebrated in Swedish Lapland with reindeer lassooing, church services, and after-church coffee in the Lapp village at Mala.

France   Brittany holds its pardon festivals in August, when women wear high lace hats and embroidered clothes and the devout seek forgiveness for their sins. At Quelven in mid August the religious festival starts with a wooden angel flying down a cable with lighted wick to start a bonfire. After penance, feasts, dancing, wrestling and other activities break out. The pardons are said to date from the Celtic feasts of the dead and are often held in remote spots with candlelit processions. Some of the best are at St Anne d'Auray, Locronan, Le Folgoet and Rumengol. Local tourist offices and churches can give dates and details.

August

Belgium Again, Belgium has splendid events. Towards the
end of the month Bruges holds the procession of Mary of
Burgundy in the evening on two nights. Hundreds of actors,
riders, dancers and musicians enact scenes from the short life of
Mary of Burgundy, the drama heightened by the onset of night
and torchlight. Reserved and numbered seats are sold in grandstands and on benches – tickets obtainable from Tourist Office,
Markt 7, B-8000, Bruges (050/33 07 11).

At the beginning of the month, on the first Sunday at
Koksijde, a spot where artists have traditionally lived or spent
holidays, a pageant honours Flemish painting. Some 33 floats
decorated with flowers make their way through the streets of an
area known as the Flower Seaside Resort of Belgium. Details:
Tourist Office Koksijde, Gemeeentehuis, B-8460 Koksijde (058
51 63 41). On the fourth Sunday of August the city of Ath
celebrates its patron saint's festival. On the previous afternoon
at 1500 the bell of St Julian's Church peals at full strength
and an old local tune, the Grand Gouyasse, is played, accompanied by a musket volley. In the Grand Place a procession
forms headed by the 'blues', an armed company, descendants of
the 'cannoniers-arquebusiers', wearing two-horned ornamented
hats, short white breeches and the black gaiters of French
guards and carrying sabre, tinder box and cartridge pouch on
buffalo hide supports. Behind them comes a band followed by
Mr and Mrs Goliath, two wickerwork figures about twelve feet
high, each borne by only one man though they weigh over 200
pounds. Other men wait nearby to take over when the bearers
get tired. Mr Goliath carries a sword and mace with sharp points
and wears a cuirass and helmet. His wife wears a black velvet
bodice with a white veil and carries orange flowers. Dating from
the mid fifteenth century, Goliath was the hero of the cross-
bowmen but his wife only dates from 1715. David also marches
near Goliath, in white with a shepherd's crook, and a devil
figure darts about threatening the spectators with an inflated
bladder. He is assisted in this by men dressed entirely in ivy
leaves armed with wicker bludgeons. The procession is followed
by city leaders and citizens. At various points along the route,
the giants dance, waltzing and embracing. In front of the city
hall David tries to slay Goliath with his sling while old rhymes
are recited. In the evening a concert is given in the Grand Place
and the following morning another procession takes place.

Food

Sweden The crayfish season begins around 7–8 August. In
Stockholm, all restaurants and households hold crayfish supper

164

parties. It is estimated that 1½ million crayfish are eaten in Stockholm each day until the end of September. Tables are decorated with coloured lights and paper lanterns and Kraftor pottery for these feasts. In the villages, evening crayfish festivals are held. The crayfish, 5–6 inches long, served with beer and shots of aquavit, are boiled with dill and eaten well guarded with bibs and napkins. There is a mussel festival in Tanum.

Finland The freshwater crayfish are cooked with dill, salt, beer, sugar and vinegar, preferably marinated overnight to get the full flavour and washed down with beer or vodka. Also wearing bibs, Finns eat every crayfish morsel with hot buttered toast. Some houses have what is called 'a crayfish terrace' – balconies, usually facing the sunset, on which family and friends gather to eat and unwind. These summer suppers usually follow a sauna.

Norway Prawns are prized, often eaten in the late sunset on platforms stilted out over the water and consumed with mayonnaise and beer. In the late north Scandinavian nights of August, fish can be caught and grilled over a fjordside fire in a midnight feast of firm-fleshed fish served with melted butter, potatoes or thin crisp flotbrod. In Sweden char and trout are grilled by the lakeside with a sprig of dill, butter and salt wrapped in foil over birchwood fires. The portable picnic accompaniment in Sweden is tunnbrod – a pancake rolled round a spreading of Swedish goat's-milk butter. It is also the time in Scandinavia to take a plastic bucket and pick berries, cloud (served with fudge sauce in some Helsinki restaurants), and bilberries which are made into preserves or eaten with cream or yoghurt. In Finland arctic bramble, whortleberry, rowan, blue, ligon and cranberries accompany meat dishes, are served as desserts or are made into liqueurs.

UK The grouse season starts on 12 August with a race to bring the first samples down to top London hotel tables, though pundits say a little hanging around would help the flavour. Blackberries begin to ripen in the south and in the north rowanberries (till November) are made into jelly and served with game. Wild duck, pheasant, hare and venison also become available. Dublin Bay prawns are at their peak.

Musseling: Wexford in Ireland holds a mussel and seafood festival.

The Netherlands Each year Zeeland produces a million tonnes of mussels and oysters. Traditional mussel festivals take place at Yerseke and Philippine near the Oosterschelde estuary. In late August Yerseke celebrates its harvest, still a mainstay of the economy, with free mussel-tasting.

Sweden   In Turku there are medieval banquets (held in several languages) in memory of Duke John, which are typical sixteenth-century meals served in the castle (details Hamburger Bors, Kauppiaskatu 6, 20100 Turku (9 21 511 211)). Grosbous in Luxembourg has a popular pig fete with spit-roasted pig, concerts and dancing and in Belgium at Veurne in mid month the park and streets go back to the year 1900 with costumes and old crafts presented in historic settings. Traditional games are played by children and cheeses, meats, sweets and beers of the region can be tasted. The programme begins in the afternoon but the feast lasts till midnight and an old style ball starts at 2000 in the park. Details, Tourist Office, Grote Markt 29, B-8480 Veurne (058 31 21 54).

Germany   At Worms on Rhine in late August and early September there is the Backfish Festival. Backfish is a kind of mackerel caught and eaten in great quantities during the festival. Worms also offers wine and is the home of Liebfraumilch. Lamplight parades, concerts, water sports and fireworks all part of the festival. Details from Worms Tourist Office, 14 Neu Markt, 6520 Worms (06241 25045).

France   In Deauville at the Normandy Hotel set in the Norman courtyard one can, during this month, have a simple 'autour d'un plat' menu with a glass of wine of the day for about 100 francs including service. The hotel also offers a number of theme dinners during August.

Wine

Germany opens the wine festival season with events in Wiesbaden, Rudesheim, a Mosel wine market at Mainz and a wine village at Stuttgart. In the Belgium Ardennes there is La Gleize Wine Festival. In Spain in Pontevedra at Salvaterra de Mino the wine festival is held on the first Sunday of August to publicise some excellent white wines. Since 1976 the *Noche del Vino* (night of Wine) has been held at Competa in the Malaga region. From nightfall on 15 August to dawn the next day, free wine is supplied to all and there is theatre, singing, dancing and poetry reading. At the end of August the fiesta in Requena (Valencia) is considered to be the oldest in Spain. It features wine competitions, heaviest grape competition, an exhibition of wine growing and making equipment, wine tasting and discussions on wine. There is free wine tasting in various parts of the town during the fair.

Arts

There is still plenty to choose from, with the accent on open air performances.

Italy   Rome has opera in the baths of Caracalla and at Torre del Lago near Lucca, the last home of Puccini, there are performances of his opera in the open air, with seating set up near the lakeside.

Verona's festival, held in the Roman arena, is one of the most popular in summer (tours are run from the UK by companies like Swan Hellenic, 77 New Oxford Street, London WC1A 1PP (01–831 1616) and also by Heritage. The Verona festival of opera runs during July and August in an arena seating 25,000 and acoustics perfect to the last row. Opera fans can stay in the city or on Lake Garda, travelling to Verona from London on the Venice Simplon Orient Express train which takes 30 hours. Milan is the nearest airport for Verona. The festival, which has been held for nearly 70 years, features works by Verdi and Puccini: *Aida* is a particularly popular opera, though *La Boheme* is performed with equally stunning effect.

Austria   The Salzburg Festival predominates, booked out well ahead and described as international and elitist. Begun at the end of the First World War with the help of Richard Strauss, Max Reinhardt and others, it was intended to heal the scars of war and move culture away from Vienna to a more peaceful setting. In 1920, for the first time, receipts went to charity and performers received gifts rather than salaries. The festival hall was built by Clemens Holzmeister, a famous Austrian architect. Recently Herbert von Karajan has been the festival's leading figure. The programme includes concerts, opera and performances at the city's Marionettentheater.

The Mozart and Haydn Festival is held in Vienna from the beginning of August to mid September in the church of St Charles Borromeo, a baroque building, and in the Palais Liechtenstein as well as in the recently restored and reopened Palais Ferstel. Information and tickets from Haydn Sinfonetta, Preindlgasse 1, A-1130 Vienna (222 82 52 08).

Switzerland On the shores of Lake Constance, the Bregenz festival dates from 1946 with performances on floating platforms in the middle of the lake. If it rains the event moves to the recently-built festival hall. Held at the same time as Salzburg, the mood is light with operettas, two operas, symphony concerts and recitals. The city's setting, between the Voralberg mountains and the lakeshore is delightful, and events also move out to the surrounding villages.

Switzerland: Montreux–Vevey has a classical music festival at the end of August into October with the participation of top international artists. Information from The Festival de Montreux, Avenue des Alpes 14, PO Box 124, Ch-1820 Montreux (021 63 54 50). Lucerne from mid August has an international music festival of concerts of chamber, symphonic, old music and lieder with exhibitions on composers and their music. Bookings from Central Music Dept, Hischmattstrasse 13, PO Box B Ch-6002 (041 23 52 72).

Saanen near Gstaad: The Yehudi Menuhin Festival runs through August. The festival, over 30 years old, supports young performers and many composers have had their works premiered in Saanen. Not surprisingly, the accent is on the violin, with Menuhin himself often performing. The Gstaad tourist office arranges packages for the festival of seven nights with half board, two concerts in the church of Saanen, excursions and folklore evening. Information and bookings from Verkehrsbuero, 3780 Gstaad, Switzerland (030 4 10 55).

Germany An enchanting evening can be had staying at the Goldener Pflug (golden plough) at Ising on Lake Chiemsee in Bavaria. From the lakeside there are boat trips to the island on which stands the summer palace of Ludwig II in the gilded long hall of which summer concerts of baroque chamber music are performed.

Oberammargau Passion Play. In gratitude for surviving the plague in 1634 the citizens of this small German village fulfilled a promise to put on a play about the agony and passion of Christ every ten years; the next performance will be in 1990. The whole village joins in the play, using a text dating from 1850; in the intervals it is possible to spot the leading actors going about their normal daily lives in the village.

Belgium A quiet West Flemish village, Dranouter, hosts an international folk festival with a weekend offering not only folk but country, bluegrass, blues, folk-pop, folk rock, funk and jazz. Groups from around 15 countries perform. Free camping near the festival field is available for this first weekend in August with food services on the spot. Details: Piet Lesage, Schomminkelstraat 8, 8961 Westouter-Heuvelland (057 44 61 02).

Finland   The Helsinki Festival, started in 1967, continues the traditions of the Sibelius weeks of the 1950s and 1960s. The programme has much expanded since then, to include concerts, opera, ballet, jazz, pop, theatre, films, literature and exhibitions. Details from Helsingen Juhlaviikot, Unioninkatu 28, 00100 Helsinki (90 659688).

UK   The Edinburgh Festival dominates in August, and attracts crowds of visitors to the city.

Over 40 years old, it runs from about 10 to 30 August and, ever growing, has recently spread out to suburbs and housing estates, all within five miles of the city centre. Opera, symphony, theatre are the main attractions, featuring international performers. There are over 500 companies and groups in the Fringe Festival, featuring professionals and amateurs. Jazz and film festivals are also staged. A spine-tingling event (and chilling, if the night is cold) is the military tattoo at the end of the month at night in the floodlit parade ground in front of Edinburgh Castle (take a rug and Thermos comforter). The tattoo, though mainly comprising skirling pipe bands and regiments from Scotland, is also international. Information and bookings (for all Edinburgh's festivals and the tattoo), Edinburgh Capital Group, Queen's Hall Box Office, Clerk Street, Edinburgh EH8 9JG for postal bookings. For individual events; Edinburgh Festival, 21 Market Street, Edinburgh EH1 1BN (031 226 4001); International Festival Fringe, The Netherbow Arts Centre, 43 High Street, Edinburgh EH1 1SR (031 556 9579); Tattoo Office, 22 Market Street, Edinburgh EH6 1QB (031 225 1188).

Wales: in the first week of August the National Eisteddfod (not to be confused with the international musical gathering at Llangollen, see page 141. Almost every community in Wales has its own small annual Eisteddfod, an amateur festival of poetry and music. At most there are three sessions starting with young children and rising in age groups. The National Eisteddfod alternates between north and south Wales and aims to preserve and foster Welsh culture. The Archdruid is ceremoniously proclaimed in the June of the preceding year in a 30-foot stone circle specially set up. The Archdruid is attended by Bards in ceremonial robes. In its present form the Eisteddfod dates only from the mid nineteenth century but in the Middle Ages many Welsh princes held Eisteddfods at their courts: the first recorded was held in Cardigan Castle in 1176. On the Tuesday and Thursday of the Eisteddfod the ceremony of chairing and crowning of the Bards takes place, with the presentation of literature gold medals and traditional welcomes to overseas visitors. The chair is awarded to the writer of the winning poem on a set theme written in a special Welsh verse form. The crown is awarded for the best free verse poem. The Eisteddfod is attended by 20,000 to 30,000 people.

Three Choirs Festival: the oldest of them all in Europe, dating from the early 1700s. It is held in the third week of August, a musical festival that moves between Gloucester, Hereford and Worcester bringing together the choirs of these three cathedrals. Information from Publicity Secretary, The Gables, South Street, Leominster, Herefordshire HR6 8JN (0568 5223).

Arundel: has its festival in the last week of August. The tilting yard of Arundel Castle becomes an open-air theatre for Shakespeare, music and jazz. Events include sculpture exhibitions, literary luncheons, puppet plays and a children's 'colossal paintin'. Sports, revues, craft markets and open air events give the festival a family air. Box office: Mill Road, Arundel, West Sussex (0903 883474).

Lake District Summer Music – a summer school and festival attracting artists and students from all over the world with nightly concerts at venues throughout the Lake District given by the concert artists who form the tutorial staff of the school. Exhibitions of painting, sculpture and crafts are also included. The school is based at Charlotte Mason College in Ambleside with daily tuition for string players and pianists with an emphasis on chamber music. Master classes are open to the public. Children between the ages of 7 and 13 can have string tuition. Information from the Administrator, The Grange, Clay Lane, Handforth, Wilmslow, Cheshire SK9 3NR (0625 522968).

Sport

Horses: the Swedish Derby takes place near Malmoat Jagersro; in Vienna there is the *Concours d'elegance* at the end of August, an international tournament for horse-drawn carriages held at the Freudenau grounds of the Viennese horse racing association. Dressage, obstacle races and team contests begin with a decorated carriage parade. A ball, of course, is held for the occasion at the Palais Auersperg. London replies on the first Sunday of the month with the London Riding Horse parade in Rotten Row in Hyde Park, beginning at 1400 with the aim of finding the best turned-out horse and rider. There are classes for ladies both astride and side saddle, children, gentlemen and riding clubs or school teams of three. The overall winner receives a cup and each entrant of suitable standard gets a merit rosette. Admission is free, details from the Hon. Secretary, London Riding Horse Parade, 10a The Pavement, Chapel Road, West Norwood, SE27 0UN (01–761 5651) (evenings and weekends).

There are the National Championship horse trials held at Gatcombe Park, the country home of the Princess Royal, Baden Baden runs a chic race meeting comparable in elegance with Royal Ascot. The rodeos held in France's Camargue area are more casual. But the big horse event of the month is the Dublin Horse Show, held over five days at a permanent 60-acre showground in Ballsbridge. Some 2,000 horses and 150,000 people gather to see and take part in two top show-jumping events – the Aga Khan team trophy on the Friday and the Irish Grand Prix on the Saturday. The show is sponsored by the Royal Dublin Society, founded in 1731 to improve the quality of agricultural life. Called the biggest horse fair in the world, sales of horses are also made. All types of horses are on show – polo ponies, children's mounts, draught horses, hunters and even a parade of donkeys. Music, dancing, fashion shows and hunt balls in the Dublin hotels form the backup to the horseflesh.

Boats: in the first nine days of the month the top event is Cowes week, held on the Isle of Wight (information on 0983 295744). But spectators need a boat or a good spot on the beach to follow the action. First held in 1826, the regatta hosts the Admiral's Cup on certain years when the worlds' latest in boat design converges on Cowes. The narrow streets of Cowes have pubs, souvenir shops and chandlers and people wear oil skins, yachtie caps and yellow wellies. Clubs on the waterfront, such as the Royal London, the Island Sailing Club and Cowes Corinthian, offer vantage points for race watching for a lucky few. The Royal Yacht Squadron is the most prestigious of all, housed in a castle built by Henry VIII in 1568 which became the Royal Yacht Squadron in June 1815. The first members had to own a yacht of at least ten tons and pay 3 guineas annually. Cowes was then a fashionable summer resort – the Prince Regent had a house there – and the club set began to race and live on their yachts. Edward VII, as Prince of Wales, granted the royal title to the squadron and the reigning king is the club's admiral, the Queen is the Patron. Even today ladies are classed as 'associate' members and must be wives or unmarried daughters of members; they have their own separate entrance.

The final evening of the regatta ends with a firework display. Around 500 boats of all types race to win, and there are often

Royal Navy ships to visit. Every other year (on uneven numbered years) the Fastnet Race takes place.

Flat-bottomed sailing barges are much more sedate as a form
of water transport. In the first two weeks of August, in Holland's Friesland, the 'skutjesilen' takes place, a race for these
barges which in the past used to carry goods along the shallow
waterways. The race starts from Grouw and ends two weeks later
in Sneek. Part of the race involves the towing of the 14 barges
taking part by a fleet of other vessels. Windsurfing, on the
smallest 'boat' of all, can be enjoyed in marathon form on Lake
Sila near St Moritz, where there are also sailing events.

Helsinki has its city marathon in August, Denmark has cycle
races, and Cyprus has its open tennis tournament in Troodos
during the first two weeks of August. This is open to all
including foreign visitors and professionals. The month's most
offbeat sport is Bog Snorkelling. The world bog snorkelling
championships are held at the end of August at Llanwrtyd
Wells, Powys, in Wales – fittingly in a town known for its
'stinking well' of sulphur water. Competitors swim lengths of a
fourteen by six foot ditch of dirty water in a wet suit, snorkel
and flippers.

Wales also hosts the grass skiing championships this month.
The British grass skiing season is roughly from April till
October, for a sport invented around 1969 by a German frus-
trated at the lack of skiing in summer. Since then Italy, Switzerland, Austria, France and Britain have adopted it. Grass skiing
has been described as a cross between snow skiing and roller
skating. It is similar to parallel or fall line skiing but on short skis
which consist of rollers set in a kind of caterpillar track like a vast
bicycle chain. All you need are the skis, snow ski boots and
sticks (broom sticks are much used). Clothing is jeans, gloves,
and tee shirt or sweater best with long sleeves to minimise grass
burns in falling; speeds of up to 55 mph can be achieved. The
grass slope needed is a field with a run of about 300 yards wide
and a slope of 12–15 degrees down a 600-foot length. The grass
should be about 4 inches long, though downland cropped by
grazing is perfect. Skiing through long grass is akin to deep
snow skiing. There are about ten permanent slopes in Britain
and places like London's Primrose Hill can be used. The Lake
District's Limefitt Park is where it began in the UK. In Britain
details can be obtained from the Ski Club of Great Britain, 118
Eaton Square, London SW1W 9AF, who also issue a calendar of
competitive events.

Shopping

Bookworms will make for Edinburgh at the beginning of August for the Edinburgh Book Fair, which began in 1984 and is held every other year. Authors give talks and readings, meet their readers and sign books. Books are also on sale. The visitor can browse, watch book-binding demonstrations, paper-making and desktop publishing, take refreshment or relax over a read in the Charlotte Square gardens, where a chef may also give demonstrations. Children's books are in separate marquees where competitions, collages and shows are organised. In Belgium the Ardennes village of Redu, twinned with Hay on Wye, Britain's book town, has 24 bookshops, several of which stock English works and can be found around the church or in a narrow street alongside a local cafe. Information from Redu Initiatives, Maison Communale, B-6914 Redu (Libin) (061 65 59 97). In Knokke there is an art and antiques fair including English dealers offering a wide range of articles such as traditional crafts and collections covering furniture, paintings, sculpture, objets d'art in glass, copper, pewter, decorated earthenware and porcelain dating from the Middle Ages. Displays with a museum approach are included and the fair is held at Scharpoord cultuurcentrum, Meerland, 32, Knokke – open from 1500–2100. Information from G. and C. Tuteleers, Gemeneweideweg noord 9, B-8310 Bruges (050 35 40 07).

During Regatta Week in Cowes (see above), Bonhams holds an annual auction of fine marine paintings, prints and models at 84 High Street, Cowes for viewing; these are then sold in the London Montpelier Street sale rooms.

In Luxembourg the Braderie annual sidewalk sales are held on the last Monday of August. The avenues and streets of Luxembourg city centre and around the railway station are closed to traffic and crowds shop and eat grilled sausages in a festive atmosphere.

Horticultural

There are lots of flower parades and flower festivals around Europe. There are begonias on show at Belgium's Blankenberg; flower days in Germany's Trier; a heather blossom festival in Luxembourg; a rose festival in Scotland's Aberdeen; and in North Brittany, at Pampol, flowers are flung at the waves on the first Sunday in August to celebrate a naval victory. In Cyprus, August is the month for village festivals with local food, exhibitions of folk art and flowers. In Spain, at Torrelavega in

Santander province, a floral gala has been held since 1956 centring round a competitive parade of flower-decorated floats and a battle of flowers. On the last Monday Laredo, also in Santander province, has a battle of flowers dating from 1908 that takes place along the main street with a parade of floral floats and prizes for the best decorated.

Holland has flower parades in August and at the beginning of the month the Delta Flora parade is held from Rijnsburg via Oegstgeest and Katwijk aan Zee to Noordwijk. A week later one is held in Katwijk and the major parade is that from Aalsmeer to Amsterdam at the beginning of September. Belgium's Blankenberg floral parade is at the month end, with private cars decorated with flowers, costumed actors, dance and choreography shows, brass bands and majorette groups from Belgium and other countries and an annual theme for decorations. Information from Tourist Office, Leopold III plein, B-8370 Blankenberg (050 41 22 27).

In Jersey on the second Thursday of the month is the great Battle of Flowers. It has been run for nearly 90 years and tickets

Battle of Flowers, Jersey Flower Festival

to see the parade of intricately decorated floats are available from 1 January from the executive secretary, Jersey Battle of Flowers Association, Meadow Bank, St Peter's Valley, St Lawrence, Jersey (0534 30178). If you miss the parade there is the Battle of Flowers museum at La Robeline, Mont des Corvees, St Ouen, which contains floats decorated in wild flowers, all past entries of the battle.

Sweden is a good place for August gardens. At the beginning of the month there is the Day of the Garden (Ortagardens Dag). At Visingso, in Smaland, there is the country's finest baroque garden with over 500 different plants and flowers shown at their best. Music and entertainment are provided as well as information on plants.

Near Rome, the Tivoli Gardens, created about 1552 by Cardinal d'Este, are cooling, hung in the middle of hills with avenues of 300 fountains, organ pipe fountains, jets and cascades including an egg-shaped fountain where one can walk round dry under the fountain overhang to 'earn' a long life. The gardens are formal in style, with trees and shrubs, and tend to get overcrowded with tourists with three tour bus departure times a day from Rome.

Kew Gardens, London, has a fete at the beginning of August on Kew Green which includes plants and produce for sale. Information from Richmond upon Thames Tourist Association, Twickenham TW1 3AA (01–892 8696).

Leeds Castle in Kent on August bank holiday has a flower festival with the interior of the castle acting as a display area for flower arrangement societies who depict themes such as fairy tales and nursery rhymes.

On Show

Ships ahoy at the Navy Days at Portsmouth; Greenwich has its clipper weeks with information from the London Tourist Board; there are sheep dog trials in Ambleside and Brecon in Wales, international jousting at Leeds Castle and in Germany's Kassel the Documenta modern (very) art exhibition – one exhibit was of 7,000 oak tree trunks – which has been called an innovative restless showcase. Information from Documenta GmbH, Friederich Engels strasse 20, Kassel (0561 777500). For five nights in Knokke-Heist in Belgium things certainly go with a bang when the International Firework Festival is held with displays at 2300 from the Beach Casino. From five different countries, firework makers battle with Bengal fire, Roman candles and crackers, all synchronised with music. A professional and public jury choose the prizewinners. Information from the tourist office, Stadhuis, B-8300 Knokke-Heist (050 60 61 85).

Seasonal Discounts

As well as the lower season prices and quiet in Scandinavia, capital city hotels such as the Intercontinentals and Hilton offer weekend bargains at special rates. In Vienna up to 50 per cent off prices can be obtained for small groups at the Marriott Hotel any day and the SAS Palais hotel till the end of August has cheaper last minute bookings made within 24 hours of arrival. Through August the Hilton has special weekend rates for couples. In Britain north Devon is not always booked out and it's possible to plan last minute holidays there.

Public Holidays

1 August, public holiday in Scotland, Ireland, National Day in Switzerland with a holiday afternoon.
Assumption Day, mid month, Belgium, France, Germany, Italy, Luxembourg, Portugal, Spain.
Last Monday in month, Bank Holiday UK (except Scotland).

SEPTEMBER

THE MIDAS TOUCH

THOUGH June is the liveliest season when the sap is still rising, my favourite month is September, a gentle, soothing, fulfilled month when the fruits ripen, the sun-soaked stones of summer give back a gentle warmth. The days may be shorter but it is usually a warm, dry month, still time to get south for a tan, and for women that delightful time when the rich, glowing colours of the new fashion wools and knits fill the shops and one can buy knowing plenty of wear will be possible – not always the case with light summer cottons. September is a gilded month when fruit, trees and walls glow with warmth; the last of the summer wine flows. It is a month light in tone before the heavier and more sombre feel of October and November.

Go for Gold

September is a Midas miracle: man's search for the philosopher's stone that turns all to gold comes true in nature; even the harvest moon rises large and tinged yellow, echoing the sun. In travelling round Europe one can go for gold in scenery and produce, feasting at festivals, eating outside in stone-sheltered spots. Gold medal winners are the scarlets, rich russets and magnificent mustard hues of tree leaves. The Scandivanian birch forests are magnificent, Germany and France too still possess large unspoilt forests in which to see September colours; collect the fruits of autumn and relax.

In France the chestnuts of the Auvergne can be seen while exploring old volcanic craters and Le Mont Dore near Clermont Ferrand. In Italy the chestnut forests rising back from Viareggio around Carrara and the wild valleys near Pisa attracted nineteenth-century poets. Back in France, Limousin is another wooded autumn colour picture and Sweden's Varmland has birch forests with deep valleys best seen from the canoeing trails on the area's 600 lakes. Tuscany's wooded Chianti hills can be seen while based in Florence and there are plenty of short break packages offered in autumn. A wine exploration in this area can start at the Cantinetta Antinori in the palazzo home of the noted wine family. The Cantinetta is near the Pitti Palace in Florence and a section of the vast entrance of the palace has been partitioned off to create a wine bar where in autumn huge bunches of grapes hang over the bar and local dishes are the fare. From the excellent Florence tourist office one can get a special map to guide one along the Chianti classico routes of stone villages and castles, where wines can be bought direct from the producers, in the way the Florentines shop for sips. The best Chiantis are distinguished by a black cockerel neck label or, around Pisa, a putto cherub symbol. A lovely September soother is to sit in the formal lemon and orange, olive and vine garden of Machiavelli's house at San Andrea in Percussina. Opposite the house is a small inn, L'Albergacio del Machiavelli.

This is the time for wine festivals in Germany. When the season is becoming 'low' in most parts of Europe, this month, the Rhine Palatinate region of Germany is enjoying its high season. The area covers the Eiffel mountains near the French border and the beautiful wooded Aar valley, and the volcanic craters and peaks around the little town of Daun with a fairy tale twelfth-century castle, set deep in a wooded crater. Eltz is all towers, turrets and courts; it is a 20-minute walk down to it from the rim. The queues on September weekends to get in underline the popularity of visits at this time of year. Inside the rooms contain weapons, fifteenth- and sixteenth-century furniture and paintings on wood, the 'built in toilets' in every third room, the sewage shafts leading into the valley and rain water from the roofs channelled through the shafts to flush them. The medieval kitchen includes a tufa volcanic stone oven heated with wood to cook bread on its stones; the thick-walled closet acted as a primitive cooling room.

The area is pinnacled with castles, many ruined but apart from Eltz all having superb views, usually down over a river valley. A particularly enchanting one is the castle above Cochen on the Mosel, one to inspire the fairy tale writer with charming flowered courtyards, herb garden and grim witches tower from which the unfortunate ladies were cast down. If they lived, as the excellent English-speaking guide remarked, 'they were put together again and rejoined society'.

A large number of the castles have a courtyard wine garden cafe bright with geraniums and gingham cloths. In the area one is never far from a glass of wine either in the inns or in tasting (wine probe) bars or weingut where the producers' own wine is on offer.

The Mosel is a magnificent river. In 1964 it was raised to the status of first class river and boats can travel from France into the Rhine at Koblenz. The Mosel loops and twists round on itself amid great spurs of land topped with towers and monasteries. One of the most dramatic curves is at Marienberg near Zell (which has its wine festival at the end of September). The Marienberg tower has been there for 800 years and one can sit on its terraces and watch the barges and pleasure craft straining round the great bend below the vineyards.

The looping provides extra south-facing vineyards and the valley retains the sun well through September. The land is of slate and slate piled round the wines soaks heat in by day and lets it out at night, protecting the vines from frost. This enables the very late harvested wines like Trockenauselese and even 'ice wine', sweet and rich in sugar, to be produced.

The vineyards are so steep in places that ski lifts were once considered as an aid to the hand tilling of the slopes. The different places have rather jokey names for wines: Neckarsche, smack bottom, Schwartz katz (black cat from Zell), Wheler Sonnehem – a vineyard indicated by a huge sundial. Piesport and Goldtropfchen are other wine names from the area. In Bernkastel, a pretty town with a small square of half-timbered houses round an angel fountain, is the scene of the biggest Mosel wine festival at the first weekend in September, beginning on the Friday with the naming of the wine queen. On Saturday evening there are fireworks from the Landshut Castle, built in the twelfth century by the Archbishop of Trier. On the Sunday morning a parade goes through the narrow streets and over the bridge to Cues the sister town. Around 40 wine houses have stalls in the streets selling wine, there is a fairground at Cues and some 200,000 visitors come to the festival. Just above the town is Mosel's most expensive vineyard, the Doktor. One can check out the health-giving properties of this wine in little bars near the bridge, where outside walls are marked with the high flood levels of the Mosel. The name Doktor is said to come from the curing of an Electoral prince's fever, though another story says it was recommended to Edward VII by his physician.

The German Wine Academy, PO Box 1705, 6500 Mainz, runs seminars and courses each year at different levels, some in English. Details are available in leaflet form from the German National Tourist Offices. One can learn about wine production, ancient and modern, while touring in the Mosel. At the Roman-founded (the locals say Mosel wines were originally grown to provide the occupying Roman soldiers with their daily allowance) city of Trier, dating from 1500 and Germany's oldest, there is the Landesmuseum with old wine relics of that time, and a charming carving of a stone wine ship from the third century from a wine merchant's tomb. Trier is a gentle place in which to sip wine in creeper-clad courtyards by the Porta Negra and buy wooden stemmed pokal glasses, the characteristic Mosel shape.

At Bernkastel's twin town of Cues (named for a sixteenth-century theologian) across the bridge there is the Mosel wine museum in part of the old monastery, with wine-tasting halls and courtyard cafe. Old types of machinery and the colourful labels of yesteryear are among the exhibits.

A good spot to see present day viticulture is the Kloster Machem near Zell. Here Michael Schneider and his family have lovingly restored a ruined abbey where noble ladies including Maria von Metternich retreated in the eighteenth century and have made it a base for wine-tasting, tours and sampling. A huge vaulted hall which overlooks the baroque altar of the old church is now the setting for evening concerts during summer with top international musicians. Saint Cornelius, the patron of the abbey's day on 16 September, is celebrated with a Mass, wine festival and a spectacular musical performance with fireworks accompaniment in the extensive vineyards, the biggest on the Mosel.

The grape harvest does not start in the Mosel till well into autumn, usually around 20 October. This means that September is a time when the wine producers can be convivial. The calendar is packed with wine festivals: every small town has its own, mostly consisting of informal wine stalls, sausages and foods in the market place round a fountain that once ran wine at these times. Now, for reasons of hygiene, this is forbidden – though the fountains may be drained and young girls in local costume stand in the fountain bowl selling wine. At Cochem there are games in the streets, wrestling, tugs of war, and jazz played on cafe terraces overlooking the river. By day there is music, wine queens and processions and at night fireworks and yet more wine. A complete list of festivals on the Mosel and Rhine is available each year from the German National Tourist Office. Book accommodation very early on for these times or perhaps stay on a vineyard farm. DER Travel Service, 18 Conduit Street, London WIR 9TD (tel. 01–408 0111) can arrange stays in and around the wine towns and have special tours to the wine villages of the Rhine and Mosel. The Rhine Palatinate tourist office also has a programme of wine and vineyard holiday ideas, including cycling tours.

English is widely understood by the tourist officials in this area and on the Rhine, which has similar wine festivals in its little towns. British tourists are the number one foreign group with 70,000 to 80,000 visiting Boppard alone. Boppard has its wine festival on the last weekend of September and another at the beginning of October, with wine in the market square and fireworks on the river. On the second Wednesday/Thursday of September there is an onion market.

September is the time the British come to the area by car, coach or flying on a Lufthansa fly-drive scheme via Dusseldorf or Frankfurt. A car is probably not necessary unless one wants to cut across the high Hunsruck road over the plateau country to the Mosel area. Otherwise the river pleasure boats are better than buses. Timetables and tickets are available by the jetty of each little town which displays its name on the river bank so one can cross by ferry or journey up and down the rivers, stopping on and off at will. Most of the larger boats have restaurants or cafes on board. On the Rhine this is the best way to see the cliff sides topped with castles, where the vineyards, little towns and railway tunnels are distinguished by turreted or cathedral like entrances. One can depart from Boppard, one of the prettiest of the Rhine towns with its riverside promenade below the hotels. The gracious century-old Bellevue hotel is the place to stay here where one dines well in the river facing restaurant.

In addition to its wine festival, the Rhine has a very special event on the third Saturday of September (there is also a similar 'manifestation' to use the French term, earlier in the summer). This is the Rhine in Flames. If you can, book ahead on a dinner boat cruise or best of all a cruise on one of the KD (Koln-Dusseldorf) hotel boats – the cruise listed as being in Rudesheim on that Saturday; this is the most luxurious and expensive way of seeing the show and a serene way of seeing the whole (or sections, as wished) of the Rhine and Mosel.

Failing this, just go down to the Rhine banks at St Goar or on the opposite banks at St Goarhausen in late afternoon and stand on the banks in the crowds. There are avenues of stalls selling wine, beer, sausages and snack foods and plenty to occupy one till the river traffic is stopped with about 70 boats nosing the current grouped across the river. The town lights go out at 2030 and the ruined windows of the Rheinfeld Castle above St Goar burn red, flicker and smoke billows to the stars. At the same time on the opposite banks, the Katz Castle burns and all along the banks, houses appear to be in flames, the lurid effect heightened by strings of red lights hung from the riverside houses and night lights flickering on balconies. Hundreds of people buy lights set in plastic floats and set these off down river, the flames bobbing and swirling between the boats so that even the river seems ablaze.

The 'fires' are doused and into the night first from one castle then the other, across the river, fireworks soar, like big bursting umbrella shapes of glittering colours, the tips exploding into yet more colours. The crowds applaud the best. The colours and noise create a crescendo at the finale, after which all the boats blare their horns and the crowds turn to a few more glasses of wine before drifting away.

Clocking on in the Black Forest

Not too far away is the Black Forest, ideal for walking holidays at this time of year. From November to May in the old days the forest people were cut off by winter and spent their time indoors carving, making clocks and straw items. The farmhouses were huge, animals lived within the house in stables, there were workshops, threshing rooms, and heat from a big stove which rose to a family bathroom. There were no chimneys and the fire's smoke cured the wood of the houses and killed any insects. Hams, bacons and sausages were also cured in the house. A pond outside supplied water and a cooling system for home-made butter and cheeses. Often there was a little chapel and a 'trying' house next door, where the heir would sleep with his girl friend to test if she could become pregnant before they married.

Such self-sufficient farmhouses can be seen at the open air museum at Vogtsbauerhof in the Gutach valley. Though modernised now, farmhouses are still built big and are now becoming popular and inexpensive accommodation bases for visitors. Cycles hired from railway stations – and feet – are the best means of seeing the Black Forest.

A comfortable hotel, such as those in Triberg and Titisee, can be chosen as a hiking base. Triberg is the clock-makers' town, set high in the hills, with a long steep main street seemingly mainly of clock shops cuckooing madly, set off by the booming church clock. The Parkhotel Wehrle has been owned by the same family since 1707. Hemingway was a guest when he was trout fishing and there is a menu consisting solely of trout specialities. The main rooms are traditionally decorated in pine and regional and nouvelle cuisine style food is served in a stube dining room, part of which was once a smithy. The owner has set up a series of packages for walkers in the area following 'the trail of the cuckoo clock traders'. Nine different hotels are linked in a circular route providing 12 to 17 miles a day walking. Unlike the clock traders who struggled to Switzerland, France and beyond with a hefty back pack of clocks, hikers carry no more than a map, a picnic and money for a drink in inns along the way. Luggage is moved from one hotel to the next by car, to await the arrival of walkers. The trails are signed and mapped in English, and holiday length can be tailored as one wishes. To appreciate the work of the clockmakers one should visit the Museum of the Black Forest in Triberg, with its remarkable collection of locally-made clocks and orchestrion. One can hear cuckoo clocks with an echo, highland soldiers playing a bagpipe style tune, clocks that play six different melodies and one with a cock that crows the hour. Clock watchers can also visit the clock museum at Furtwangen and the largest cuckoo clock in the world (according to the Guinness Book of Records) created by Jozef Dold in a cottage-sized building at Schonach which houses the massive wooden machinery and the bellows to create the cuckooing from a parrot-sized bird over the clock face on the exterior. Details of walking holidays from Claus Blum, Parkhotel Wehrle, 7740 Triberg im Schwarzwald (tel. 077 22/8 60 20).

A Baltic Bolthole

Bornholm Island belongs to Denmark but is 83 miles away, and only twelve miles from the Polish coast. It is a cheap flight from Copenhagen or there is an overnight ferry from Copenhagen's Nyhavn harbour to Ronne, Bornholm's chief city. The island offers a tranquil rural scene with superb white beaches in the south, on which amber is sometimes found washed up after a storm. The calmness has attracted many Danish artists and ceramicists, whose studios can be visited. Farming or fishing are the main occupations and the only factory chimneys to be seen are the tall stacks of the herring smokeries. At Svaneke the smokery offers lunches of lightly and freshly smoked herring sprinkled with rough rock salt served with beer and schnaaps. Smoked salmon sides are another bargain buy.

Bornholm is slow to warm up in spring but the summer heat absorbed in the granite rocks and skerries keeps the island warm in September. Granite was quarried here to build the public buildings of Copenhagen. The rock-released heat gives a rich autumn harvest. In the small, neat gardens, sunflowers grow tall, and peaches, figs, grapes, and mulberries ripen along with the many apple trees. July is the high season for tourism here: in September accommodation discounts are between 30 and 50 per cent. Most of the hotels close from the end of September till April.

Colour is immediately striking in Bornholm. The houses are low, neat, wooden-timbered and painted in bright yellow, blue, ochre and rust, with white- or black-framed windows filled with geraniums and plants. There are comfortable hotels with Danish-style food but most of the accommodation is in chalet-style self-catering cottages based round a central restaurant, shop, swimming pool and children's play area. The central point can be an old farmhouse complete with rooms furnished in the style of the past centuries as at Dams pa Bakken near Aakirkby in the island's centre. On the south coast at Dueodde, little log cabins are set among trees backing the fine white sand beach. On the north coast at Gudhjem long lines of linked accommodation have patios for eating out and sleep up to six in comfortable, if simple, surroundings. Accommodation can be booked through Dan Center, Falkonercentret, Falkoner Alle 7, 2000 Copenhagen F.

A healthy and intimate way of exploring the 100-mile circumference island, only 25 miles wide at most, is by walking or cycling and there are packages of accommodation and cycle hire. The north coast is more rugged, with a dramatic castle, Hammershus. The east coast is rocky with little coves, beaches and fishing villages and in the south-east there are huge sand dunes. To the north there are small satellite islands, with bird sanctuaries, reached by an hour-long ferry trip. White windmills and farmhouses dot the interior and one can walk in the Almindingen forest in the south centre part of the island. Nearly 20 per cent of Bornholm's surface is covered with natural woods and in the north-east, around Vang, the typical scenery is of small fields, birch and beech woods, streams, heather and rocks.

British Colours

In September the English vineyards have special tours and tastings – details available from the English Tourist Board. Lying in bed and watching the trees turn colour this month is an offer from Derek Tongs, owner of Raleigh Manor Hotel at Wheddon Cross on the edge of Exmoor, which is furnished with antiques and a half tester bed in the squire's bedroom. Here beech hedges, 12–15 feet high, are used as snow breaks and form golden tunnels in the autumn as the oaks change colour. Watch this from around the wood fire in the lounge or take a foot path to Dunkery Beacon, the highest point on Exmoor, to see the moorland purple with heather in late summer. The colours stay bright until the end of October.

The hotel runs week-long packages with guided inclusive day sorties for groups of eight to nine at a time to see the Exmoor National Park. In Devon, the Coombe Cross Hotel at Bovey Tracey has a 'glorious autumn' colours holiday with visits to houses and gardens in the area. In Cornwall, autumn gardens are the theme for tours, with visits to the National Trust property Glendurgan, a valley garden with specimen trees and flowering shrubs running down to the Helford River.

Commercial forests cover 9 per cent of the UK and the Forestry Commission encourages the public to visit, providing trails, picnic sites and rentable chalets and old cottages in spots like the Scottish glens and Snowdonia, where cottages are reached on forest roads and have, of course, big log fires. The Forest of Arden was the haunt of that diary-keeping Edwardian lady, Edith Holden, and today one can be guided round the autumn colours that she loved in a special leaflet issued by the Heart of England Tourist Board.

Knowing Your Place

Coastal resorts are getting a little weary of the season and visitors, but also gradually becoming less crowded, though inland places like Florence continue to be packed well into the late autumn. Alpine and inland lake areas are more serene and gentle in the sun. The cities are beginning to awaken again, but the full arts programmes have not started up as yet and the best places to be are where there are gardens, parks and trees for colour and sheltered spots from which to admire them.

Old Customs

In September these are much concentrated on food and wine festivals (see below), harvest festivals in some areas and fairs.

Italy In Venice on the first Sunday of September since 1300 there has been the historical regatta on the Grand Canal with a procession of old ships; two-oared gondolas are decorated and take part in races with the gondoliers in special costume. Each of the gondolas represents one of Venice's districts.

At Arezzo, early in September, the Saracen Joust takes place with a historical procession of representatives of the city led by a herald, who reads a proclamation. In the afternoon there is a parade, then a joust of horsemen who attempt to lance the 'Saracen', a large dummy figure with its head on a pivot, holding a shield in one hand and a whip in the other. Once the horseman has hit the target he has to turn quickly to avoid being hit by the whip. In Foligna in Perugia, the Quintain joust is held mid month over two days. On the first there is a historical procession and on the second, ten knights in seventeenth-century costume compete for the *palio*, banner. The 'Quintain' is a wooden figure dating from the 1600s of a Roman soldier with a ring in its right hand which the knight on a galloping horse must catch with his lance and take away. The knight who gets all the rings in the shortest time is the winner.

Holland Utrecht windmill day. Every year in September the Utrecht board of tourism and Utrecht Mill Foundation and Voluntary Millers Guild organise a windmill day. Two routes to the mills are signposted for cars and a shorter cycle route. The route can also be followed by bus. Visitors are taken past a large number of windmills, several of which will be open to the public. Various events also take place at the start and finish of the routes. The Utrecht Tourist Board, Vredenburg 90 (tel. 030 3141132) also issues a list of mills which are open to visit in its general information booklet.

On or round about 15 September Prinsjesdag is celebrated in the Hague, when the Queen welcomes back both houses of parliament from the summer recess and outlines the business of government for the coming year. The ceremony is in the thirteenth-century Ridderzaal, Knight's Hall, where the Queen arrives in a golden coach escorted by units of the armed forces.

UK   In London on Primrose Hill on the Autumn Equinox the Druid order celebrates the coming of the harvest season at 1300. The Lady of Autumn scatters fruit on the ground to carry seeds for the next spring equinox back into the earth. The election of the Lord Mayor of the City of London dates back in an unbroken line to 1192. The ceremony is know as Common Hall and takes place on or near St Michaelmas Day (29 September). The reigning Lord Mayor travels at noon to Guildhall from Mansion House to the election and is presented with a nosegay of garden flowers. Tickets are available free of charge from the Keeper of the Guildhall, London EC2. Before the election a service attended by the Court of Alderman is held at the Church of St Lawrence Jewry in Gresham Street and visitors can participate.

St Michaelmas Day is also celebrated in Coventry Cathedral, which is dedicated to St Michael; events include a service of thanksgiving. A Michaelmas craft fair is held in Kentwell Hall, Long Melford in Suffolk (details from Sudbury Tourist Office, 0787 72092) and Colyford in Devon has a medieval Michaelmas goose fair with procession of villagers in medieval costume, crafts, food, sports and mummers play. Details from Seaton Tourist Office tel. 0297 21600).

Other fairs include the St Giles fair at Oxford, with two days of stalls and side shows; Barnet's three-day horse fair; Widdecombe fair in Devon on the second Tuesday in September with sheep dog trials, pony shows, slippery pole games, cross country races and a Master of Ceremonies dressed in a smock and armed with a crook who announces events in dialect.

Mop fairs are common this month and next. The mop was a symbol of trade of a maid and was exchanged for a ribbon and shilling by maids when hired by their new employer at the mop fairs at which maids were hired for the year. Mop fairs are still held at Stratford upon Avon, followed a week later by the

Runaway mop fair: those unhappy with their new masters could run away and have a second chance at employment.

In the Heart of England at Abbots Bromley near Uttoxeter in Staffordshire, there is the Horn Dance, one of England's oldest, held on the first Monday after the first Sunday after the 4 September (but never on 5 September!). In a ritual said to come from hunting or fertility rites, the dancers carry reindeer horns and are accompanied by a fool, hobby horse, male/female, Robin Hood and his merry men, and musicians. The procession goes through the parish visiting cottages and farmhouses where they are greeted as bringers of good luck. Details from Horn Dance Day Promotion Group, 31 Goose Lane, Abbots Bromley, Rugeley, Staffs (tel. 0283 840558).

In Lichfield on 20 September they celebrate Dr Johnson's birthday: mayor and corporation go in state at noon to the Johnson Monument in the Market Square where a laurel wreath is placed and Johnson's anthem and other hymns are sung. In the evening a Dr Johnson supper takes place at the Guildhall, with tickets available on application to the Supper Secretary, Dr Johnson Museum, Breadmarket Street, Lichfield.

Food

Germany   The country celebrates this rich plentiful month with its Black Forest plum festival and, like Belgium and Luxembourg, makes onion tarts to be eaten traditionally with the new wine. But the biggest event is the Durkheim Sausage Fair, held on the Friday to Tuesday of the second weekend and Friday to Monday on the third weekend of September. It begins with an open-air concert in the Schlossplatz, followed by a procession of bands, wine-growers and council leaders to the festival ground with a parade of decorated wine floats complete with serving staff. The mayor and the German Wine Queen officially open the fair and on the Monday of the second part and Tuesday of the first there are firework displays at 2100. The Wurstmarkt (sausage fair) goes back 550 years, originating in a religious pilgrimage that became a wine drinker's tour. The religious part was associated with the payment of a large sum of repentance money on St Michaelmas Day. The citizens would use a wheelbarrow as a stall for the wine cask, a pan to heat sausages and offer homemade bread to the pilgrims. Now 36 booths maintain the tradition – small roofed wine taverns open at the sides and fitted with narrow tables and benches for wine drinking. There are also large pavilions called 'halls' where bands play on elevated platforms below which people dance into the small hours. The wine served is in glasses which hold half a litre called

Schoppen: over 400,000 are served during the eight days of the festival. Forty sausage and fried chicken stands serve all kinds of meat and complete meals are available in the halls. The festival has its funfair and there is a market with a household goods and fashion exhibition.

Scandinavia   In Norway there is a salmon festival and in Finland they welcome harvest with a porridge feast, the traditional harvest festival at Kesalahti; details from Kyllikki Paajanen, Norotic 3, 59800 Kesalahti (tel. 9 57 371063). In Helsinki's market square the Baltic herring market takes place towards the beginning of October in this open-air market with the gulls wheeling over head and the stalls and big chip baskets of produce ranged along the quayside. It is backed by empire-style buildings in soft pinks and blues. There is also an indoor market more protected from the autumnal winds where one can buy delicacies like reindeer tongue and fish roes which make excellent toast toppings. At the end of the summer, the evening markets cease, the last berries go on sale and the mushroom season starts with korvasieni (morel) and chanterelle on sale. The traditional herring week takes place at the end of the month and at the beginning of October with pickled herrings and the dark bread brought from the Aland Islands. The harbour is full of fishing boats selling produce. Shoppers and sellers alike can buy coffee, doughnuts and hot meat pies from the cafe tent which is heated by a gas burner, and hung with pictures of royalty and the VIPs who have also eaten there. Details from City Tourist Office, Pohjoisesplanadi 19,00100 Helsinki (tel. 9 0 15 091).

Belgium   Breughel painted some powerful pictures of feasting and one can have the experience of such an event at the Breughel Festival at Wingene which has been run for over 30 years. Held every other year on a Sunday from 1400 in a decorated village setting, a Breughel feast is served with brass bands and dancing; at 1600 there is a pageant with 1,000 actors and a dozen brass brands and after this a Breughel meal is served in the church square which spectators can pay to join. After this the festival continues with brass bands, dance groups and a torchlight procession at 2000. Information and stand reservation from Gemeentehuis Wingene, Secretariat Breughel Feesten, Oude Bruggestraat 13, B-8050 Wingene (tel. 051 65 70 71).

West Flanders offers visitors a series of historical style meals in castle settings and the Breughel feast in the town hall of Damme has artists painting diners' portraits while they consume rabbit terrine and a suckling pig, black pudding and white sausage with garden cress mousse, cod cooked Flemish style, brown mousse with cold ice cream, coffee and beer in earthen-ware mugs. These historical banquets are for groups of a hundred people and details are from Westtoer vzw, Kasteel Tillegem, B-8200 Bruges 2 (tel. 050 38 02 96).

Spain A National paella contest is held at Sueca in Valencia province. This is part of the rice festival at which the new rice stalks are offered to Our Lady of Sales with a procession to her shrine.

France In Provence wild mushrooms are sold at Aix en Provence shops, along with a selection of olive oils at the Saturday morning market. White nectarines and charcuterie from Corsica, where the pigs eat acorns and chestnuts, are other seasonal delights and at Ampus, north west of Draguignan, there is an olive museum with olive breads and sales of the oils.

UK In Keats' 'Ode to Autumn' he talks of the autumn time 'to bend with apples the mossed cottage trees, And fill all fruit with ripeness to the core'. Many fruit shows are held around the country mainly in September. The English Tourist Board has an apple trail leaflet showing where traditional apples with glorious names like D'Arcy Smith or Peasgood Nonsuch can be found on farms. The Worcester Pearmain apple is a particularly brilliant red one in September and October. In Scotland at Prior's Wood in the shade of Melrose Abbey is a National Trust garden noted for its autumn dried flowers and also an orchard which shows the changing vogue in apples since the eleventh century. In mid September for two weeks there is an exhibition and tasting of old-fashioned English apples with historical details, how to grow, trees to buy and apple juices to try; details from The Garden Centre, Alexander Park, London (tel. 01–444 2555).

Goose is still much eaten for Michaelmas and goose fairs to sell them are held round the country. An old superstition says it is unlucky to eat blackberries on or after Michaelmas because the Devil spits on them. But this month berries are booming with blackberries, rowan, elderberries, hips and haws to make jellies to go with the game of autumn: grouse, mallard, venison, snipe and teal. The season for native oysters begins in September, hyped at the beginning of the month in restaurants and hotels rather as the arrival of grouse or Nouveau Beaujolais. Farmed oysters can in fact be found year round and oyster bars increasingly offer takeaway packs which you have to open yourself. Ireland celebrates with the Galway Oyster Festival at which the title of World Champion Oyster Opener is competed for.

Wine

Germany   The big month for wine festivals, though the biggest
booze up of the year is undoubtedly Munich's 16-day Oktoberfest – mostly held in September though it overflows, literally,
a day or so into October. Tour operators organise packages
and this is strictly for the gregarious, sturdy stomached and
powerful throated. Germany claims 40 per cent of the world's
breweries and the stronger Marzenbier is made for this celebration of a fourteenth-century tax exemption. Between six million
and seven million visitors go to the Oktoberfest and during the
festival 1,345,000 gallons of beer are downed from Bavaria's 800
breweries and 5,000 different beers; 698,137 roast chicken,
800,000 pairs of sausage, 75 spit roasted oxen and 75,539 roast
pork knuckles are eaten.

Oompah bands help the steins go down in the huge marquees.
Alternative evening music and food are found in the Schwabing
district with discos and restuarants serving 88 varieties of
dumpling, which should see you through to Frushoppen
'elevenses' which could be taken at Valentin's in one of the old
city gates, a spot dedicated to a local comedian where tea with
rum or mulled wine or light beer with a slice of lemon can be
bought. In the mornings, a beer with fresh rolls, cheese or
sausage can be bought from stalls around the maypole in the
Victuelien market. One can escape the madding crowd of the
Oktoberfest and take an S bahn train an hour out to Herrsching
for a short walk to Lake Ammersee to eat at lakeside cafes, swim
or go boating. At Andrechs there is a Benedictine monastery
where a strong dark beer is brewed. The monks run an open-air
terrace restaurant with views over the fields (as well as an
indoor cafe), which is a favourite meeting point for walkers. A
picnic can be brought to go with the beer or cheeses, white
sausage, curling strands of white radish, dark rye breads;
platters of obazder, creamy light cheese mixed with herbs, garlic
and other flavourings, can be ordered.

But back at the beer festival: the Hofbrauhaus of the Hitler
meeting fame seats 5,000 and has relays of oompah bands to
back daily intakes of 20,000 litres of beer. The smallest measure
sold is a litre stein. The festival, held on the Theresienwiese,
was created to honour the wedding of a prince in 1810. Each of
Munich's half-dozen top breweries takes over a marquee hall
housing thousands at tables and benches which can be booked
in advance. As well as beer swilling there is plenty of other
entertainment: a crossbow marksmen's tent, a flea circus, a
snake show, traffic education playgrounds for children, and a
huge rollercoaster.

Another large German knees up held this month is the Stuttgarter Weindorf and Cannstatter Volksfest. The former runs between the last Friday in August and the first Sunday in September with a wine village made up of 100 stalls and booths on the market square, Schillerplatz and Kitchstrasse where over 300 Baden Wurtemberg wines are served and Swabian specialities offered. The Cannstatter Volksfest has taken place since 1818 on a meadow on the Neckar banks open for 16 days from the end of September. It has 4 million to 5 million visitors to the huge beer tents and gigantic amusement park.

A more peaceful festival is Heidleberg's Herbst, a harvest festival held on the last weekend of September. The warmth of this southerly city in Germany is mirrored in the russet of trees along the Philosopher's Path above the Neckar River and one can walk here and sip wines with onion tart at outside cafes. During the herbst it is fun to take wine and a different meal course in the studentenlokale such as Sepply, Schookenloch, Schnizelbank with its decor of workmen's tools and benches, Vater Rhien and Hirchgasse where they say duels are still occasionally fought.

During the herbst, girls stand in emptied fountains and sell wine. There is oompah and jazz music in the streets, children dress up and hold pageants, and their own toy-selling flea market, one buys suckling pig, onion pie or sausage from street stalls and finally the castle ruin overlooking the town is 'burnt' in a late night blaze of illuminations and fireworks. Dates of all the German Wine Festivals can be obtained from Deutsche Weininformation Postfach 1707, 6500 Mainz 1.

Luxembourg During September the duchy holds many wine festivals, including one at Schwebsange with wine flowing from a fountain; Wormeldange has a concert and dance and Grevenmacher a grape and wine festival with fireworks, a parade with floats, majorettes and bands. Wine is sold in the public squares and there is dancing in the evening. A second festival at the same town later in September includes a marathon long distance run along the Mosel from Remich to Grevenmacher.

Belgium Poperinge in the south-west of West Flanders, which is known for its hops, has a hop festival once every three years. The national hop museum is open and guides explain the world of hops, ending the visit with tastings of a local beer. In the afternoon hop picking by hand is demonstrated on the market square and at 1500 the hop pageant of 40 groups of 1,400 costumed actors and 10 horse-drawn floats moves off. A festival beer tent on the Oudstrijdersplein sells beer and provides a brass band. Packages for the whole day with meals and stand ticket or stand tickets only can be obtained through the tourist office, Stadhuis, Markt 1, B-8970 Poperinge (tel. 057 3340 81).

Spain Though the Jerez Sherry Festival is now more of a trade event with less of the fiesta spirit of the spring fair, September is a lovely time to visit this area, especially when the grapes are being harvested from the neat chalky white vineyards around the town.

The harvest festival began in 1948 and each year is dedicated to one of the countries importing sherry; Britain is still tops with 60 million barrels. The grapes are blessed before the cathedral with ceremonial grape-treading and the release of white racing pigeons with poems about the new vintage attached to their legs. The first wine 'must' is blessed before the statue of San Gines de la Jara, the patron saint of this region's wine-growers. There are processions, flamenco competitions and contests, bullfights and livestock exhibitions.

At any time of the year Jerez is a friendly place to visit. One can see the bodegas (cellars) and the biggest tours are around the Williams and Humbert, Gonzalez and Sandeman. The cellars close at 1500. Phone ahead to make an appointment to visit. Gonzalez Byass has about 80,000 visitors a year and passing in from the creeper clad courtyard one is guided to see the ironwork 'concha' shell building designed by Eiffel in 1865. Las Copas has around 60,000 barrels including some of the world's largest. One sees the original cellar where Tio Pepe (Uncle Joseph) started work. Tio Pepe introduced the fino or very dry sherry from the neighbouring village of San Lucar to Jerez. An enchanting sight (perhaps not for some!) is to see trained mice climb little rope ladders to drink a copita (little narrow necked glass) of sweet sherry. Or there may be a performance by a champion 'veneciando', using the long flexible handled measure to slip into the narrow bungs of the barrels to test and sample the sherry. The expert veneciando can hold a fistful of nine glasses with their narrow necks and flick in the sherry without spilling a drop. The sherry producers are generous with sampling and some have splendid sampling rooms and bars.

The leading producers have maps and city information and after a tour one can explore the tiny squares and gardens at the back of the orange tree lined main street or visit the big sherry bars where the traditional Andalucian tapa (hors d'oeuvres) are served; mountain ham and olives, grilled prawns, deep fried fish. Jerez, though swiftly modernising, is still a very traditional place: meals come very late and the siesta pervades. One can move out then to Jerez's port and seaside outlet Puerto de Santa Maria where firms like Terry and Osborne are situated. In Puerto in particular the bars automatically serve tapas of squid, shellfish or spiced kebabed meat. At Valdegrana, the beach area of Puerto has the cooking of Lala MacPherson, a Spanish lady married to a fifth generation Scots family of sherry agents in Cadiz, who is Chef at the El Fogon restaurant. She uses the local brew generously in her recipes (and has written a cook book in Spanish) ; her chicken liver paté with oloroso sherry and brandy is superb.

Another local drink is the manzanilla wine from San Lucar on the Atlantic coast near the Guadalquivir estuary; walk the wide flat sands and eat at restaurants like Bajo de Guia, taking the ferry across the river to see a little of the Cota Donana wild life reserve. Details of festivals and visits from the Sherry Institute of Spain, 23 Manchester Square, London WIN 5AP (tel. 01–487 5826).

Spain also has the Rioja grape harvest festival at Logrono in September on San Matteo's day, with a week-long celebration of parades, a special Mass and the offering of the must to the local patron saint, with cookery competitions and folklore. At Alella near Barcelona on the third Sunday in September a blown glass porron (drinking vessel) is made to a new design each year and sold during the festival, which coincides with the pressing of the first must.

Cyprus In the first half of the month Limassol holds its well established 12-day delightfully informal wine festival with parades, music and dancing under the pine trees, the festivities fuelled by free wine in the Limassol Municipal gardens and local food, such as open air snacks of kebab or grilled chicken, sold at low prices. At this time of year the grapes are left drying by hill and roadside and on roof tops for 12 to 15 days to make the traditional dessert wine, Commandaria.

Switzerland At Neuchatel the vintage festival is held in late September with costume parades and restaurants open all night.

France The early autumn months are quiet in the Beaujolais region and September is the hard working month of the grape harvest. Horse chestnuts are scattered on the roads which are full of tractors loaded with bins of grapes. Beaujolais is unusual in France as a region where harvesters still gather the grapes by hand, slow and more expensive but a way of ensuring that the black Gamay grape retains its juices. The harvesters come from all over Europe and work hard to gather the grapes.

England   The English Vineyard Festival is held over a weekend in early September. Held for the last 14 years, the festival offers tastings of over 70 English wines as well as cider, real ale and traditional English foods. There is country-style entertainment, with wine tours, a wine museum and a grape-treading competition to find who can tread the most juice in three minutes. The festival is held at the English Wine Centre, Valley Wine Cellars, Drusillas Corner, Alfriston, E. Sussex BN26 5QS (tel. 0323 870532). During September, English vineyards particularly welcome visitors and arrange tours. In the East Sussex area vineyards are included in the 'English Vineyards Open to the Public' leaflet available from the English Vineyards Association, The Ridge, Lamberhurst Down, Kent TW3 8ER (tel. 0892 890734).

Arts

Cyprus   At the beginning of September, the Nicosia festival is held at the Famagusta gate in the old town with music, drama and dance performances by Cypriot and Greek performers as well as exhibitions and an open air market.

Italy   Pesaro holds the Rossini Festival in early September (starting at the end of August) in the composer's birthplace and it is now becoming a fashionable rival to Bayreuth and Salzburg. The town is now a modern seaside resort but it is surrounded by woods and Urbina and Ravenna are not far for visits. The music of Rossini is performed in a small opera house rebuilt in Rossini's time and renovated in the 1930s. Concerts in Teatro Rossini and the main hall of the Conservatario are relayed by TV to the Piazza del Popolo, which is used for al fresco recitals. In 1986 Pavarotti sang here. The festival began in the 1970s, using the edited texts of Rossini's works, some of which had not been seen since the 1830s.

Switzerland   The Alpengala is held at Wengen in mid September, a relatively new musical festival at the foot of the Jungfrau. The theme is the harmony of music and nature. Wagner spoke of the Swiss 'golden summits' after a visit to the Jungfrau area in 1859. The concerts are non-profit-making, supported by public institutions, sponsorships and membership fees. Annual concerts have been planned each September until 1990. Members throughout the world (fees are in some cases tax deductible) are given ticket priority. Founded and directed by Andrea Cova, who points out that Brahms, Tchaikovsky, Mendelssohn and Wagner all summered in the area – 'so why not honour their memory in a magic place where the air is pure?' Tickets and accommodation c/o Director Andrea Cova, Hotel Falken, 3823 Wengen, Switzerland (tel. 036 551905/55 36 66).

Wales Swansea's end of September festival is best known for its range of symphony concerts with international orchestras as well as contemporary music, opera, theatre, dance, films, jazz exhibitions and literary events, as well as a programme for children and a fringe festival. Swansea is the principal arts festival of Wales, over 40 years old. Its Grand Theatre was renovated in 1987 and concerts take place in the Brangwyn Hall, which houses the Frank Brangwyn empire panels. The programme is published in May and booking and accommodation can be organised from 1 May. Information from Civic Information Centre, PO Box 59, Singleton Street, Swansea (tel. 0792 468321).

In North Wales a programme of morning and evening concerts is held in the sixth-century St Asaph's cathedral in the third week of the month. Information: North Wales Music Festival, The Cathedral, St Asaph, Clwyd (tel. 0745 584508).

In early September there is a festival of a different sort at Llandrindod Wells, where a Victorian festival has been run for the past seven years. The whole town gets into the period spirit with costumed events, Victorian window displays, competitions, morris dancing (well pre-Victorian), Victorian meals, carnival parades, fêtes, teddy bears and a dolls' picnic, Gilbert and Sullivan opera, Victorian music, costumed bowls match, beer tasting, taking the waters in the Rock Park spa, Victorian church services, farmhouse visits for morning coffee by 'motor vehicle', country walks, Victorian fashion parades, bandstand concerts, tea dances, male voice choir concerts, old films, harp recitals, town walks, wheelbarrow races, a parade of vintage vehicles, traction rally, Grand Victorian ball and fireworks and a torchlight procession to finish it all off. Throughout the festival there are Victorian street entertainers, competitions, horse carriages can be hired and punch and judy shows are given – each day has a full and varied programme. Details including accommodation from Festival Office, Old Town Hall, Memorial Gardens, Llandrindod Wells, Powys, LD1 5DL (tel. 0597 3441).

Ireland Waterford International Festival of light opera at the Theatre Royal, the only surviving rotunda theatre in Ireland, lasts for 17 nights and is 30 years old. Entries come from all over Ireland and the UK. Details: Theatre Royal, The Mall, Waterford (tel. 051 75788).

In Greece there is the song festival at Thessalonika with folk singers from all over Greece taking part; in Spain there is the San Sebastian International Film Festival, one of the world's top film events; and in Deauville, France, the American Film Festival. The Flanders Festival spreads itself over a number of Belgian towns this month including Antwerp, Brussels and Ghent, with a programme of concerts held in halls, castles, churches and historical buildings. A folder details the events in different towns and packages with accommodation and tickets are arranged. Information from Belgian Tourist Reservations, Rue de Toulouse 44, 1040 Brussels (tel. 02/230 50 29).

Sport

Ireland: All-Ireland Hurling Finals are held. Hurling is considered the fastest field game in the world, played on a grass pitch by two teams of 15 players each. The teams contest for possession of a small leather ball with hurley sticks about three feet long. A large amount of body contact is allowed but technical expertise is more important. Camogie is a woman's game based on hurling. Also held in September at Croke Park in Dublin is the finals of All-Ireland Gaelic Football, a game more closely allied to the Australian rules game with high catching, body charging and fielding the ball in flight.

Cricket: when the cricket season is coming to an end in England, the addicted (and it is an addict's game) can move to the more predictable warmth of Corfu in Greece for the September week of cricket matches held in Corfu town square with visiting overseas teams. The setting is pleasant, with cafes in the cool stone-arched arcades surrounding the pitch.

Engines: the Monza Car Race is held in Milan, at le Castelet in Provence there are motor cycle races and France also holds world sailing championships. In Cork, Ireland there are sea angling festivals.

Horses: the St Leger race is run at Doncaster, one of the great classic races and one of the oldest, at which Derby winners and some of Europe's leading horses compete. The Burghley horse trials also take place and in London love of horses is manifested in Horseman's Sunday, held on the second last Sunday since 1968. Horses assemble at the Church of St John and St Michael, Hyde Park Crescent, London W2 at 1130 and the service starts at noon. The service is taken by the vicar on horseback, lasts about 25 minutes and is followed by a procession of the horses to receive commemorative rosettes when the horses go onto Hyde Park to ride the 2½ miles of tracks. In addition there is a horse show in Kensington Paddock (the western end of the gardens) from 1330 with show classes, jumping and gymkhana (details from originator Ross Nye on 01–262 3791).

Walking: Wales organises four-days of non-competitive walking with a choice of three distances, 10, 15 or 25 miles each day through superb scenery in mid Wales. A medal and certificate are given to all who finish. Details from the Secretary, Llanwrtyd Wells, Powys (tel. 05913 236).

Shopping

At the end of the month, as Mediterranean resorts start to think about closing down somewhat, look for sales in shops particularly in southern Spain where leather goods and shoes are bargains. In London the Jermyn Street Festival runs for a week in the first half of the month. In this street of perfumiers, royal appointment cheese shop and shirt makers, to the south of and parallel with Piccadilly, there are special shop displays, competitions, film reviews and fireworks. The Chelsea Antiques Fair, Chelsea Old Town Hall, Kings Road, London SW3 has been held twice a year for 35 years and is attended by collectors and trade buyers from around the world. Quality antiques, mostly pre-1830, are on show. The Burlington House Fair is held in the Royal Academy of Arts in Piccadilly, where over 60 top dealers from eight countries fill thirteen galleries with jewellery and silver and items of historical interest for sale, as well as furniture, paintings and pieces for exhibition only.

Horticultural

In Ireland the wild fuschia along the hedgerows of many areas, especially the south west, is scarlet with blooms this month and lasts into October. Autumn gardens to visit in England include Wakehurst Place in West Sussex with 250 acres of woodland, ponds, shrubs, gentians in autumn, maples and beeches. The gardens are now run for the National Trust by the Royal Botanical Gardens at Kew. Scotney Castle, Kent, is a romantic garden around a fourteenth-century moated ruin with red and yellow creepers and browning royal ferns reflected in the water. And there is an unusual heather-thatched ice well. Sheffield Park in East Sussex, 100 acres originally laid out by Capability Brown, has autumn flowers, leaves and berries.

In London there is the Great Autumn Flower Show at the Royal Horticultural Society Halls, Greycoat Street and Vincent Square SW1 with roses, dahlias, trees, shrubs, an orchid glasshouse and rock garden plants. The two-day City of London Flower Show, Guildhall, Gresham Street, EC2 is a display of flowers, fruit, vegetables, crafts, home made wines, beer, honey and an ideal gnome exhibition. The Clog and Apron Race is usually held on the last Thursday of September at Kew Gardens beginning at 1730 with a race along the Broad Walk, a wide avenue between the Palm House Pond and the Orangery. It originates in the custom for all first-year horticultural students and gardeners working under glass to be issued with a pair of wooden-soled leather clogs and navy blue gardening apron; even today some clogs are issued as they are better for keeping feet dry on wet greenhouse floors. The race competitors are students working at the gardens and women are given a 50-yard start. The clogs are heavy but the fastest time is 60 seconds. Details from Kew Gardens (tel. 01–940 1171).

On Show

The Farnborough Air Show in Surrey gives aviation buffs a chance to see the latest in plane design on the ground and in the air. A fun time is had at the beginning of September in Blackpool when a VIP switches on 700 tons or £2.5 million worth of lights and traffic slows to a rubber-necking crawl along the promenades of this Lancashire seaside resort, extending its season with the viewers. The resort, which boasts more visitor beds, 200,000, than the whole of Portugal or the Greek islands, loves its lights with over 500 featured figures and tableaux. There are floral lights, romantic designs, each year something different. It takes 80 people all year to maintain, erect and operate the illuminations which include about 375,000 light bulbs, lasers and 75 miles of wire and cable. After struggling among the crowds to see the lights, a good refresher pit stop is Yates Wine Bar where champagne can be bought on draught and wines by the half pint.

Public Holidays

8 September, Malta, Our Lady of Victories, a holiday commemorating the lifting of three historical sieges in 1565, 1800 and 1943 with regatta and boat races in the Grand Harbour.
21 September, Independence Day, Malta.

OCTOBER

FOR HARVEST HOMING

O
CTOBER is a month of gathering in; a final outdoor fling before the inward-looking atmosphere of November and December, the trees turn their deepest gold and finally fade and Europe is busy harvesting the food ready for winter's eating, in an ancient urge still pursued in spite of deep freezing and international fast jet freighting. It is Keats's season of mellow fruitfulness, the time to slip into a church and see the golden harvest piled up with sheaves of corn, big loaves baked in the pattern of corn, polished tomatoes, round red apples shined for God, big marrows, fat pumpkins, yellow and orange dahlias, bunches of purple Michaelmas daisies from gardens, scarlet hips and haws from the hedgerow.

In Britain harvest festival is supposed to have originated in North Cornwall where in little churches the choir sang to bass viol, flute and pipe by candlelight with wild thyme and wormwood strewn on the floor. At this parish of Morwenstow, Stephen Hawker the vicar is said to have invented harvest home. He died in 1875, an eccentric in the best Anglican tradition who when young wore seaweed and pretended to be a mermaid. He buried shipwrecked sailors, paid for a school and built a lonely hut on a cliff, still to be visited, where Tennyson spent much time in 1848 before going to Tintagel to write *Idylls of the King*.

The Scarlet Season

Red is the colour of October and Bologna in Northern Italy has the nickname 'red' for the terracotta and reddened stucco on palazzo walls and turrets, which gives an impression of warmth and comfort even in deepest winter. Cynics called the city red for its communist mayor.

The buildings of Bologna are not the only attraction in early winter. The weather protective arcaded streets shelter one from rain while window shopping for leather goods, silks and superb shoes and Bologna is also Italy's food capital: the many restaurants and cafes have excellent regional food and in October there are wild mushrooms, particularly the prized porcini, named for its pig's ear shape, and the white truffle (see below) that is generously proffered whole to grate over pasta. Meals can be accompanied with the Lambrusca and Sangiovese wines grown and made around the city.

Sightsee before eating – the city has culture a-plenty to offer, with richly endowed art galleries, churches and evening concerts. In winter there are three or four concerts a night, many free, in Bologna's concert halls in addition to church music recitals. As it is a walking city (take comfortable shoes) it is best reached by air to

Milan and a train ride across the Lombard plains. One can stay centrally at the Baglioni in the main street, overlooked by the stone saints of the huge church opposite. Buses enable one to ride to the San Michele Bosco hill, from which there is an ideal vista of this rose red city of Europe. From the hill terrace, the church domes are dominated by San Petronio, intended to be the world's largest church. A Pope, jealous for Rome's St Peter's reputation stopped the building however, and it now has to be content with being merely the seventh largest. However, the Pope did encourage the building of the university on church land.

San Petronio and the university, now a public library, are both worthwhile visits. San Petronio has side chapels with fifteenth-century paintings of heaven and hell and gorilla-like depictions of the devil. A sundial is set in the floor: in the seventeenth century, the astronomer Cassini spent ten years perched each day in a church window above watching the sun in order to perfect this sundial.

The university is across the square from the church and a tip to the gate keeper gains admittance. The anatomical theatre is a restored wooden building dating from the days when medicine was considered an arts subject and the church's inquisitor had a spy hole to make sure the taboo subjects of the brain and reproductive organs were not discussed as the bodies of condemned criminals were dissected. There are carved wood figures showing men without skin. The figure of Tagliacozzi, a thirteenth-century 'plastic surgeon', holds a nose to be grafted with skin from the arm, a useful art in days of duelling. The library nearby has 2,500 handwritten books and above the bookcase are the coats of arms of pupils from all over the known world, from Scotland to India. Dante and Copernicus were among the students at Bologna. Enchanting is the bust of Laura Bassi, an eighteenth-century lady lecturer who was so beautiful she was forced to teach hidden by a curtain in order that her pupils would not be distracted.

Bologna, also nicknmamed 'the wise' from the eminence of its university, also had its school of painters. Their works and those of others can be seen in the modern Galleria delle belle arte. Modern painters still inhabit two of the city's medieval towers and today's students can be seen at the Friday and Saturday street markets or walking in the gas-lit cobbled streets behind the Via Independenzia, which seems little changed since Dante walked there.

Only a handful remain of the 200 tower houses of the twelfth and thirteenth centuries that were then raised as family status symbols – getting higher meant getting ahead of the Joneses. The tallest now is the 300-foot Asinella tower, slender and

elegant, next to the Garisenda, stubbier and slanted precarious-
ly, as a result of subsidence when it was built. Those two towers
are now the city symbol. Another tower, the Alto Bello,
pushes its foot into the side of a leading restaurant, Brunetti's.
Lucianao's is another noted eating spot which names a rich
pasta dish after the Garisenda tower. Eating is good in Bologna
the wise – a sausage, spaghetti sauce and a way of cooking veal
cutlets bear the city name – and the city runs a big food fair in
spring.

D'Artagnan's Town

Toulouse in France, another notable gourmet city, is the gateway airport for the little town of Auch, its old golden stone walls
radiating the sun's warmth in October. It is in the department of
Gers, better known historically as Gascony, a beautiful unspoilt
agricultural region, the least populated 'department' in France
with only 28 people per square kilometre. The home of the
proud D'Artagnan, Auch is set in a gentle, timeless area with
flocks of geese and ducks in the river meadows, beneath hill-
topped (so many hills, the area is described as a 'mer des
collines') villages of golden stone fortified originally against the
troops of the Black Prince. To the south rise the Pyrenees:
according to the locals, when they can be clearly seen, it is going
to rain.

 Auch (pronounced Ohsh) is a good base for exploration. It is a
pile of stone buildings up a steep hill rising from the River Gers.
City wall and gatehouse remnants can still be seen as well as the
'pousterles', narrow steep lamp-lit alleys of steps up which
those living outside the protection of the city could clamber
quickly for supplies and safety. In summer, the efficient local
tourist office in a half-timbered fifteenth-century house in
Auch's heart, arranges guided walks around the pousterles.

 Shell motifs on some buildings show Auch was on the
pilgrimage route to Compostela and the town dates from Roman
days. It is a compact cobble wander down to the river terraces
from the top of the Place de la Liberation, with its nineteenth-
century municipal theatre and gardens from which the twin-
tower renaissance facade can be seen turning apricot in tone at
sunset. This cathedral was 200 years in the building and its
sixteenth-century windows are described as a bible in glass. It
charges a 3-franc entry to see the carved choir stalls which form
a church within a church. The wood used was soaked for 20
years in the Gers, hardened for 30 years and finally carved for
over 40 years to make 1,500 different characters.

The city is preserving and restoring its old balconied buildings and the past lifestyle can be viewed in an old monastery setting of the Musée des Jacobins with an unexpected array of Inca artefacts and, less surprisingly, Roman relics. The D'Artagnan collection has been moved to Paris. The local son's statue however still stands, rapier in hand, on the Escalier Monumental leading down to the river. On Thursday mornings below the steps is a good market with local mushrooms, garlic and foie gras on sale as well as coastal vans with oysters, sea food and Bayonne ham.

In Auch, Andre Daguin, an ex rugby player, is the leading chef, something of a D'Artagnan of today in looks. His hotel and Restaurant de France in the Place de la Liberation is a member of the Relais et Chateaux organisation. The bar/lobby becomes a local club in which to drink coffee, champagne or a light white wine, Le Colombard, which Daguin discovered, Le Floc a pinot noir wine or a pousse rapier, the Gascon aperitif of champagne, armagnac and an orange peel twist. Daguin is consultant to the De Montal armagnac firm and a descendant of D'Artagnan is married to one of the De Montal family, which stills owns the beautiful private chateau of the Duc de Montesquieu, seen near Auch from the main road to Toulouse and containing historical relics of D'Artagnan and Napoleon.

Daguin serves a simple but substantial menu in his bar, an alternative to the restaurant, which should be booked ahead as the Michelin starring draws in crowds. Foie gras features strongly among the dishes. Halfway through the menu a trou Gascon, a shot of young and fiery armagnac, served in a glass without a base, blasts some stomach space. Daguin gives some three-day cookery courses which include tours of the local foie gras markets at Samartan, Gimont or Mirande. His 30-plus hotel rooms are individually and flamboyantly furnished and very comfortable. Continental breakfast in the room is memorable. A trolley arrives bearing fresh jugs of coffee, a huge crusty Gascon loaf, butter – about a kilo in a wooden tub – a basket of fresh croissants and brioches and five full-sized jars of local fruit preserves and honey. Daguin is generous in spirit and has set up what he calls the Ronde des Mousketeers with a choice of about 14 hotels and restaurants in the area which the visitor can tour for four days or so, enjoying the best of Gascon food and hospitality.

One can also get a tourist office leaflet and sample Gascon food in the fermes auberges, farmhouses offering reasonable set menu prices. Driving is pleasant on roads that curl past chateaux, vineyards and little bastide villages, the houses concentric round a central 'place' usually with a covered market hall. Among places to see are the Roman founded Lectoure for its valley views from the walls, Roquelaure and Lavardens perched on hillsides. Condom has old cloisters where banquets are held and the Table des Cordeliers restaurant is in a fourteenth-century chapel. Larresingle is called the Carcassonne of Gers, a thirteenth-century circular fortified village with a few houses where old ladies sell wine in summer from their houses grouped round a ruined church.

Flying the Wine Lists

Burgundy has given its name to the wine and a colour beloved of autumn. Around Beaune, with a hospice and old wine cellars in its stone-walled heart, are famed vineyards – Mersault, Savigny, Volnay, Pouligny and Montrachet. An unusual and gentle way of seeing these vineyards at vintage time and taking in some of the 600 plus chateaux of the area, many still private, is by hot air balloon. New Yorker Buddy Bombard has based his balloon fleet – the largest in Europe – near Beaune for many years and finds the area the best for flying. He runs short balloon breaks, not cheap for four days, collecting guests from Paris. These are carefully and well run and entirely inclusive, and can be booked through Abercrombie and Kent, Sloane Square House, Holbein Place, London SW1W 8NS.

The holidays run from May to October and in October, with the shorter days, the flights take place in the afternoon whereas in June they are in the long still evenings. Buddy has painted his balloons, which are the height of a nine-storey building, with flowers and butterflies to show friendship and certainly the Burgundians welcome them with waving arms, greetings and invitations to share wine and food. Swirling low over the vineyards at harvest time, the pickers throw bunches of grapes into the traditional style passenger baskets till they run red with juice.

The balloon passengers stay at the Hotel de la Poste in Beaune and here sample typical Burgundian dishes and wines to match. Buddy Bombard's colleague, Libby Dunton, takes them on wine sampling and learning tours in the morning with talks and tastings in the candlelit cellars of the old church of Cordeliers, now a leading vintners establishment. The wines are discussed over meals and visits made to wine chateaux like Mersault or to see other chateaux like the fourteenth-century Chateau Rochepot, a chequered mosaic-roofed castle with multiple towers and turrets. In the evening what Buddy terms a candlelit picnic is in reality a substantial well-cooked buffet with again plenty of good wine in another private chateau, perhaps that of Philip Le Hardi at Santenay or at Savigny les Beaune. The group sits round an open fire with the pilots and chefs, all talking late into the night.

Buddy calls his flights aerial nature walks and one can see birds and wild life from tree top heights. The balloons can be landed on narrow parapets, as they do occasionally at the chateaux, or on paths, but the back-up teams on the ground are well organised and equipped and nothing is left to chance.

Five passengers go in the armpit-high balloon basket and Buddy will also take the elderly and disabled, lifting them into the basket. The pilots are all licensed, mostly British or American, and many spend their winter flying balloons on safari in Africa. The balloons are extremely manoeuvrable, moving along suspended in their air mass at eight knots per hour. The balloons are taken to a chateau courtyard or field, having first launched a toy balloon to check wind direction and speed and to determine which route to take. The balloon envelope is spread out, fanned open and filled with propane, hauled upright by ropes and passengers loaded. With no jarring, noise or alarm, the whole rises serenely above the pepper pot chateau turrets and drifts out over the Burgundian vineyards. On landing, curious locals appear and help wrestle the air out of the balloon so it can be packed quite small. When all is neatly stowed, a small table, glasses and a bottle of champagne are produced to toast the success of the flight. The last evening's supper is held at Chateau Laborde which is owned by Bombard; he keeps the balloon fleet and spares in the stables. Here a meal is served in the candlelit eighteenth-century orangerie and next morning the twentieth century takes over with a ride on the 165 mph Train de Grande Vitesse back to Paris.

Places

Stone sponge places which have absorbed the sun are good for visits this month. France has Rocamadour also near Toulouse. Above this hill-clinging village is a rock sanctuary, reached by many of the pilgrims on their knees. The Hotel Beau Site, like the rest of the village, is snugged into rock scoops high above the valley and has huge beds swagged with silk and fairytale casement windows. Venice's stones are less crowded towards the end of the month and the Venice opera season starts in October. Sun gilded mists rise from the lagoon in the morning and Venetians run a winter hospitality programme with heavily discounted hotel prices and free afternoon tea in the Palazzo Mocinigo. An hour's drive from Venice is a favourite place of mine, Asolo. Discovered by Browning and many a Briton since, the little medieval stone town perches on a hill with little squares and courts for coffee sipping. Gardens and tree-lined walks terrace down from a fortified summit. Here the Villa Cipriani, once the holiday home of the Guinness family, is a welcoming hotel with delightful gardens and rooms looking out across the valley. One can sit under the pomegranates gazing across the blue hazed Paduan plain or look back to the Dolomites, make tours to see these mountains, Palladian villas, buy leather goods from factory shops, walk through the vines and cyprus scenery echoed in Giorgione's paintings or just sit like a cat in the warm wall niches and look.

Old Customs

Harvests and halloween are highlights this month. Halloween, 31 October, was considered the time when the dead walked. It originates in the Druid's festival of the dead and the Celtic end of summer celebration. In Hungary the cemetery is alive on this day when families go to honour their dead; in the evening flowers are placed on every grave and everyone brings candles to light and place on the graves. In other countries children dress up in sheets as ghosts or as witches and hold parties lit by hollowed out pumpkin 'lamps', though the American habit (originally from Scotland) of tricking and treating is growing.

In London there are some charming harvest customs to follow. At St Martin's in the Fields WC2 on the first Sunday in the month, the Pearly Harvest festival is held attended by the Pearly Kings and Queens (originally street traders). The service starts at 1500 and altar and pulpit are decorated with produce. Harvest festival hymns are sung and a Pearly King reads one of the lessons. Members of the public are welcome to attend this service, as they are at the Harvest of the Sea service on the second Sunday of October at St Mary at Hill, Lovat Lane, Eastcheap EC3. This has been held since the seventeenth century and is the church of the Billingsgate fish market. On a big slab placed in the church porch the Billingsgate market merchants (now based on the Isle of Dogs) display a wide variety of fish which is later donated to church army hostels for the aged. The service, attended by Aldermen in state, starts at 1100. Also in EC3 is St Olave's Church, Hart Street, the parish church of the wine and spirit trade who have their festival service at noon on the first Tuesday of the month attended by members of the Worshipful Company of Vintners and Distillers in full regalia. The public are welcomed and afterwards there is a buffet lunch and wine served in the church for which no tickets are required but for which a small charge is made.

October is also another month for holding mop fairs. The Tewkesbury mop fair in Gloucestershire dates from a grant by Queen Elizabeth although now a fun fair replaces more traditional entertainment; Cirencester holds its fair on the Monday before and Monday after 11 October (if this falls on an eleventh day, there are three) with fun fair and stalls. Other mop fairs are held at Stratford upon Avon and Warwick, which also features a roast ox with the first slice auctioned in aid of the Mayor's charity fund. Both towns follow up with a runaway mop fair a little later in the month. This is also the month of the great Nottingham Goose Fair, though the traditional delights of balloons, stalls and foods still recalled by locals have now been replaced by a modern fun fair with stalls held, as it has been since 1155, in the market square. The geese have gone but it has an imposing opening ceremony performed by the city's Lord Mayor.

In Spain, Zaragosa has its festival of the Virgin of Pilar dating from the nineteenth century. It starts with a cavalcade then the proclamation of the queen of the festival and her court of honour takes place in the Longa Palace. The heart of the festival is an offering of flowers to the Virgin in the Basilica of the Pilar by women in regional dress and there is also the procession of the Patroness of Spain. There are folklore parades of decorated floats and regional dance competitions.

Food

Truffles, considered a powerful aphrodisiac by many, are in Italy the food of October. One of the world's more expensive edibles, they have been prized since Babylonian days. In Italy and France (the latter beginning next month), professional truffle hunters work alone and in secrecy at night aided by pigs or truffle hounds. In Roddi in Italy there is a kind of university to train truffle hounds, traditionally a cross between a poodle and a beagle. In Alba, hunters work with old maps to get the white truffle and in October in Florence (even now still crowded with visitors) try a truffle sandwich at Doneys in the Via Tournabuoni. The truffle smell is strong and they are also used raw thinly sliced on a risotto or salad dish. Truffles can also be found sliced thinly in the hot dip, bagna calda, with fresh vegetable pieces for dunking, and they can be added to scrambled eggs or potted in layers with Parmesan cheese and baked till the cheese is just melting. This mixture can then be spread on toast. They can also be layered with anchovies, garlic and parsley in a pot, covered with olive oil and chilled, covered for a few days.

In Northern Italy the best white truffles are found around centres like Albi, Spoleto and Norcia. In mid October Alba, near Turin, has its Fair of St Martin paying homage to the truffle and every Saturday there is a truffle market with much selling done surreptiously from car boots to avoid the 38 per cent VAT duty. (France considers truffles a windfall and no VAT is added.) The fair lasts for weeks till every truffle has been prepared or eaten. Alba has a truffle museum and what is boasted as the world's largest truffle preserving factory. At the beginning of October in France in the Perigord region the local car clubs sometimes organise the Truffle Race Rally ending near Avignon and taking in gastronomic delights en route.

Another expensive delicacy in peak production from October (till February) is foie gras. Perigord is again a leading French region where increasingly duck liver is used. Rival Strasbourg has been making paté de foie gras since 1784 when a cook, Jean Pierre Clause, invented it. The Reverend Sydney Smith in the last century declared that heaven was eating paté de foie gras to the sound of trumpets. The traveller in his heaven can sample some of the 30 tonnes each year used by Air France on its Concorde and first class services.

As well as the foie gras markets near Auch mentioned above, in France it is customary for restaurants to sell foie gras and in Strasbourg Georges Sengel, a restaurateur, sells 200 kilos over the Christmas period. Visiting Strasbourg, a delightfully traditional town, one can stay in the shadow of the cathedral with its narrow surrounding streets decorated with old coats of arms and indulge at the two-star Michelin restaurant Le Crocodile, where chef Emile Jung serves foie gras as an hors d'oeuvre with an acidic counterpart; pineapple or apple. Georges Sengel, at the Zimmer Sengel restaurant, cooks escalopes of duck liver with caramelised apples and a sherry sauce. The helpful local tourist board has maps enabling visitors to follow the Alsace wine route around the city and stays can be arranged in farm houses and villages around.

Still in France on the last weekend of October, a culinary festival is held at Romarantin-Lanthenay, south-east of Blois. Cooks compete fiercely and display their creations and there are plenty of tasting stalls. The grand place to eat here is the Lion d'Or, 69 Rue Clemenceau. Make hotel bookings a year ahead or stay outside Blois.

Spain: yet another top-priced comestible is in season with
the mauve sativus crocus blooming. Since the days of the
Phoenicians, saffron has been culled from the dried stamins of
this flower, requiring a quarter of a million to make a pound of
saffron. The real stuff should be dark orange and evenly
coloured. The redder types are often dyed and adulterated with
safflower. Saffron is much used in Spain in paella.

In Italy October is the time to hang up your hams, the Parma
type in the Langhirano area. The curing process is long – six
months hanging after salting in a cool place. The pigs have been
fattened on whey left over from making Parma cheeses and the
Parma area has a dry even temperature and a medium altitude
considered ideal for curing. About 150,000 Parma hams are
cured each year.

In Britain the pheasant shooting season begins. Pursuit of the
bird, named for the River Phasis by ancient Greeks, has become
the sport of nobles through the centuries in Europe. Celery is at
its best at the end of the month, fruit and nuts are in season –

Pheasant shooting in England

211

hazelnuts and plums till the middle of the month, and even late raspberries and strawberries, pears, courgettes, marrows and beans. Rose hips and rowan are gathered: October is the best month to make them into jellies. Partridge is also good in October.

October is the month for apples. Worcester Permain is tailing off but Egremont Russet and, by the end of the month, Cox's Orange are available. From the end of the month Bramley's Seedling, the best known cooking apple, is widely available. A tree which grew from the branch of the original fruiting tree can be seen in a garden at Church Street, Southwell in Nottinghamshire. The Heart of England Tourist Board has a food and drink leaflet detailing vineyards and cider makers to visit at this time of year. Seasonal cider-making is carried out in an original horse-drawn mill usually in October at the Cider Mill Gallery, Blanchworth Farm, Stinchcombe, Gloucestershire (tel. 0453 2352). Other cider outings can be made to the Museum of Cider, Pomona Place, Whitecross Road, Hereford (tel. 0432 54207) which tells the story of cider-making, and there are tours of the original champagne cider cellars, and demonstrations by a resident cooper. Tastings and tours are offered at Dunkertons Cider Company, Luntley, Pembridge, Herefordshire (tel. 054 47 653) and H. Easton and Sons, Much Marcle, Ledbury, Herefordshire (tel. 053 184 233).

Still on apples, a tourist office has produced a Cider Trail in mini guide form for those who are interested in the history of cider production, to sample and buy varieties of local ciders and to follow the theme while travelling in Herefordshire and Worcestershire. All the producers are within easy driving distance of Malvern and along the way inns will be serving meals with cider. Copies of the guide from Tourism and Leisure Services Officer, Winter Gardens Complex, Grange Road, Malvern WR14 3HB (tel. 0684 892700).

Sweetness is all at the National Honey Show, Porchester Hall, London W2 (tel. 0732 883163 for information).

Luxembourg: usually on the second weekend of October, Vianden holds its nutmarket selling fresh nuts, nutcakes, nut candy and nut liqueur. Bands play in the narrow streets of the old town with its dominating castle.

Wine

Switzerland Zurich holds Expovina, an international wine festival with tastings held aboard eight lake steamers. There is a small entrance fee and 886 wines on exhibition for tasting. On the first Sunday of the month Lugano holds its vintage festival of sparkling nostrano wines with folklore performances and local food.

Germany   After Munich, it is the turn of Berlin for a mid October beer festival. This includes fairground entertainment and is open each day from 1500 till midnight. Wednesday is half price day and every Friday a Berlin brewery raffles three tons of barrelled beer. A Wine harvest festival is held in Klotten on the Mosel near Cochem and at Cochem itself there is a Mosel wine ramble.

Luxembourg   In Mosel, Wormeldange at the end of the month holds its Bacchus festival of wine.

Spain   In Barcelona province after the local harvest is over a Ball del Most is held on a Sunday in El Pla de Penedes with muscatel and coca, a kind of pizza, served halfway through. At Cadiar in Granada a wine fountain is installed which runs through the festival from about 5–8 October. A local firm of beef producers donates meat to make tapas on 9 October.

Arts

Ireland   The Wexford festival is unpretentious yet produces rare operas with seriousness and flair. Evening dress is the rule for the audience at the Theatre Royal. During the day there are recitals that go on even in series at midnight, and choral performances. The music mad can take in four performances a day if wished, though meals should be booked and consumed before the opera starts. The surrounding scenery of river estuary, beaches and mountains makes a refreshing counter-point to the festival intake. 'Opera scenes' are programmes of excerpts from a wide range of opera staged with a handful of props and minimal lighting. These are put on in White's Barn for several hundred people, usually in the mornings. If you cannot get accommodation in Wexford itself, stay in Dublin, Cork, Waterford or Kilkenny and take an opera coach to Wexford each afternoon for dinner, then the opera; light refreshment can be consumed before departure. Postal and personal ticket applications from the end of June at the Theatre Royal, Wexford (tel. 053 22240) or through McCullough Pigott Ltd, 11–13 Suffolk Street, Dublin 2, and phone bookings to 053 22240. Accommodation lists from Tourist Office, Crescent Quay, Wexford (tel. 053 23111).

The Dublin Theatre Festival runs from the end of September into October. Organ and choral music is also performed in churches during the festival. Bookings 47, Nassau Street, Dublin 2 (tel. Dublin 778439)

Greece   Saint Demetrius is the patron saint of Demetria in Thessalonika and celebrates with religious and artistic events including ballet, music, songs and art exhibitions.

Luxembourg   In Luxembourg city and Esch sur Alzette the municipal theatres reopen for the season of theatre, concerts, ballet and opera.

Germany   Berlin holds its festival of arts from the end of September at the opera house. The Berlin Philharmonic under von Karajan gives performances and there is also operetta, pop music, rock and jazz.

UK   Cheltenham Festival of Literature is said to be the biggest literary festival in Europe. Authors participate, many talks are given and events are held throughout the city and in the surrounding countryside in houses associated with particular writers. The festival ends with a literary ball in Cheltenham Town Hall. Details from Town Hall, Imperial Square, Cheltenham, Glos. GL50 1QA (tel. 0242 521621).

Punch and Judy Festival, Covent Garden, London. The Punch and Judy Fellowship hold a festival in the Covent Garden Piazza on the first Sunday in October (sometimes the last in September) which attracts different Punch and Judy shows from all over Britain and Europe. The performances continue all day. (Information tel. 01–802 4656).

Sport

Horses: Wembley Arena, Middlesex, hosts the Horse of the Year show which attracts the best show jumpers from Europe) (information on 01–235 6431). In Helsinki there is the international horse show for the Volvo world cup, held at the Helsinki fair centre. Details from Oy Scanhorse, Ab Eerikinkatu 43,D 00180 Helsinki (tel. 90 694 99 11).

Horsing about: an unusual sport on view in London is the London Private Fire Brigades competition. There are 66 brigades in this association which since 1904 have held a competition which mainly involves target spraying with hoses and is held in Guildhall Yard, EC2. Teams of six compete for a Silver

Challenge Shield. Usually held on Saturday from noon, spectators welcome – but take a rain coat.

Racing: the Prix de l'Arc de Triomphe is held at Longchamps, Paris. This is one of France's major classic races and Paris Travel Service arrange day trips from central Paris by coach, with entrance to the race. The Houghton meeting at Newmarket is held in mid month and the Dublin racing calendar now features the Cartier Million race, billed as the richest in Europe. First run in 1988, it is run at Phoenix Park, the Saturday before the Prix de l'Arc de Triomphe. St Moritz has a guests' tennis tournament at Corviglia, Paris has a six-hour motorboat race, Berlin has a six-day cycling race in mid October with about 25 international stars taking part at the Deutschlandhalle which continues well into the evenings; food and drinks are available at the hall. Finland has a 21-mile jogging race from Valkeakoski to Tampere; details from Pirkan Kierros, PB 19, 33101 Tampere (tel. 9 31 37 410).

The Suntory matchplay golf championship has been held at Wentworth near London for nearly a quarter of a century. Keith Prowse Travel will arrange packages for this event.

Shooting and fishing: in Scotland visitors who seek up to date information on where to hunt or fish can call Dial a Stag or Dial a Fish (tel. 031 220 1800) at Finlayson Hughes Sporting Department, 51 Queen Street, Edinburgh EH2 3NS. This company can provide instant details on sporting facilities on estates throughout Scotland and make reservations through a computer booking service. For pheasant shooting, which begins on 1 October (till 1 February), commercial estate agencies in the UK can make arrangements – for example, Strutt and Parker, (tel. 01–629 7282) – for places on syndicate days. Anyone shooting needs a shot gun certificate from the local police station and, for pheasants, a game licence which can be obtained from post offices. General information from the British Association for Shooting and Conservation, Marford Mill, Rossett, Clwyd LL12 0HL (tel. 0244 570881).

Shopping

London, Chelsea Crafts Fair, Old Town Hall, King's Road, SW3 (information on 01–930 4811). Here 200 selected designers from all over the UK show their work and sell their products such as furniture, rugs, leather, jewellery, clothing, knitwear, ceramics, glass and toys, baskets, textiles and scarves. Prices run from £5 to £5,000 and the fair is divided into two sessions, with different exhibitions in each half, with a Sunday gap between them. An entrance fee is charged.

Scottish Book Fortnight is held in the two weeks from the last week in October into November. Scottish books are focused on in 60 Scottish bookshops and programmes of Meet the Author, events and readings are arranged. Libraries join in with exhibitions of books. Books featured suit all ages and tastes and 20 per cent are new titles launched during the two weeks of the fair. English bookshop chains also participate by featuring Scottish books. Details from the Scottish Book Marketing Group, 25a S.W. Thistle Street, Lane, Edinburgh EH2 1EW.

Horticulture

A good time for trees and arboretum visiting to enjoy the autumn colours. In England's West Country, autumn colour holidays are offered from mid month at the Coombe Cross Hotel, Bovey Tracey, Devon TQ13 9EY which include two visits a day to gardens which are not usually open to the public such as Andrews Corner at Belstone, 1,000 feet up on Dartmoor, Marwood Hill, Barnstaple, with its arboretum, and Rosemoor at Torrington for ornamental trees and shrubs. In mid October in southern England the countryside can be seen on walking tours organised by Sussex Scene, 14 Maltravers Street, Arundel, W. Sussex BN18 9BU. A weekend autumn colour walk explores the Arun valley covering ten to twenty miles a day over Downs and through woods. Forest lovers can rent self-catering cottages deep among the trees from the Forestry Commission.

The Forestry Commission's 116-acre Westonburt arboretum near Tetbury in Gloucestershire is open year round but is particularly good in October for its many maples. Maples can be seen at their firey best in mid October at the 95-acre Winkworth arboretum near Godalming, south of London, reflected in two lakes. Berries and rare oaks can also be seen here. Batsford Park in Gloucestershire near Moreton in the Marsh is 50 acres of Britain's largest private tree collection with specimens from around the world. The seasonal bronzes and golds are complemented by Japanese bronze buddhas and mythical Chinese animal figures. Windsor Great Park's Savill Gardens have a restaurant open till the end of the month and 35 acres of woodlands. The Valley Gardens of 400 acres on the north bank of Virginia Water include 100 acres of heather; the Japanese maples, red oaks, cherries and liquid ambers are a bright sight till the beginning of November in most years.

Autumn Leaves

In Italy, the majority of good resort hotels close till spring but in the UK, from the beginning of October, winter rates for out of city centre hotels (and many of these too at weekends) fall by 20 per cent and the hotel groups and tourist offices offer an almost bewildering brochure plethora of bargain breaks of every kind, price level and hobby interest. Weekend breaks are low priced at this time in London; a good time to get ahead with Christmas shopping and shows. The London Tourist Bureau (tel. 01–730 3488) has a round up list of offers in town, some including theatre ticket offers; the regional tourist boards also publish directories. Statistically, October is Britain's driest month, though 1987 may have done something to disprove this! (The winter bargain breaks run through to around April.)

Public Holidays

12 October; Columbus Day, Spain
28 October; National Anniversary Day, Greece
31 October; All Souls Day, Sweden

11 NOVEMBER

FOR MUNICIPALITIES
IN THE MIST

NOVEMBER is a much maligned month. Thomas Hood gave it a bad press in his poem that ends 'No fruits, no flowers, no leaves, no birds – November'. A little unfair, although kaamos starts on 14 November and lasts till 20 January. This is polar night in Lapland when the sun never gets over the horizon and the moon by day sheds a pale, opalescent light. Along with February, November is probably Europe's least favourite month. In November, mists take over from mellowness and the fog often disrupts airline schedules and driving plans. In the French revolutionary calendar, November was called Brumaire, the foggy month. The clocks have gone back by the end of October and the afternoons are dark. November, then, is a time for city visiting, to cling to cosy cafes, bright-lit shops selling Christmas gifts by now and in countries like Germany and Austria to join the start of the carnival season and in big cities enjoy the full range of theatre, opera and concert programmes.

Municipal Mists

Mists can be very attractive viewed from a warm restaurant or snug hotel room. The most romantic are in Venice. It is heady in November to possess St Mark's Square, at other times of the year usually living up to Napoleon's description of it as 'the drawing room of Europe', overcrowded and impossible to move. Though the orchestras move inside, the pigeons and duck boards take over and tea at Florians, perched on the little red banquettes peering out at gilded domes and the skirts of towers piercing up through the mist, is enchanting.

I have taken the 24-hour boat service across from the Cipriani Hotel after dinner in November to see the last waiter hurry home across St Mark's Square, his footsteps echoing. The bars were all closed and while at first it was exhilarating to walk the empty city, slipping through alleys and arches, knee deep in mist moving in from the canals, it was all too easy to get lost and see every building shuttered tight as against some unknown calamity. No one walked the streets, not even a cat, and a sense of panic crept up with the sucking of the water along the eroded steps of empty palazzos. My companion recalled the *Don't Look Now, Darling* film, based on the Daphne du Maurier story of the murderous dwarf in Venice. Evenutally the Grand Canal bank was rediscovered and from a water bus conductor came the cheery Italian equivalent of 'There'll be a number 9 along in five minutes'. Humanity was restored and the route back to St Mark's Square and comforts of the hotel attainable again.

By day, it is magic to take one of the ferries or a private hotel boat and go out into the lagoon following the guiding lines of the pallio channel posts; the sun above, the mists around and the sound of the hollow fog horns. One can visit Torcello to eat at the Locanda Cipriani, where Churchill painted and Hemingway drank, and see mosaics in the churches showing in this dripping month their problems of ceiling level rising damp. Burano, the artists' island, has soft Turneresque skies and water effects and brightly coloured houses where lace is still made. Murano, the glass blowers' island, is brightest around the blazing ovens as the workers produce garish little horses or animals as souvenirs.

Amsterdam is another city of canals, perhaps more chilled than misted in November – just the time to slip into a tasting house for a shot of jenever or thaw out in one of the many 'brown cafes', one of the most traditional meeting places where locals gather to meet, sip, snack and read the papers provided. Late at night Amsterdamers also meet to discuss the performance of the national theatre in the Cafe American next door. This is part of the American Hotel on Leidsekade built at the end of the nineteenth century and recently renovated in its original art nouveau style. It is now a national monument and makes a good base in which to stay near the museum area. The Cafe, open from 9.30 to 1 am, has kept its 1920s lights and faded, yellowed walls stuck with old theatre posters and there's a central reading table piled with daily papers. The cafe serves coffee, drinks and light snacks all day.

'Gezeluge' (cosy) is the right word for the city's brown cafes. They are found thickest along the canals round the harbour or Leidesplein and Rembrandtsplein where coffee, papers, gossip, snacks and alcohol are dispensed. Amsterdam is a great city for snackers, ideal for the tourist taking in the sights, particularly the richly endowed museums. Amsterdam has 40 such weather insulators, including the massive Rijksmuseum for Rembrandts, the Van Gogh museum, modern art in the Stedelijk with special tours, films, discussion sessions and a restaurant terrace overlooking the sculpture gardens. The Schuttergalerij, the Civic Guards gallery, has paintings displayed in what was once a street.

Snacking about, one can eat on the heated boats that make year-round daily tours of the harbour, and pick from street stalls (some have large marquee-like constructions edged with fun fair lighting), as seen beside the Westerkirk near Anne Frank's house. Here poffertjes are sold, also found in many cafes. They are penny sized pancakes, sweet and puffed up, served with rum butter and icing sugar, and delicious with coffee.

The mid-morning cup of coffee is essential to the Dutch taken with the papers by regulars in small canal-side cafes or in offices or restaurants accompanied by a sweet biscuit. This can be the *syropwafflen* from Gouda, wafer-style biscuits rich in syrup or perhaps *boter mopen* (butter biscuits), round vanilla-flavoured rich biscuits.

In winter, the Dutch cafes move inside from their summer terraces and little squares. Beems, near Kalverstraat and the Singel flower market, serves lovely big slices of apple pie and fruit flans as well as poffertjes and with the typical welcome of Dutch cafes has a side shelf-like table where books and papers can be propped to read while sipping. Coffee can be taken with a view of the royal palace at the Krasserie in the Krasnapolsky Hotel on Dam Square. By late morning the sandwich shops are doing good business that continues all day. Broodje van Winkel has three branches in Amsterdam selling every kind of sandwich filling for 2-6 guilders. A well loved Dutch light lunch or anytime sustainer is the *uitsmijter*. The name means 'chucker out' and it consists of an open sandwich of roast beef or ham with fried eggs on bread and butter. At the Cafe American, the uitsmijter comes with ham or veal topped with three fried eggs.

With drinks in tasting houses and bars, little snacks will often be served. As well as cheese and sausage, there will be *bitterballen*, a kind of round meat croquette eaten with Zaanse mustard, a spicey, peppery, vinegar mustard. Amsterdam has some old and beautiful tasting houses like the roomy Bols Tavern and the seventeenth-century De Drie Felschjes.

The winter drink is a slug of jenever (gin), instantly heart and body warming. The barman at the American Hotel says a Beerenburg gin in the winter 'brings up the temperature'. Gin is traditionally drunk from a small flute glass in one gulp with a beer chaser but it can be used as a mix with Cola or tonic. The jonge (young) gin is considered best but some prefer oude (old). To a non Dutch throat, it tastes something like aquavit, nothing like London gin, and is inexpensive.

As well as young and old gins, there are bessenjenever made with blackcurrants and redcurrants and Citroenjenever with lemon flavouring. Corenwyn should be drunk ice cold from the freezer, preferably with a herring snack. Women often go for the cherry-based gin which can be drunk with orange and lots of ice.

It was in 1645 on Amsterdam's Kattengat that Hendrik Beerenburg created his jenever made with herbs that was introduced as a health drink. Today it can still be drunk young or old near its original home in the Koepel Cafe of the Sonesta Hotel, created from two seventeenth-century houses. The Koepel has much of a brown cafe atmosphere with bulletin boards bursting with information and is decorated with antique prints of the area and art and folk objects.

The Koepel is an old copper cupola of a seventeenth-century Lutheran church with its Great Round Hall with an organ on which Sunday morning coffee concerts are given with jazz in the afternoons. A Sunday brunch follows the Sonesta's cafe concerts in the church which forms part of their complex.

Lisbon, the Dowager Lady

Lisbon, switchbacking over seven hills on the banks of the River Tagus, can be misty in November when sea fogs seep up the estuary. A wonderful winter sight in the old Moorish quarter of Alfama is of Lisbon's old and stately trams, like ships sailing on mist swathes out of the narrow high cobbled streets. Their way is cleared of cars by officials who wave either a red or green bat in winter, hugging into the warmest doorway in the slim streets.

In the Alfama are the fado houses, their sad songs seemingly suitable to this time of year, listening over coffee and port in a candlelit restaurant. Lisbon is a wonderful city in which to eat out; one of the cheapest in Europe, with inexpensive taxis too. Her native foods are warming and hearty in winter. One can of course pay the highest prices at Tavares or Aviz, the enduring top spots, or choose the rarely found nouvelle cuisine style of Michel Costa's restaurant in a tiny square, Largo de Santa Cruz do Castelo, below the ramparts of the Castle of St Jorge; a place to take a morning walk in the company of white peacocks, view the city or inside the castle, and look at English prints which show Lisbon in ruins after its disastrous 1755 earthquake. Michel Costa's vegetables, in deference to the colours of the Portuguese flag, are sometimes presented in combinations of red, white and green.

Some of the best meals are found in modest pensaos in the Bairro Alto area, which is crowded with restaurants. All walks of life eat together. Primavera, Traversa Espera 34 is one such. The narrow hill streets of the Madragoa, an area of art galleries, is another good eating spot. Varinha da Madragoa, Rua Madres 36 is a white tiled, gingham clothed, candlelit, simple place where a meal will cost 500 to 600 escudos. On a budget, the visitor can eat at a tasca (tavern), a third-class restaurant with a bar, which offers typical small dishes based on chicken, meat, offal and eaten with wine or beer. A light but nourishing and inexpensive dish that makes a good winter warmer, is a bitoque or a prego, found in most simpler style restaurants. Bitoque is a thin, juicy steak cooked in an earthenware dish topped with a fried egg and surrounded by fried potatoes. A prego is sliced beef in a sandwich or on a plate. Often veal is used in this dish and prego na plate means a plated version served with chips.

Lisboans love to hop on a snub nosed ferry, cross the Tagus and eat in one of the fish restaurants at Cacilhas. The fish is superbly fresh and sole grilled plainly and served with spinach and a light vinho verde wine is superb. Lisboans make the trip as much to admire their much loved city skyline, as the russet tiled roofs undulate across the opposite banks interspersed with plumes of palm trees. In November a breath of sea air is afforded by taking the coastal train or the fast dual carriage road to Cascais to eat in what was once a fishermen's village but is now a chic resort or beyond to Guincho for sea food at the beach restaurants on this sweep of Atlantic pounded strand.

Or one can drive south over the soaring Tagus bridge that in a mist is suspended in the sky and on clear days makes ships below look like dinky toys. Beyond is the Arrabida of high cliffs and little quiet beaches around San Martinho. A meal can be taken at the castle São Felipe above Setubal a rather dismal sardine canning town. The castle has its own chapel tiled in typical blue azulejos and a terrace with views out to Troia, where oysters come from. An even lovelier setting is the castle once owned by the Dukes of Palmela atop the traditional village of Palmela where a sweet dessert wine is produced. Now a pousada (state-run inn), the castle has a large sheltered courtyard where drinks may be taken even this late and a formal dining hall with traditional dishes including some of the old and often secret recipes for puddings from convent sources, usually served in tiny earthenware bowls.

Another high castellated place just outside Lisbon is Sintra. Byron's 'other Eden'. Sintra has two contrasting palaces, the hill topping Pena, which has been inflicted with nineteenth-century gargoyling and turreting, and the old Moorish palace below, with the huge dunce's cap chimneys of the kitchen. Sintra is a cool damp place of tall trees, little green hung twisting roads that suddenly debauch onto sweeping headland above the Fim del Mundo, the most westerly point of Europe. At Sintra one can explore the regal gardens of Monserrat with its superb tree collection and stay at Seteais, the palatial ancient house of a diamond dealer.

Back in the city on days when rain lashes Lisbon's open air drawing rooms of Praca do Commercio (known as Black Horse Square because of an equestrian statue there), Praca Rossio and Praca dos Restauradores and the artery of the Avenida da Liberdade and flower sellers wrap themselves and their pampas grasses and flowers in plastic, the old-fashioned, lady-like tone of Lisbon's life comes into its own. The shelter of the tea rooms, casa da cha, is gratefully welcomed. Many of the traditional ones are around the Rua Garrett area, the main shopping street, and as well as snacks and light meals, the tea shops sell alcohol and the sweetmeats the Portuguese adore. Here in Rua Garrett Ferrari, Caravela and Bernard and on Rato Square, Vicentinas are the most popular. The coffee rooms where rich Brazilian coffee is served are mainly round Rossio Square and the Avenida. On winter afternoons, tea with thick fingers of hot buttered toast are downed along with pastries and cakes. A little language course helps when ordering coffee. Bica, the mid morning energiser, is strong and served in a tiny cup. Espresso is as elsewhere, café is strong in small cups; com leite with milk. Garato (little boy) is hot milk with strong coffee in a small cup. Galao is strong with hot milk in a tall glass. Carioca is a mix of hot water and strong coffee in a glass or larger cup.

The British wintered in Lisbon and stayed at York House in Rua das Janelas Verdes, an early seventeenth-century convent, traces of which remain in the old chapel lower dining room, still with its font; the noviciates' rooms are the smallest and cheapest. Azulejos tiles, Arraiolos rugs in blue and white, dark wood cupboards and white walls supply the decorative themes of this hotel. Across the street, in contrast, is the annexe built in turn of the century belle epoque style. Views are out over the cranes of the docks and the hotel is near the national art museum.

Lisbon does not have a foot-defeating plethora of museums and monuments but one or two gems are enjoyable and not to be missed. Museums and churches defined as such are closed on Mondays and public holidays. The Museum of Popular Arts near Belem on the river is a delight of regional crafts and life-styles. Not far from here is the Coach Museum, set in two eighteenth-century halls which were once the royal riding school. The old noble and royal coaches are ranged in gilded solemnity. They are monsters of painted wood and thick leather suspensions that took two years to rumble to Rome. One coach has a toilet, others tables and chairs; the most impressive are three giants made in 1716 for a pope's journey. With winged cherubs and statuary they look like baroque chapels on wheels. In the Praca de Espanha is the Gulbenkian Foundation collection in a modern block which also has a concert hall, where one can see superbly arranged objects from ancient civilisations and an extensive array of paintings.

Of Lisbon's churches one can go to the Pantheon to see the royal Braganza family, joined together in death and including Catherine, wife of Britain's Charles II. The richest church is Sao

Roque, Largo Trindade Coelho. One of its side chapels is described as the richest in Europe; it cost £25,000 back in the 1700s, when it was dedicated to John the Baptist; and has an altar of lapis lazuli, surrounded by amethyst, with supporting pillars and steps of agate. Carrara marble, porphyry, jade and gilded bronze stud the rest of the chapel. The whole was made in Rome, blessed by the pope, pulled apart and shipped to Lisbon in three caravels.

Still in the Iberian peninsula, Madrid is a cooler and easier place to explore in winter. The best way to enjoy a winter weekend is to take a Ritz Crown weekend. The package includes accommodation at the lovely hotel (lovingly restored to its original regal glory) next to the Prado museum. A chauffered car greets one at the airport, and brings one to the hotel; sherry and chocolates greet the visitor in the elegant bedrooms, meals are arranged, and theatres, flamenco show visits to the Prado and sightseeing to Toledo and El Escorial by chauffered car are organised as required. From November to February the Ritz will arrange shooting weekends for groups of 10–12 on the estate of the Duke of Fernan Nunez at Aranjuez with lunch at the eighteenth-century manor house there. The Ritz is close to the Retiro Park housing the Royal Botanical Gardens, inaugurated in 1781, with displays of medicinal plants, herbs, old roses and an eighteenth-century greenhouse, the Villanueva pavilion.

The Ritz and other central Madrid hotels make a good base for day visits to the historic cities, tours around which can be accomplished in a day each with careful planning of sightseeing in advance. The Spanish have a habit, even in winter, of closing top sightseeing spots, including churches, from 1300 to 1600, which can be irritating, especially in Toledo with so much to see. Avoid weekends and holidays like the plague. The Spanish are allowed into museums and monuments free, but the tourist has to pay; £2 a the Prado, £1.75 at El Escorial and 50p or £1 in most other places. The Spanish often come in just to get warm or dry: El Escorial on a Saturday is a struggling mass and visitors won't get in unless they can form a group or get one of the official guides to help them fight their way round. If the crowded palace of Philip II, all 400,000 square feet of it, is a turn away, go to the Valley of the Fallen about five miles away in the same hill group. A mountain-side tunnel in honour of Spain's civil war dead does not seem appealing. Built in 1959 it is reached up a long pinewood-lined drive and shadowed by a simple 492-foot stone cross on a tumble of rocks. The basilica has a huge stone terrace looking towards Madrid. The entrance is guarded by immense angels of death but the length of the aisle tunnel is warm with old tapestries and little scarlet and gold alcove chapels edged with gloomy marble figures. The dome before the altar is a dazzling mosaic of crowds of people drifting up to heaven and Christ. Below, Franco is buried.

Toledo, the ancient capital, is encircled by the Tago River and has a parador, the place for lunch, looking out at the city. One can eat the Toledo speciality of partridge or fill in the siesta hours in the Zocodover main square and sample the Toledo marzipan. Toledo's craft of damascene work is all too evident. The thirteenth-century cathedral has a heavily carved choir, and paintings by Van Dyck, Goya and El Greco. The old Jewish synagogue of Santa Maria La Blanca has moorish styling, and the Transito synagogue has a rich moorish ceiling and a musuem. The church of San Juan de Los Reyes has superb cloisters with gargoyles of cats, dogs, bagpipe player and an upside down boy. The Tansito is near El Greco's house, more enjoyable as an example of domestic architecture round its little courtyard than the least superb of the master's paintings. Toledo's highlight El Greco is probably the splendid Burial of Count Orgas housed in a side chapel of San Tome. More long and gloomy faces can be seen in photos in the mighty, but rebuilt, Alcazar, the site of a lengthy civil war siege of particular horror.

Aranjuez is more relaxing, the eighteenth-century summer palace, and its massive gardens on the Tajo banks. The royal boat collection can be admired and one can walk in the Jardin de la Isla, which has 1,699 plane trees, and in the other gardens. Strawberries and cream can be bought at any time of year from little stalls by the park entrance.

North from Madrid over the Navacerrada pass, the road descends to the bare plains of Castille and the calmer and more instantly friendly town of Segovia. Views of the whole can be had from the modern parador where local meals can include garlic soup, crayfish and trout from the Eresma and Clamores rivers that wash round Segovia's rock base. Segovia's two stunning architectural features are the Roman aqueduct and the Alcazar. The aqueduct prances across the city's edge forming a gateway to the main street with its 118 arches up to 93½ feet high. In its shadow is Candido's restuarant, offering sucking pig and Castillian cooking. The Alcazar looks as if it has inspired many a Disney castle with its golden stone walls, ramparts and pointed turrets rising sheer from a solid rock rampart spur. It has Moorish or possibly Roman foundations and was extended in the fourteenth and fifteenth centuries, damaged in the nineteenth century and restored in 1882. Inside the royal rooms are warm and charming with carved ceilings, old furniture, paintings and a fine collection of well displayed armour. The steep climb up the uneven stone steps of the great tower earns the reward of sweeping views of the city dominated by the great roofs of the cathedral.

Crossing the plain where mules still pull the plough, Avila is guarded by immense, sturdy and little restored walls rebuilt in the eleventh century by Raymond of Burgundy, after whom the parador is named. There are 88 cylindrical towers and nine gates in Avila's walls and storks nest in arches above the walls. The best view of the huge battlements is outside the city from Los Cuatros Postes, four stone pillars in the valley. Avila is a compact city to walk, with plenty of churches including the twelfth-century cathedral and those associated with St Theresa. The convent of St Theresa, created in her original home, shows her tiny garden and birthroom – now a small brightly gilded baroque chapel. Next door, beyond the saintly souvenir shop, is a small collection (with entrance actually free) of her relics, including a rather furry looking ring finger in a phial. In the royal monastery built by Ferdinand and Isabella in the fifteenth century is an oriental museum off the upper cloisters. The visitor can also see huge Gregorian chant books of the sixteenth and seventeenth centuries and a room of natural history containing a seven legged small buffalo and a vampire bat. The choir is set over the rear of the church and affords a good view of the tomb of the only son of Ferdinand and Isabella; a slab in the sacristy marks the burial place of Torquemada, the inquisitor. One can walk between the churches admiring the fine old house facades, many with balconies glassed in against the winter cold. A snack sweetmeat made from egg yolks and called Yemas de Santa Theresa can be tried in several places.

Kicking off Carnival

Germany's industrial Ruhr does not sound in the least appealing for a winter visit. Yet Dusseldorf, reached from Britain with direct Lufthansa flights, is a delightful, sophisticated city, the centre of German high fashion, yet one unique in teaching children how to cartwheel and having an impressive start to the carnival season in November.

Fun starts on 10 November with the children going around singing and collecting gifts of sweets in the lantern decked streets. On the eleventh day of the eleventh month at the eleventh hour, carnival is officially introduced by the mayor. Everyone crowds into the tiny cobbled square in front of the town hall around the aloof statue of the Electoral prince Jan Wellem and the mayor introduces the new spirit of carnival and the beauty queen to the crowd. Guild fraternities parade in feathered velvet costumes with tall feathered hats, sporting dozens of carnival pendants round their necks, a new one made for each year. There are torchlight parades, bands and singing and huge feasts. Girls parade dressed like bewigged majorettes.

After watching a winter's night procession, Dusseldorf has a warm welcome in the dozens of small night spots in its narrow old quarter streets near the Rhine's banks. Whole streets seem to exist of nothing but small beer houses, restaurants, dance and night clubs, coffee houses and even local style chicken, fish and chip shops. They stay open well into the night. Dusseldorfers love their food and produce excellent local beer, Dussel and Alt draught beers, as well as sausages and mustard. A local speciality is rubekuchen, a fried cake made from grated potato. Thick vegetable soups, veal dishes with good sauces and ice cream confections are popular dishes. The Dusseldorfer is never far from a source of food. On some of the intercity trams to Duisberg, half an hour's run away, there are small dining cars where hot snacks can be bought and eaten. A tram tour is one way of seeing a little of the rich surroundings of the city cheaply and quickly. The trams depart from the terminus outside the Park Hotel. After passing through some of the industrial area you come to the pink and white Schloss Benrath built in 1756 for the Elector Palatine. Classical gardens stretch away on one side and on the other is the duck pond and village of Benrath. The ruins of Frederick II's palace at Kaiserworth can be visited, more easily until October with Rhine boats. A visit to Wuppertal can include a ride on its suspension railway. In the forests nearby there is a cathedral in splendid isolation, the Schloss Burg, Tasperre dykes and Lake Baldeney in the wooded hills of Essen has a forest restaurant and good views of the Ruhr Valley. The nearby Villa Hugel, formerly the home of the Krupp family, is open to the public. From Ratingen, the 'gateway to the Bergisch country', the Blue Lake set in beech woods can be reached by tram from Dusseldorf's Jan Wellem Square. Also near and tram accessible are the Grafenberg and Aaper woods, a large game park stocked with deer and wild boar. A bus from Dusseldorf's main station takes one to the spot where Neanderthal man was discovered in 1856, where there is now a museum and bison, primitive horned cattle and wild horses can also be seen.

Dussledorf itself has its elegant Konigsallee, a wide central street with ornamental canal in its centre and Triton fountain at one end. In summer the broad pavements are covered with boulevard cafes where eveyone meets to walk and gossip.

The name Dusseldorf means 'little village on the Rhine' – a village that now has tall skyscrapers like the Thyssen building and stately ancient churches. The centre is well planned with trees, parks, vistas of water and fountains that soften industrial-isation. A non city note is struck by local lads who cartwheel on the pavements at the drop of a mark. It is an old custom and is commemorated in a statue in the old town, annual cartwheel competitions are held. Children at the Old Town school get proper tuition – cartwheels are part of the physical culture course. Culture is also upheld in the well patronised opera house and in the many city museum collections and exhibitions; notable are the assemblages of china and porcelain. German Tourist Facilities Ltd, 182–186 Kensington Church Street, London W8 4DP (tel. 01–229 2474) have winter city breaks to Dusseldorf for three of four nights. DER also have three- and seven-night Dusseldorf packages throughout the year.

The Last of the Summer Sun

The places to be this month are either enjoying city comforts or catching the last of the sun. The south of France, the Greek islands and Costa del Sol are some of the best hunting grounds, along with Majorca. The sea stills retains some of its warmth and around the toe of Italy and Sicily and Malta is quite swimmable almost until Christmas. On my first wedding anniversary in mid November we swam every day for a week in Malta, not just in the hotel pool but off the rocks and beaches and acquired a fine tan. Majorca too has been the scene of warm November holidays; I recall boiling in clothes more suited to London than Palma and sunbathing happily on my balcony or on the decks of yachts in the harbour. Evenings at this time of year do call for sweaters and jackets. Cyprus in November boasts a 73°F temperature with six hours of sunshine and has plenty of evening entertainment; apartments for hire are available through the year and, as on Malta, prices are cheaper from November.

Naples is a good November city, even though it can rain a lot, but I have lunched outdoors on a sunny terrace overlooking the sea on Capri in early November and sunbathed in deckchairs on the terraces of Sorrento. Naples has its waterside pasta and pizza restaurants to visit, the narrow washing-swagged jungle of streets of the old quarter behind Santa Lucia and many churches and art museums, including the archaeological museum with treasures from Pompeii. Ferries can be taken to visit the islands and the Sorrento coast. The San Carlo opera house has magnificent eighteenth-century interior decoration. Pegasus Holidays, 24a Earls Court Gardens, London SW5 0TA (tel. 01–370 6851) have packages to Naples and Sorrento through November, as well as many other European cities.

It may seem an unlikely choice but I found Finland in November, crisp, bright and frosted, much more appealing than in August, when it rained persistently. Finland is well equipped to cope with winter: the cosy houses and hotels and the always warming sauna are welcoming and the tall birch trees in gardens are carefully spot lit by hotels and restaurants so that one can appreciate the etching of ice along branches from inside. Sauna windows often also have similar, lit views of nature.

Jyvaskyla is a city in the lake area with the Rantasipi Hotel near the town. The city is a place of architectural pilgrimage with buildings designed by Alvar Aalto. There is a museum to his work and the tourist office offers an architectural map of the town. But the joy of the winter countryside is about an hour's drive away on Summassaari island at Saarijarvi, where there is another Rantasipi hotel. This chain encourages outdoor sports, walking and trailing through the forests and arranges barbecues and picnics even in the winter.

A fond memory is of walking through the frozen forest to an iced-over lake side where an old hunter's log cabin stood. Inside a long pine table gleamed under scarlet candles and was laid with an informal lunch. The food was cooked over a blazing birch log fire; wild mushroom soup culled from the forest, grilled salmon trout served with a dill and mayonnaise sauce and boiled potatoes, home-made wholemeal bread and home-made herb beer. The Finn likes the masculine approach to eating and many dishes are cooked by the men with an accent on the great outdoors. In winter holes are cut in the ice to get at the fish, particularly turbot, which is made into fish soup, each man boasting of his personal recipe variations. Fish soup with pieces of butttered black bread on top is another November warmer. Scanscape Holidays, 197–199 City Road, London EC1V 1JN (tel. 01–251 2500) have winter city breaks to Scandinavia including Helsinki.

Old Customs

Bonfire Night in Britain is 5 November and only the British would want to stage outdoor parties on what is usually a cold, damp evening. The event commemorates the seventeenth-century attempt by Guy Fawkes and colleagues to blow up Parliament. Children collect 'pennies for the guy' well before-hand, pushing a scarecrow of old clothes around the streets in an old pram. Families and friends arrange the bonfire in gardens

and village greens and city parks with fireworks and suitable
warming food and drink and it is a night to keep pets safely
inside. In some places, the event has become much larger and
more formal in style. At Ottery St Mary in Devon, huge ignited
barrels of tar are borne in a race through the town and home-
made cannons are set off at dawn to wake the town. At Tichfield
in Hertfordshire there is an afternoon carnival-style procession
followed by bonfire and fireworks and an evening torch-lit
procession. Lewes in Sussex has probably the biggest bash
which also commemorates the burning of Protestant martyrs in
Lewes in the reign of Mary I. There are half a dozen bonfire
societies in Lewes and each holds a torchlight procession with
fireworks and tableaux and effigies of Pope Paul V are burnt.
Leeds Castle near Maidstone, Kent, is a dramatic moated
backdrop to a big firework display held on the Saturday nearest
5 November. Bands entertain and hot food and drinks are
served such as jacket potatoes and hot broth. The fireworks start
at 1930, fired from the castle battlements, and are accompanied
by music. At the end pipers play from the battlements as the
audience leaves. Tickets are available in advance or on the night.
In London the Yeoman of the Guard arrested Guy Fawkes with
his gunpowder and every year they still search the cellars with
lanterns before the state opening of Parliament (see below). The
London Tourist Board (tel. 01–730 3488) can give details of the
public bonfires and firework displays held around the city on 5
November.

November 3 is the feast day of St Hubert, the patron saint of
hunting. In Belgium there is much blowing of hunting horns
and hunts particularly in the villages of the Ardennes. There are
special Masses said by the priests, usually by torch light. In
Brussels High Mass is celebrated at the church of Our Lady of
the Sablon and also at the basilica of St Hubert, a national
pilgrimage spot, where relics of the saint including an ivory
trumpet are preserved. As well as the sound of hunting horns
at the day's ceremonies, there is a traditional blessing of bread
and dogs. The Ardennes tourist office has a series of winter
packages which can involve hunting or walking through the
forests and sampling local dishes such as Ardennes ham and
trout. Guided walks in the woods and outdoor barbecues are
included as well as river kayaking, alpine and cross-country
skiing and other sports. Details from Belsud, Rue Marche aux
herbes 61, 1000 Brussels (tel. 2 230 57 30).

November 11 is St Martin of Tours Day, principally celebrated
in France and also in Lisbon (see under food). St Martin was the
patron saint of beggars, drunkards and outcasts. Feasts were
held as animals were killed for winter about that time. Today

the date is better known as Remembrance Day, when services are held on the nearest Sunday in honour of the dead of two world wars.

Germany celebrates St Martin's day with processions of children carrying their own lanterns. Originally all these processions took place on 11 November but now they are more spread through the autumn.

State Opening of Parliament, London. This can be held at the end of October or early November. The ceremony at the House of Lords is not open to the public, but the procession with the Queen and the Duke of Edinburgh in the Irish state coach leaves Buckingham Palace around 1100 passing down the Mall, Horse Guards Parade and on to Whitehall. The imperial state crown precedes the Queen from the palace in its own carriage at 1037; a gun salute is fired in Hyde Park at 1115 and at 1200 at the Tower of London.

Lord Mayor's Show; London. Since the charter of King John of 1215, a procession has been held to show off the new Lord Mayor on the second Saturday of November from 1100. The Lord Mayor travels in a gilded coach drawn by six shire horses with his own bodyguard of pikemen and musketeers of the Honourable Artillery Company. The coach forms part of a procession of floats decorated to a theme chosen by the new Lord Mayor and accompanied by military bands. A route map of the procession can be obtained from the London Tourist Board.

Luxembourg: at Vianden, usually in the middle of November, there is the Miertchen, an old harvest custom with two big bonfires and a torchlight parade through the streets.

Santa Claus comes early to Holland, usually on 14 November, his birthday. He arrives on a steamship (more suitable to a seafaring nation than a reindeer sleigh) in Amsterdam, changes to horseback and tours the city followed by his assistants, the 'Black Peters', who scatter gingerbread to children in the crowd.

Food

France   In the first week of November there is the Dijon food fair. Cordon Bleu awards are announced and visitors can taste the foods on display, a wide range from sausages to sweetmeats.

Switzerland   Onion lovers should make for Berne, for the Ziebelmarit, the onion market festival. This is a winter fair with merry-go-rounds, confetti battles, music and street dancing.

UK   Fish, scallops, woodcock, plover, snipe, wild duck, wild goose and parsnips are fresh and varieties of small oranges start arriving for the Christmas period. Chestnuts roasted at home or on street braziers a custom common to many countries.

Portugal   In Lisbon, 11 November, St Martin's Day is marked with the eating of roast chestnuts washed down with new wine. It is good to try the custom at Golega where there is a St Martin's Day horse fair with horse parades and competitions.

Spain   On 11 November at the Festa de Maogosto in Orense new wine and chestnuts are offered up to symbolise the fruits of the earth. Queimada, a kind of flambé distilled wine, is handed out around the fire while chestnuts and chorizo sausages are roasted and a lot of wine-drinking and singing completes the celebration. Also on 11 November, as part of the Feria de San Martino at Teo and Puentevea in La Coruna region, lots of red Ribeiro wine is drunk. The white wines go well with the octopus and local pies traditionally eaten on that day.

Finland   Reindeer is available fresh and steaks are served with a berry sauce or mushrooms and cream. It is also smoked and served with salad as an hors d'oeuvre or, like lightly smoked salmon, with creamy scrambled eggs. The most prized delicacy is the reindeer tongue. Elk can be found roast, fried, stewed or sauna smoked.

Wine

At midnight on 14 November the first Beaujolais of the season is released and heralds an amazing if not lunatic race to get it from Beaune in Burgundy back to Britain so that 15 November often starts with a Beaujolais breakfast party. The Beaujolais nouveau is also rushed to other wine-drinking countries to be drunk chilled in order to bring out its fruity flavour. But for more serious wine buffs, the big Beaune date of the month is the third Sunday, when a few hundred barrels of new wine are auctioned for charity. The weekend begins on the Friday when there is a tasting in the cellars under the Hospices to which all take their tickets and a glass or tastevin as none are provided. About three dozen wines are tasted. There are three great feasts, for which it is hard and expensive to get tickets; the feasts are lengthy, punctuated by Burgundian drinking songs, all part of Beaune's answer to harvest festival. At the town hall there are stands from each village in Burgundy dispensing samples of the new wine. On Sunday the auction is held in the afternoon, with details relayed to bars and through the town. The sealing of a bid is made by the auctioneer blowing out a first and then a final candle.

Luxembourg celebrates its new wine at the Fiederwaissen at Wormeldange, usually on the first or second weekend in November, depending on the date of the harvest; in Spain, wine festivals run as late as 30 November in Tenerife at Icod de los Vinos, where they celebrate San Andres Day by running through the streets carrying burning torches leading up to the opening of the bodegas and roasting of chestnuts in the streets. At Aviemore in Scotland many wee drams thaw one out at Scotland's whisky festival.

Not so gigantic as the great German beer festivals is the Mid Wales Beer festival held at inns and pubs around Llanwrtyd Wells in mid November. The festival is held in free houses with about 30 different real ales to be sampled; nightly entertainment includes oompah bands and country and western music as well as male voice choirs. The festival includes real ale rambles and a real ale wobble. Doing it yourself, the Real Ale Trail in Cumbria leads the visitor round suitable pubs, starting at Cockermouth Brewery. The trail is detailed in a leaflet and map created by Jennings Breweries and available from the Cumbria Tourist Board, Ashleigh, Holly Road, Windermere, Cumbria LA23 2AQ (tel. 09662 4444).

Arts

France   Paris has plenty of offerings, including a Paris jazz festival, concerts in churches on the Ile de France, a church festival of sacred art, and an autumn festival that runs through to mid January with music, dance and exhibitions involving a number of theatres. Details from Bureau Central of the Paris Tourist Office, 127 Avenue des Champs Elysee, Paris 8e (tel. 47 23 61 72; a 24-hour information service in English is on 47 20 88 98).

Holland   Amsterdam has an international puppet theatre festival in various theatres. Details from VVV Amsterdam Tourist Office, PO Box 3901, 1001 AS Amsterdam (tel. 020 26 64 44).

Northern Ireland   In Belfast a festival is held at Queen's University in the second half of the month. Opera, concerts, theatre, films, jazz, literary events, folk music, architectural tours, children's and fringe events are included in the biggest arts festival in Ireland, with over 80,000 seats sold annually for the internationally performed events (the Royal Shakespeare company often appears for the festival). Most events take place round the university campus which includes a grand opera house built in 1895. The programme is published in September and booking opens in mid September. Details and bookings: Festival House, 8 Malone Road, Belfast BT9 5BN (tel. 0232 667687).

Wales Cardiff has its festival from the second half of November to the beginning of December. It has been going over 20 years and features symphony concerts, chamber music, choirs and soloists as well as an 'orchestra in residence' and visiting orchestras. The main venue is the recently built and very central St David's Hall; the university concert hall is also used. Music for Christmas is one of the festival's most popular concerts. The programme is published in August and booking starts at the beginning of September. Details: Festival Administrator, Fox Hollows, Maendy, Near Cowbridge, South Glamorgan (tel. 04463 3474).

Austria On Wednesdays, till the last one in November, international musicians play on the grand organ at St Stephen's cathedral, from 1900–2000.

Sport

Cars: on the first Sunday in November the London/Brighton Veteran car run from Hyde Park Corner to Madeira Drive in Brighton is organised and was made famous by the film *Genevieve*. Elegance rather than speed is the theme with costumed drivers in clothes sometimes as old as their cars. International enthusiasts compete and there are usually around 300 entrants; not all finish the course. The race starts from between 8 am and 9 am and the cars go down the A23 road, starting to arrive in Brighton around 11 am. The run has been held since 1896 when the law, which said that motorists had to have a man carrying a red flag walking in front of their cars, was abolished. Motorists celebrated by burning their red flags and driving off to Brighton. The first organised run was in 1933 and only cars made between 1895 and 1905 can compete. It is as well to arrive early for space to see the start or finish, but anywhere by the A23 gives a good vantage point, and the RAC can give more details (tel. 01–839 7050). In Cologne in mid month they hold the international motor cross races indoors at the Sporthalle.
    Horses: at the end of the month, the Hennessy Cognac Gold Cup is run at Newbury, which is easily accessible from London

Brighton veteran car rally

with its own railway station. The course is popular with trainers and stables at nearby Lambourn. Packages with London hotels, race admission and rail travel can be arranged by Keith Prowse Travel. In Berlin in mid month there is the International Riding and Show Jumping Tournament. Here the power jumping event involves rider and mount getting over 6½-ft hurdles. The Grand Prix de Dressage tests the art of horsemanship fully. The show includes a costume jumping event and the whole ends on Sunday with World Cup show jumping. The finale of taps is played by the Berlin police band. The venue is Berlin's Deutsch-landhalle. In England the hunting season starts in November (and ends in March). Rutland, now part of Leicestershire, is a leading area. The Belvoir Castle foxhound pack dates from 1750 and Uppingham is the place to buy antique hunting prints. Melton Mowbray is the meeting point of three hunts, Belvoir, Quorn and Cottesmore. The town is also know for pork pie,

Stilton and Hunt cake; the latter made and offered to hunts with their stirrup cup.

Skating: in Berlin at the end of the month there are international speed skating competitions at the Wilmersdorf skating rink. The Hotel Quellenhof in Bad Ragaz, Switzerland, offers tennis weeks from 1 November to 20 December and golf weeks till the end of the month. Packages are available through Leading Hotels of the World, 15 New Bridge Street, London EC4V 6AU (tel. 01–583 4211).

Shopping

The month to get to grips with the needs of Christmas, already well underway in stores around Britain. In London special street Christmas lights are switched on from mid November and stay on till Twelfth Night in Oxford Street, Regent Street – usually the most spectacular – and Bond Street. Shops stay open later on Thursday evenings in the run up to Christmas.

A day out can be mixed with some less pressurised buys by visiting some of the china and glass companies in the Midlands, particularly around Stoke on Trent, where companies have museums. Wedgwood has a particularly fine one and a visitor centre with cafe and a shop selling its products. Glass companies are found around Stourbridge; facilities and times of opening are detailed in a leaflet, 'English China and Glass', from the Heart of England Tourist Board, 2–4 Trinity Street, Worcester (tel. 0905 613132).

In Germany and Austria there are the delightful Christmas markets described in the December chapter, which start in the third week of November and continue to Christmas eve. They are fine places to stock up on small gifts, toys, decorations and sweetmeats. In Cologne there are two Christmas markets, one in Altemarkt square from 1100–2100 daily and also in Neuwmarket from 1000–2000, Saturdays till 2100 and Sundays from 1100–2100. Stores stay open till 1800 on the four Saturdays before Christmas, starting from the last in November. Parking in 24 of the 30 downtown garages is simplified at Christmas with digitally operated signs at key entry streets showing where the next available parking space or garage is situated and how many spaces are free.

In Berlin, the Kurfurstendamm or Tauerntzienstrasse (the alternative name) provides about 5 km of shopping plus side-street shops. Antique shopping is in the Elsenacherstrasse/Morzstrasse and area. Bric-à-brac style items and cheaper things can be found in junk shops at Chamissoplatz or in Neukolln around Flughafenstrasse. Good for cold or wet day exploration is the Nolle flea market in a disused underground station at Nollendorfplatz (closed Tuesdays, open otherwise 1100–1930). Tin figures are fun gifts and you can make your own or buy from the 30,000 figures in stock at the Zinnfigurenkabinett at 38 Knesebeckstrasse. Replicas of statues, reliefs and porcelain vases make unusual gifts found in Berlin at Gissformerei der Staatliche Museum (plaster moulding workshops of the state museum) at Sophie Charlotten strasse 17–18.

Horticultural

Hardly a highlight month, but evergreens stand out even more dramatically and can be seen in forests in most countries; the dark spruce of the Black Forest in Germany is particularly dramatic. Scotland's National Trust Gardens have some colour and impact this month such as a purple form of florists' foliage an impressive tree in the walled garden at Brodick Castle where Griselina Littoralis can be seen on the terrace with its cream and green variegated leaves. Branklyn Garden has hellebores with pale lime green flowers in late winter, and small crucifers with white flowers and pale green leaves. Crathes Garden has Chinese prunus trees with mahogany red bark that stands out at this time of year and at Kellie Castle garden, another Chinese originating plant, a form of Chinese rose, produces large red fruits.

Season and Discounts

In Vienna a recently added carnival calendar occasion is the Champagne Ball around the 13 November, held in the art nouveau setting of the Vienna Konzerthaus at which a highlight is the big champagne bar with bubbles from leading French producers. There is a midnight cabaret, special theatrical settings are devised and, of course, there is a lot of waltzing. Tickets cost about £50 and can be obtained from the Ball Office, Johannesgasse 22/5, A–1010 Vienna (tel. 222 75 70 42).

Vienna is the place for weekend bargain stays that run from the beginning of November till the end of March (not from 31 December – 4 January). Over 100 Viennese hotels and pensions in all grades have winter arrangements under their 'stay for three nights, pay for two'. Prices for each category are laid down (from about £6 to £100 per person in a double room) and a sightseeing tour is included. Booking through Osterreich

Incoming Club, Margaretenstrasse 1, A-1040 Vienna (tel. 222 588 66 ext. 215) or through travel agents.

In Britain, as well as cheap winter break prices for weekends, and mid-week breaks, hotels go a little winter wild with off-peak weeks at the beginning of November: a time to indulge a hobby or interest. Weekends can include Gilbert and Sullivan, regional food, four poster beds, with candlelight dinner and violin serenade and a London Hotel, the Norfolk Plaza, arranges Christmas shopping breaks. The Nelson in Norwich is known for its offbeat ideas and has 'in praise of winter' weekends, with the emphasis on eating hearty fare. One York and Edinburgh hotel group has a Spend Spend Spend idea that includes champagne to clean the teeth, caviar unlimited, fillet steak and a ten-course breakfast. The Mount Royale Hotel in York (claimed to be the birthplace of Guy Fawkes) has a Guy Fawkes break, with a list of the best bonfires and a chance to let off a giant rocket from the hotel gardens. The hotels, or the English Tourist Board, have up to date details of such breaks. Southport greets November visitors with free woolly hats and a nip of brandy if the temperature falls below 5°C, as well as providing interesting lists of things to do.

On Show

One associates visiting stately houses in Britain with summer, but the National Trust doesn't close all its properties and lists those open from 1 November to the end of March in a small booklet covering the four regions of England. The booklet details about 100 properties with opening times, special events – and those that have shops open specially for Christmas shopping.

An unusual aspect of visiting houses at this time of year is being able to see them being 'put to bed'. A section in the booklet covers this and details where the public can see the conservation of history during the winter; chandeliers being washed and bagged; precious objects cleaned and wrapped in acid-free paper; furniture being shrouded in dust covers with experts on hand to explain these finer aspects of historic housekeeping. The leaflet is available (send a 9 by 7 inch sae) from the English Tourist Board, Thames Tower, Blacks Road, Hammersmith, London W6 9EL.

Public Holidays

1 November, All Saints Day, Belgium, France, Germany, Italy, Luxembourg, Portugal, Spain

2 November, National Unity Day, Italy; day of the dead, Luxembourg

11 November, Armistice Day, France, Belgium

18 November, Repentance Day, Germany

12

DECEMBER

THE MONTH OF MERRIMENT
AND GOODWILL

D ECEMBER is a month of homecoming and thoughts of family and roots, but perversely also the month that starts the holiday calendar. With the long breaks over Christmas, more and more people travel to shorten the grey length of northern winter or just to see how the other half celebrates the big festival. A growing number of packages are now available to sample Christmas in various parts of Europe as detailed below.

A decade ago few British hotels thought of opening at Christmas. Now increasingly they offer breaks that include festive foods, carol singing and old style Dickensian fun with fancy dress parties, treasure hunts, guided walks on Boxing morning, and tours of the surrounding countryside. These are perfect for those whose family are grown up and gone or those on their own. Other hotel ideas are aimed at those who just want peace and quiet and relaxation. Others provide sports and hobby interests and even health farms like Stobo Castle in the Tweed valley on the Scottish Borders and Champneys at Tring find their Christmas health breaks are well booked up. They put on special programmes and the food, while seeming traditional, will have had some of its calories removed.

A Choice of Christmas

Northern Europe makes up for lack of sun and light around the year's shortest day, 21 December, by use of candles, coloured lights, baubles and extra special foods. Scandinavia particularly loves its traditions and follows them faithfully. Denmark issues a set of seals for Christmas cards and letters in aid of charity each year. Fifty million are sold; one year the design was of musical angels, created by Queen Margrethe. Advent's arrival is signalled by hanging a pine twig wreath set with four candles and lighting the first candle. The other candles are lit as the four Sundays of Advent proceed, until by Christmas all are lit together. Children have calendar candles marked in 24 divisions lit for each day from 1 December till Christmas and a Christmas calendar is also customary – a cardboard house with 24 windows or an embroidered tapestry with 24 hooks on which hangs a little parcel, a sweet or charm; one to remove each day.

A sheaf of corn for birds is hung in a tree or from a balcony and outdoor lighted trees are increasingly popular. The family goes out to plantations that sell trees to cut down the carefully selected tree; more fun than just buying a ready cut one. Home decoration is important; tulip and hyacinth bulbs are set on the window sills in white cones of paper to come into flower on

Christmas Day. Cut out fairies and mobiles hang everywhere. The kitchen as well as living room receives attention – red paper garlands with pictures of gnomes and goblins. Danish families and friends gather to cut out decorations – woven paper hearts are a Danish speciality. Traditional foods are prepared – gingerbread men, liverpaste, marinated herring. Over half of Danish families still do their own cooking.

Christmas Eve is the big evening. The tree is brought in and decorated, the table laid with a special cloth, candles and decorations and the traditional dinner served of a rice pudding starter containing one almond. The finder gets a prize – often a marzipan pig. Then follows roast pork, duck stuffed with apples and prunes, goose or turkey with candied potatoes, red cabbage and jelly, though now more families eat turkey and the rice and almond tradition moves to the dessert position. After dinner, the tree is lit, usually hidden next door and in darkness the door is thrown open to dazzle the children who surround it singing carols and then open the superbly wrapped gifts.

Christmas Day in Denmark is a sociable eating day with cold buffets of herring, caviar, shrimps, meat balls, warm paté, smoked leg of lamb, brawn, pressed meats, cold roast pork, salads, sausages and cheeses along with beer and schnapps to drink. The feast is repeated on 26 December. Then back to reality, though on one evening before New Year, the remaining candle ends are burnt right down with bets on which will last longest. Through Christmas, the Nisse, little devil-like creatures, are placated with a bowl of porridge in the attic – a custom dating back 4,000 years when Yule was the festival when the dead held their meetings and the living stayed well indoors.

Although Christmas is a family festival in Denmark, the ferry company DFDS has special Christmas breaks as at Odense, the home of Hans Christian Andersen, where traditional Danish dinner is served and excursions arranged. Or Christmas can be spent in Southern Jutland in a village on the German border called Rudbol, surrounded with marshes full of bird life where stays are in a 1791 inn; again, traditional fare is served. Details from DFDS on tel. 0255 554681. In Copenhagen the 71 Nyhavn Hotel has Christmas packages which must be booked direct (tel. 010 45 1 118585) with accommodation and food including a grand breakfast buffet and meals arranged in different Copenhagen restaurants and hotels.

In Copenhagen before Christmas there is the Christmas fair in Tivoli Gardens with stalls and entertainment in the Hans Christian Andersen castle. On 1 December there is a traditional Christmas parade through the city led by the Lord Mayor. Around Denmark there are Christmas exhibitions such as at

Vinderup at the Hjere Hede, an outdoor museum with old houses and workshops. At the Bangsbo Museum at Frederikshavn, the Roskilde Museum and also at Roskilde the Jeppe collective shop has a Christmas and sale fair at Farver Hammers Gard. On Christmas Day chorale singing from the Margrethe spire of Roskilde cathedral, where the Danish royals are traditionally buried, ends the morning service. Hardy Danes take part in the 26 December Hellerup/Copenhagen Christmas regatta for dinghies.

Sweden and Norway are traditionalists too, exchanging few gifts and spending less. On 24 December the bells ring, shops close around midday for 3 to 4 days and children sing 'Glade Jul', Merry Christmas, to the Silent Night tune around the tree. Hot chocolate and special home-made cakes, made from recipes carefully handed down, are served before a late afternoon service. In villages, traditional costume is worn for church. The Christmas Eve dinner includes sausages and rice, lutfisk, a fish with pepper and spices, thyme and kummel; fresh and marinated salmon and wind smoked lamb. Later nuts and spice cake, sultanas and multker, yellow berries, are served. The drinks served are beer and Linje aquavit, matured in casks on board a ship which must cross the line of the equator at least twice before returning to Sweden or Norway. Each bottle has the transporting ship's name on it.

On Christmas Day before dawn, there is the Julotta Mass with torches, candles and lamps, and sleigh horses in the snow outside. Sweden's celebrations start on 13 December, St Lucia's Day. It was once thought to be the darkest night of the year, so many lights were lit, as people sang from door to door and ale was poured over trees to propitiate evil spirits.

Young girls wear white with a wreath of whortleberry leaves and bear a circle of lighted candles, the first lights of Christmas. These 'Lucias' bear trays of cakes, sometimes cat shaped with raisin eyes, and a pot of coffee to wake the family. It is something of a beauty competition for girls to be chosen as Lucias to represent their town, particularly in Stockholm.

In the run up to Christmas, sausages of barley, pork and liver are made, hams are cured with saltpeter and brown sugar and smoked and bread is baked: rusks to go with coffee sessions and wortbread. On Christmas Eve this is dunked in a broth of boiled sausages and hams and the day is nicknamed 'dunking day'. Wheat bread is flavoured with cardomum and saffron shaded. Christmas cookies are called Nissel and Nasse, gingerbread figures. Other biscuits represent the sacred goat of Thor, the Christmas boar; cross wheel cakes are marked with the ancient sun symbol. In the yard, a pole holds a sheaf of grain and evergreen twig tips are put on the entrance hall floor and in front of the door. Young spruce trees guard the door and two days before Christmas the indoor tree, trimmed with dozens of small Swedish flags, small marzipan pigs and pure wax candles, is installed.

The Christmas Eve feast includes finding an almond foretelling marriage in a rice porridge – but only eaten after an impromptu rhyme is recited. A smorgasbrod forms part of the meal. After dinner the 'hustomten', the good luck gnome who lives under each house, bears in a sack of gifts. Then there is dancing round the tree, carols and the early morning church service to prepare for on Christmas Day, with families passing along streets lit with candles in each window. A more formal meal is served to the family on Christmas Day of roast pork, roast goose with apples and prunes, puff pastries, Christmas cheese and special Christmas ale. The celebrations continue with New Year balls, suppers, sleigh and skating parties till St Knut's day, 13 January, the twentieth day of Christmas, when they dance Christmas out.

DFDS also have Christmas packages in Sweden with choices of Christmas by Lake Vattern or in Stenungsund, on the rocky shores of the Bohuslan archipelago north of Gothenburg, with excursions and traditional fare. Details tel. 0255 554681.

Finland traditionally celebrates on Christmas Eve, beginning at midday, with the reading of a Christmas peace message while hot punch is drunk and Christmas pies eaten. After that in the hotels, guests help choose the tree on the special Lapland holidays run at Rovaniemi, just south of the Arctic circle. After choosing the tree and decorating, a sauna is followed by drinks and barbecued sausages around an open fire. The hotel at Rovaniemi puts on huge candle-lit buffets with salmon, herring, ham, pork, reindeer, salads and vegetable casseroles which are kept stocked through the night. Santa, of course, arrives on his sleigh pulled by reindeer. Christmas Day starts with another sauna and swim, and a massive breakfast followed by service at the Lutheran Log Church, though another hotel organises morning service outdoors in the forest lit by ice candles and torches and the guests are invited to church coffee by an open fire. Visits are made to Santa's village on the Arctic Circle, with log cabins and workshops where all the toys are made and a post office for special Santa stamps and mail cards. In the afternoon tobogganing, reindeer rides and snowmobile safaris are organised. Cross-country and downhill skiing is always available. In the evenings all the hotels offer dancing and a party on Christmas Eve. Snow sports and sleigh riding in the forests go on until St Stephen's Day, 26 December, before the guests leave to catch flights back to Helsinki. Several companies offer Lapland Christmas packages and British Airways' Concorde makes Christmas Day flights to Lapland for the ultimate idea in how to spend Christmas day. The day costs about £1,000 plus with Christmas banquet, visit to the Arctic Circle, drink with a Lapp family, reindeer rides, and a tour of Santa's village. Details from Goodwood Travel, St James's House, 78 Castle Street, Canterbury, Kent CT1 2QZ (tel. 0227 65967). Other companies to contact for Lapland Christmas packages are Finnair, 14 Clifford Street, London WIX 1RD (tel. 01–629 4349); Scanscape Holidays, 197–199 City Road, London EC1V 1JN (tel. 01–251 2500) with three- and five-night tours; Canterbury Travel, 248 Streatfield Road, Harrow, Middlesex HA3 9BY (tel. 01–206 0411), offers stays at Luosto among pine trees with accommodation in traditional log cabins with reindeer rides, motorised snow scooter tours, ice fishing, skiing as well as the challenges of reindeer skiing, and skidoo racing. Finlandia Travel Agency Ltd, 130 Jermyn Street, London SW1Y 4UJ (tel. 01–930 5961) has Lapland Christmas and Christmas in Helsinki.

Some of Britain's Christmas customs came from Germany with Prince Albert; Queen Victoria put up the first Christmas tree in 1840. Christmas trees as we know them originated in the Black Forest and the custom there goes back to pagan times, though it was revived about 150 years ago. Present-giving is supposed to have come from the Roman Saturnalia. The tree in Germany grows ever more popular, set near the Weihnacht-stisch, the Christmas table of presents and sweetmeats and in South Germany gradually replacing the Bethlehem crib representation. Around 1870 glass blowers in Thuringia discovered how to decorate glass balls on the inside, producing baubles for the tree that went abroad with German emigrants in the second half of the nineteenth century.

St Nicholas Day on 5 December is celebrated in Germany and Holland. German children receive fruits and sweets put in the shoes they leave out overnight. 'Good' Dutch children also have their gifts then and anyone with an eye to Christmas gift bargain buying should slip over to Holland after that date to find reduced prices in the shops. In Holland for St Nicholas Day children eat cholocate biscuits in the shape of their initials and adults eat boterletter made from almond paste and puff pastry shaped in the family initial. It is said that Martin Luther substituted Christ for St Nicholas as the bringer of Christmas gifts and today's Christmas child (Christkind) in Germany more closely resembles an angel. Weinachtsmann, Santa Claus, is gaining ground, however, in a merger of St Nicholas and his demonic companions who admonished bad children.

The Christ Child has his own market; an appealing aspect of the German pre-Christmas season, delightful to visit and now organised as a pre-Christmas break by holiday companies for an event which magically brings back the childhood delight in this season. On the way over to Nurnberg, the greatest of the Christkind markets, Lufthansa even hangs fir garlands in the front of its cabins during advent and the crowns of pine spices, especially ginger and cinnamon, pervade the German advent air.

Nürnberg's church of St Lorenz forms a backdrop to the Christmas market

Nurnberg has held its weihnachtsmarkt, Christmas market, for the past 300 years. It is set in the market square with a soaring backdrop of old buildings as a skyline stacked up past

Durer's house to the castle. Stalls line the square, roofed in red and green striped awnings, garlanded with fir and lit by lanterns at dusk. In the centre of the square is a crib. The Christ Child's fair runs through till Christmas Eve. As well as the stalls there is a music programme featuring trombone concerts, carol singing, plays and a procession of hundreds of children carrying lanterns that winds its way up to the castle walls and along its ramparts.

The stalls sell tree decorations, candles, gingerbread moulds, characteristic gold foil angels and Zwetschgenmanner, – little witch-like dolls made of dried prunes, nuts and crepe paper. Wooden toys are also sold: Nurnberg is the world toy capital, with 400 factories. At the market, gluhwein or schnapps is sold and the city's well-known pork sausages and hot chestnuts are charcoal grilled.

A special bilingual leaflet listing Nurnberg's market celebrations is available from German tourist offices. Virtually every other German town has a market of some kind or another, though Munich is better noted for its pre-Christmas opera and musical performances. Rothenburg ob der Tauber, a poster pretty place (and used as such by the tourist office), has a Christmas village specialising in tree decorations, hand-crafted music boxes, soft toys, nativity figures, wax angels and beer steins among the stalls. Details and a leaflet from Kathe Wohlfarts, Hermgasse 2, Rothenburg ob der Tauber. DER Travel has special Christmas and Nurnberg packages, the latter with stops at the Grand Hotel opposite the station and near the walls of the old town. The package is for five days by air or rail. Boppard on the Rhine has a Christmas fair and a five-night holiday with Christmas programme is available. DFDS also offer ferry travel and Christmas packages in Lubeck.

In Austria, where traditions are similar, Vienna holds its Christmas fair in the park in front of the town hall, as much an art exhibiton as shopping venue. The Adventzauber attracts over two million visitors, though it has only been in existence for three years. As well as a nineteenth-century crib with 230 figures, the park trees are decorated with designs created by leading Austrian artists, each in a different style. There is a skating rink with performances every day and fanfares from the town hall, followed by entertainment with dancing, theatre and singing. The Volkshalle in the town hall becomes a place where children can play, make handicrafts, bake Christmas sweetmeats, and paint glass, while adults wander among over 100 stalls to buy presents and foods. The Imperial hotels (Imperial and Bristol in Vienna) offer Christmas and Advent packages. The Christmas programme includes Christmas Eve punch round the Christmas tree with carols and gift giving, a special

Christmas afternoon tea at the Cafe Imperial, Cafe Sirk or the Cafe Central and – if you stay on 24 December – the third night is free. The packages can be booked through Leading Hotels of the World, 15 New Bridge Street, London EC4Y 6AU.

Salzburg too has its Christmas markets and advent and Christmas programme organised by the local tourist board, which includes visits to the market in the Cathedral square and performances of the advent singing and perhaps a concert at the Residenz or Mirabel palace (see also page 255). An English language booklet, Salzburg Package, details the options; from Salzburg City Tourist Office, A-5024 Salzburg (tel. 0 662 80 72 0).

In Spain lottery fever takes over at Christmas. El Gordo, the fat one, has 427,000 prizes and people save to buy a ticket or a portion of one. The draw is made by the orphans of San Ildefonso school and on that pre Christmas day, life stops in Spain. In Greece, on Christmas Eve children go from house to house bringing the news of Christmas and singing the kalanda, often sung by boys to a triangle and clay drum accompaniment. The kalanda vary from region to region and bear wishes of goodwill. The children are offered buns, chestnuts or walnuts. Pork is the staple dish of the Christmas meal. On Christmas Eve housewives bake christopsomo, 'Christ-bread', large sweet loaves in various shapes with designs in the crust usually depicting the house's profession. Special buns are baked in country areas for the cattle and hens. A bun may be dedicated to the land and kept nailed to the wall year round. The buns for the cattle are usually broken up into crumbs, salted and fed to the animals as a protection against illness. Various rituals are performed at Christmas to ensure good crops and oil or wine is often poured over the hearth. The dead are remembered in visits to the cemetery, and several of the many dishes eaten for the Christmas meal are taken to church to be blessed. As in Scandinavia, it is thought that goblins or sprites appear at this time of year and in the twelve days of Christmas; one such type of creature is the kallikantzaroi, whose year-round occupation is to cut down with axes the tree that supports the earth. When they have almost done this, Christ is born, the tree grows again and the spirits come up on earth in a rage, entering houses down the chimney and being a great nuisance. A fire with a big Christmas log is kept going to keep them away.

Scene of the Season

Skiers try to schuss off early to beat queues on the ski slopes but the snow can be evasive or non-existent. Changes in weather patterns are forcing tour operators to adapt their winter sports programmes to the new conditions. The snow now arrives later in the main ski resorts than it did in the 1970s. Andrew Selby, chairman of Vacations Tours, has said 'ten years ago snow conditions were generally good by mid December at the major European resorts. Because of this companies started their programmes around the 15th of the month. This is no longer the case. My advice if you want a bargain winter sports holiday is go for January, April or, if you choose the right resort, Christmas.' If you go in December choose a resort at least 1,600 metres high and remember that resorts near cities and airports get more weekend skiers; once school is out, queues start forming at the lifts. Holidays start around 23 December in France, Austria, Italy and Switzerland, but St Moritz should be allright for the skier. At the end of 1987 a 4 km piste, wide and fully snow covered, was opened in Graubuenden – the longest mechanically made snow piste. The area now offers 10 km of pistes from early winter, including the glacier runs on Corvatsch and Diavolezza and mechanically made pistes at Corviglia/Marguns. Mechanical snow facilities are also planned for the Olympic Corviglia. The popular Sunshine Ski Weeks run by the St Moritz school are now guaranteed from the end of November onwards.

Even if the snow is not around, the Victoria Jungfrau Grand Hotel at Interlaken is a good spot to sample the Swiss winter on special ski packages held from 13–20 December with accommodation half board, use of indoor swimming pool and entertainment at night. Interlaken is a good base for excursions to the Jungfrau ski area which is also a good walking centre. The hotel also has a tennis centre with four indoor courts. The package can be booked through Leading Hotels of the World, 15 New Bridge Street, London EC4Y 6AU.

Traditional Customs

These are mostly centred on Christmas, but there are other offbeat ceremonies also carried out this month.

Switzerland At Kussnacht on Lake Lucerne, 6 December is celebrated with processions of locals wearing masks and huge structures lit from inside with candles. The origin of the procession is said to be a hunt for St Nicholas, so noisy cowbells, trumpets and whip cracking are encouraged.

Geneva's Escaladeon takes place from the eleventh night till dawn of the twelfth in December. On 11 December 1602 the Duke of Savoy's army tried to scale the walls of the city. They were deterred by Mere Royaume, who threw a pot of stew over the first soldier to appear, and then cracked his skull with her empty pot. Her victory is now commemorated with bonfires, a torchlit procession in the old town and parties.

Holland   In Gouda on 16 December a candlelight festival is held. The houses are lit with candles, a huge Christmas tree is put up in the main square and street performers entertain. Being Gouda, of course, huge cheeses are trundled through the streets on carts for a traditional market.

Italy   In Bari the statue of St Nicholas is carried to the sea, and pilgrims come in boats to pray.

Spain   Las Palmas in the Canary Islands also celebrates Santa Lucia on 13 December with a procession of pilgrims bearing offerings of fruit and flowers at the church portico and boys wearing typical Canary Island costumes. The following Sunday the fiesta of the Labradores or farmers is held, with a procession of the Virgin del Rosario in carts drawn by oxen and typical local songs and dances.

At Labastida, in Alava province, there is a custom dating from the Middle Ages that brings the nativity scene delightfully to life. For a midnight Mass, twelve shepherds with a leader, a 'grandfather' carrying a lamb and a shepherdess carrying a baby Jesus, sing in front of the church and dance, beating the ground with sticks. After the Mass is over, a bonfire is lit and the shepherds pretend to make soup, which is given to Jesus.

Austria   On 5 December Bad Mittendorf puts on a play with unique figures, strange 'schab' clad in straw with long horns on their heads. They parade ahead lashing whips and are followed by colourful processions of frightening or fantastic figures in old handed-down costumes going through the village from inn to inn.

Greece   Chios, 31 December, is when the local sailors carry models of ships round the town. The models can be 6–9 feet long, hung with flags and lit with lamps. They sing local carols and end in the central square for a parade. The best ship models are given prizes. In Greece 31 December is a day for children to sing carols, exchange gifts and play cards.

UK   26 December is the traditional day for the meeting of hunts. Mummers plays, once put on in every village, are now rare but in Waterley Bottom in Gloucestershire one is still performed, with the dates and times posted outside the pubs where it will be put on. Players dress up in rags and paper-streamer-covered headgear and are announced by the Captain. The story is usually King George (the hero) versus Boneypart (the villain) with duels. The slain man is revived by the doctor clown and audience. A variation in Crookham near Aldershot involves St George fighting his enemies and a Turkish knight. The play is performed outside Chequers and Black Horse pubs at about noon on Boxing Day.

London: since 1947 the city of Oslo has donated a Norwegian spruce tree which is set up in Trafalgar Square as an expression of goodwill. The tree arrives about mid December and is decorated with white lights in Norwegian style and lit every afternoon and evening until Twelfth night. Carols are sung around it each evening by groups in aid of charity. The Queen gives two trees to St Paul's to stand outside the cathedral. An unusual procession is the carrying of a boar's head (which preceded turkey as the Christmas feast dish) on a butcher's stretcher from Butchers' Hall, 87 Bartholomew Close to Mansion House via Little Britain, St Martin le Grand and Cheapside. It commemorates the twelfth-century granting of a piece of land to the butchers' company in return for which they were to present the mayor with a boar's head. The procession is usually on the second Wednesday of December and the London tourist office will have details.

Food

The month for parties and the most indulgent bingeing of the year. Each country has its own goodies and traditional menus. Germany enjoys candied fruit and spiced Stollen cake. Wild boar is featured on German menus and Nurnberg bakes its *lebkuchen*, a spiced honey cake made into figures of men and women, houses, big hearts and sold in shops and at the Christmas market (see above). Lebkuchen has been made in Nurnberg for 600 years, since the days when spices first came to it as a trading centre. Hazelnuts, spices, candied fruits, honey and the minimum of flour are combined in a spice cake on an edible wafer. Visitors to Nurnberg can tour Germany's largest gingerbread factory, E. O. Schmidt on the outskirts of Nurnberg. Here one can buy from their shop or see a film in the visitor centre and relax in the coffee shop. Around Christmas the factory makes 1½ million lebkuchen a day in five different shapes (stars are only made for Christmas) and ten different recipes. Domino shapes are sandwiched with jelly, coated with chocolate and packed in traditional tins and boxes decorated with Christmas figures and legends.

December is a big biscuit making and eating time in Germany. Even today some housewives bake about twenty-five different types four weeks before Christmas, icing them and mixing in ginger, cardamom, anise, nutmeg and vanilla. Other Christmas preparations start back in the summer, when fruits such as raspberries and strawberries are packed in large pottery jars and marinated in rum and sugar syrup until at Christmas the 'rum pot' is opened and served with cream or ice cream. Baum-kirchen is a cake made on a spit to resemble the trunk of a tree. Layers of spiced liquid biscuit dough are poured over the turning spit, then each layer is glazed with sugar. The finished cake can be from 2–5 feet long and is served shaved in thin slices.

In Berlin jam doughnuts are made for 31 December and served with hot punch. Apples and nuts are gilded to hang on trees and marzipan fruits and figures also hang on the branches. Carp and goose are traditional Christmas Eve fare, with rice pudding containing an almond, or souffle.

Sweden   Different biscuits are piled into a yule 'pile' by each plate, the mound topped with an apple or orange at Christmas morning breakfast, and trees are hung with small iced biscuit shapes, as well as small nets of nuts and sweets.

Holland   Doll-shaped Speculaas are made with sugar and spices for St Nicholas Day on 5 December and children are often given a seaside rock-like stick to suck made with cinnamon. As a little Christmas stocking touch, candy lollies shaped like tulips are a good buy from the old style candy shop which also sells biscuits by the arts and crafts centre near Amsterdam's Sonesta Hotel.

Finland   Finns have what they call 'little Christmas' when parties are given a month prior to Christmas to build up the atmosphere, in a country that has no carnival. Traditional Christmas feasting starts on Christmas Eve with roast pork. On the day, ham baked in a rye dough is served with a carrot pudding with rice, with rice pudding and that lucky hidden almond to follow. To keep warm in the winter months, pea soup with rye bread is a popular dish, particularly on winter Thursdays.

UK   In Britain cheeses are part of the seasonal fare, with Sage Derby layered with green sage once made specially for Christmas and still available in Derby's street market. Stilton is still king and at Christmas is served with port and walnuts and perhaps some sweet apples such as Cox's Orange. The Christmas cake goes down better with a slice of Cheshire cheese and the Christmas panto season is nothing without the tang of mandarin oranges. Steam railway societies run special Christmas meal trips as does the Venice Orient Express in the UK.

The National Trust keeps many houses open (see page 239) in winter and puts on many events for the Christmas period including special Christmas meals which make a fine day out, especially as shopping for presents can be done in their shops. The Trust puts on 1920s evenings, themed children's Christmas teas in Cornwall, carol concerts with minced pies and mulled wine in Yorkshire and Christmas dinners in Surrey and Northumbria. Just before Christmas, lunches and entrancingly candlelit dinners of traditional food are given at places like Cotehele Barn in Cornwall or Lanhydrock House restaurant also in Cornwall. Details from the National Trust, 36 Queen Anne's Gate, London SW1H 9AS.

Other European goodies to note for Christmas include Panetone light dryish cakes from Italy (also sold for Easter), marron glacés from France, biscuits from Nantes and silver wrapped chocolate fish. From Portugal, sugared almonds and Elvas sugared plums in boxes. In Luxembourg hotels and restaurants prepare a selected Christmas Eve dinner: lists of these are available from the Luxembourg tourist office from November. Families gather after midnight Mass for meals of black puddings and sausages.

Wine

Plenty of it flows this month from chilled champagne to toast Christmas to mulled wine or gluhwein to keep out the cold. In Britain mulled ale was once traditional and can still be found in some small country pubs with ale heated in a can with a red hot poker. In Luxembourg on 26 December there is still a wine ceremony to take in. At Greiveldange, vinegrowers parade accompanied by the local band and carry a barrel of wine to the church where it is blessed. After the church ceremony, there is tasting of the wine on tap for all those who attend. Beer drinkers can note that the strongest beer in the world is reckoned to be Samichlaus, or Santa Claus beer brewed in Switzerland in December and kept for a year to mature.

Arts

Germany There are Christmas concerts in Regensburg cathedral by the choir and in various other churches during the Christmas fair – a custom widespread in the country. Recitals are also given in Nurnberg churches during the fair. From just before Christmas to the end of the month Berlin too has a display directed by Louis Kine of the Swiss National circus, which takes over the arena of the Deutschlandhalle for circus acts from east and west of the Iron Curtain. Information and details (tel. 000 303 81).

Italy The Milan La Scala opera season starts in December and runs through till May.

Austria Salzburg has its advent singing in the large Festival Hall and the town theatre runs through the month with operas, operettas, plays, ballet and contemporary German language theatre. Orchestral concerts are held in the Mozart circle at the Mozarteum Foundation with chamber music, master soloists and matinees. The Salzburg Society of Culture gives cycles of the great symphonies in the large Festival Hall. On 4 December, the anniversary of Mozart's death, there is a concert requiem in the church of St Peter. In the Mirabell palace and concert hall in the Residenz, the former home of the Archbishop of Salzburg, from 23 December till 3 January there is a cycle of music at Christmas and the New Year and throughout the winter there are several concerts every week. There are also performances at the end of the month at the city's marionette theatre. During Christmas and the New Year daily concerts of Mozart serenades are given at the Gothic hall of St Blazuis church.

UK The National Trust organises a series of concerts, particularly choral and carol concerts, around Christmas, including some by candlelight at places like Knightshayes in Devon. In London the full season of shows can have a seasonal theme with the possibility of buying theatre and concert vouchers as gifts through Keith Prowse, Gift Voucher Department, Banda House, Cambridge Grove, London W6 0LE (tel. 01–741 7441). The company can arrange theatre and hotel packages to London and a lovely idea for a special occasion or a Christmas get together is to reserve a private room at one of 21 of London's theatres for use during the show. Keith Prowse have a special leaflet about this. One can have the exclusive use of a VIP room before the performance and during the interval (avoiding the scrum at the bars). Often these rooms are used to entertain royalty.

Guests are greeted by the theatre manager on arrival, have a champagne reception with smoked salmon and canapés before the show and during the interval and have the attendance of a personal usher through the evening, with the best seats and free theatre programme. The leaflet details the sizes and location of these rooms which take from 6–50 people (300 in the Grand Salon of the Theatre Royal, Drury Lane). The price is about £40 per person excluding show ticket. Room examples include the Royal Retiring Room at Her Majesty's, hexagonal with fireplace and private exit (takes 16), the crimson and gilt anteroom for eight at the Garrick, and the Prince of Wales suite for fourteen, a secluded base at the Theatre Royal Drury Lane. Buffet dinners after the show at the theatre or tables reserved at nearby restaurants can also be arranged.

Arts

Carol singing brings out the best and worst singers this month. The top rated carol service of the nine lessons is at King's College Cambridge, which is broadcast and televised each year. In London on an early December Tuesday evening at St Martin's in the Fields, the same traditional festival of the nine lessons is put on with the church choir and well-known actors and authors reading the lessons. A collection is made for Bookrest, a publishing charity, and afterwards mulled wine and mince pies are served for a small charge in the crypt below. Details from the *Bookseller* magazine (also for all book-related events in the year), 12 Dyott Street, London WC1A 1DF (tel. 01–836 8911). A new spot to note if in London at Christmas and listening to carols around Trafalgar Square is a new restaurant, Fields, in the crypt of St Martin's in the Fields. Seating 200 with modern furniture against the original vault brickwork, the brasserie style food is reasonably priced with vegetarian selections, light snacks and full meals with an evening fixed price menu – open from 1000 till midnight and fine for after-theatre suppers. The new complex also includes a 46-strong craft stall market in the courtyard of high quality goods. With bookshop and visitors' centre, the complex will raise money for the church work especially for the homeless.

Sport

UK Early in the month there is the Rugby Varsity match at Twickenham. It is ostensibly a match between Oxford and

Cambridge, but it acts as an excuse for city gent graduates and old boys and corporate entertainers to have a day out. The ground has a museum with historical video show and there are tours each weekday. Information from The Secretary, Rugby Football Union, Twickenham, Middlesex TW2 7RQ (tel. 01–892 8161). Summer comes indoors with the Nabisco masters men's tennis doubles in the Royal Albert Hall for five days in mid month. There are Boxing Day horse race meetings at Kempton Park near London, but the horsey highlight of the month is the International Horse Show in mid month at Olympia, with show jumping championships given a touch of Christmas magic.

Wales without snow has torchlit road races based on the legend of Guto Nyth Drau, the fastest runner in the world. These races are held at midnight on New Year's Eve at the Town Centre, Mountain Ash, Mid Glamorgan (information from the Wales Tourist Board).

Switzerland The country concentrates on skiing, snow or not. At Davos there is the Spengler Cup ice hockey championships. Ski swiss packages are available at the high altitude Saas Fee at 2,550–3,500 metres with three packages before Christmas. Information from Verkehrsverein, 3906 Saas Fee, Switzerland (tel. 028 57 14 57). In December, January and spring St Moritz has bargain priced sunshine ski courses including special ski/ tennis weeks.

Davos runs the international cross-country ski competition and men's cross-country world cup.

France The ski resorts put on extra attractions over Christmas with children's costume parades, exhibitions, world cup free-style in La Plagne, downhill races at Les Menuires, freestyle world cup races at Tignes, as well as a symposium on monoski, surfing and, for the really macho, scubadiving under the ice of Lac de Tignes in the week of Christmas; divers must be qualified.

Germany The Teufelsberg hill near Berlin at 328 feet is the city's highest point and at the end of December becomes an alpine slope, transformed by snow cannon if the weather is too warm for real snow, on which the best skiers compete in a parallel slalom race. This world cup race takes place on two equally long parallel slalom courses and the event attracts about 15,000 spectators.

Shopping

The most seasonal places to shop are the German and Austrian Christmas markets running through to 24 December. Helsinki also has a Christmas park and charity market held on the Esplanade Park, which is specially decorated; handicrafts are sold for charity. In Salzburg, stalls with sweets and cakes are set round high Christmas trees. Berlin has its Christmas fair in the eastern part between the two S Bahn stations Alexander Platz and Jannowitzbrucke in the city's historical centre. It is the city's oldest Christmas fair with booths and stalls selling food frippery like candy floss and roasted almonds near fairground carousels. Border crossing points are at Friedrichstrasse or Checkpoint Charlie.

Britons and Continentals use ferry systems to cross the Channel to stock up on the other goodies, the shopping grass seeming much greener. Continentals plunge into Marks and Spencer while Brits head for Calais and Boulogne on cheap-day shopping tickets issued just before Christmas and buy up French foods and wines in the hypermarkets and duty frees are added on the trip back.

In London's Richmond area they have a Victorian late night Christmas shopping time which is better than fighting for survival in the Oxford Street stores. Or one can buy easy-to-post gifts of prints at the London Original Print Fair at the Royal Academy in Piccadilly where top dealers exhibit and sell prints from the fifteenth century till today. The National Trust has shops in various parts of the country with Christmas fairs at Brodie Castle, Crathes Castle, Falkland Place and Inverewe and Threave gardens in Scotland. Many of the original gifts on sale are inspired by design details from the Trust's properties and artists are commissioned to produce new ideas and ranges.

In London shopping details are available from the London Tourist Board. They include the Barbican Centre, with a programme of Christmas music, an art gallery offering a special seasonal exhibition, traditional meals and a charity Christmas card shop as well as a range of shops. The Endell Street Place, 27–29 Endell Street WC2 (tel. 01–240 1069) has ranges of handmade craft items for sale with special craft demonstrations. Hamley's, 188–196 Regent Street, W1 (tel. 01–734 3161), London's leading toy store, is packed this month, with customers visiting the Father Christmas grotto on the fifth floor (£2 entrance fee). Harrods, 87–135 Brompton Road, SW1 (tel. 01–730 1234) also have a Father Christmas grotto or magic forest on the fourth floor, while at Heals, 196 Tottenham Court Road, W1 (tel. 01–636 1666) has a jester to entertain in the store on December Saturdays. St Christopher Place off Oxford Street has lovely Victorian-style street illuminations. This is near Selfridges which always makes a big show with Christmas decorations starting early in November. There is a big, spectacular Father Christmas grotto on the third floor hosted by professional entertainers. The twelve main Oxford Street windows have specially created Christmas scenes with moving characters. Christmas shopping events include a Christmas fair at the Kensington Town Hall, Kensington High Street, with stalls, tombolas, raffles, clothes market, Christmas gifts and foods sold in aid of the Sightline charity for the Greater London blind. The Contemporary Applied Arts, 43 Earlham Street, Covent Garden WC2 (tel. 01–836 6993) has a wide range of items from silk scarves to bird tables in its Christmas show. The Crafts Council Gallery, 12 Waterloo Place, SW1 (tel. 01–930 4811), has its Christmas collection – Crafts to Buy or Borrow – with an exhibition of crafts to be bought or borrowed, such as glass, textiles, jewellery, ceramics and tableware. Greenwich covered market is decorated with Christmas lights and many of the stallholders, shopkeepers and locals will dress in historic costume to celebrate the market's birthday; the market includes craft stalls. Crafts are also on show and sale at the Alexandra Palace Christmas craft fair at Wood Green, with over 200 craftworkers showing goods for sale and demonstrating how they are made. Morris dancing and puppet shows are among the entertainments.

The spend spend syndrome of the month is not allowed to die with the candles on the Christmas tree in Britain. Although termed January (of which more in that month's chapter), sales start around 27 or 28 December, depending on the day of the week. In Germany as soon as the Christmas decorations are cleared out, shops put in New Year goods to sell such as streamers, squeakers, crackers, fireworks and the krapfen doughnuts made specially for this season.

Horticultural

Hardly the best season to go out garden sightseeing, but a good time to bring into the house holly, conifer and mistletoe. Mistletoe's magic dates from the druid's cult in Britain and was considered a magic plant as it was supposed to have supplied the wood for the Cross as well as curative properties for itching, sores, toothache and bites. The oak groves of Anglesey in north-west Wales were favourite pilgrimage routes of the druids, who came from the Celtic strongholds of Europe to enact a ritual there. In Amsterdam there is a month-long kerst flora—exhibition of flowering bulbs.

On Show

Belgium has a diamond exhibition, Naples at the end of the month puts on a display of local Christmas cribs and Helsinki holds an international dog show at the city fair centre. Details from the Finish Fair Corporation, PB21 00521 Helsinki (tel. 9 0 15091).

London on the other hand goes for cats, with the century-old National Cat Show at the National Hall Olympia in mid month. Claimed to be the world's largest cat show, 2,000 moggies converge upon the hall including breeds such as tiny Rex kittens, Golden Persians with hippy lengthy hair, and more modest housepets, superbly groomed, who come with their owners to show off. The show is said to have been inspired by a cat show held at Crystal Palace in 1871 after which cat fanciers got together to form the National Cat Club which registers pedigrees. In 1871 there were 16 types of cat on show, now there are 80.

Livestock get their chance to parade the ring in the Royal Smithfield Show, held early in the month at Earls Court with an agricultural exhibition which draws farmers from all over the country. But although only a day or so is open to the public, the World Travel Market at Olympia at the beginning of the month is the place to work out the venue for next year's holiday, with companies and countries from all over the world putting over their messages with food, wine, local drinks and folklore exhibitions on central stages.

Seasonal Discounts

In the UK many hotels offer very low room rates at the end of the month and around Christmas, particularly outside main cities. Escaping from crowds and the parking problems and traffic jams of central London, Richmond is peaceful and traditional on the River Thames and its Tourism Association, Twickenham TW1 3AA (tel. 01–892 8696) produces a well thought out and lively 'Winter in Richmond' leaflet detailing offerings from antique markets, historic houses, including Ham House and Hampton Court, Kew Gardens with its cosy hot houses or the year-round wild water slides at old Deer Park to ice rink spots. Christmas lights are detailed, churches and carols, and Christmas services, concerts, guided walks and hotels with special winter weekend packages. During the Victorian late night shopping evening, with street entertainment and horse-drawn traffic in Victorian decorated streets, there are competitions, mulled wine, hot potatoes, muffins and carols. The shops are open till 9.00 pm. Visitors are invited to come in Victorian costume.

Heading north, Yorkshire is a very traditional country and has a Dickens festival in Malton and Norton in the Ryedale district in the week running up to Christmas Eve. A building in Malton is believed to be the prototype for Scrooge's office in *A Christmas Carol* and festival events include steam train tours from York to Scarborough, stage coach rides, Christmas lights, costumed locals depicting characters from that book with period buskers, brass bands, Victorian-style refreshments such as hot chestnuts to Pickwickian breakfasts and Dickensian banquets. Readings, talks, antiques events and children's entertainment are also featured. Hotel packages include the events and there is a choice of five hotels. Details from the Ryedale District Council, Ryedale House, Malton, North Yorkshire YO17 0HH (tel. 0653 600666).

Rome for Christmas is made accessible and festive by Ciga Hotels' deluxe Christmas packages based on their Grand and Excelsior hotels. Four nights accommodation are offered with breakfast, Christmas lunch, sparkling wine with traditional Italian panetone cake, guided sightseeing tours of ancient Rome and the Vatican. A highlight of the package is reserved seats for Midnight Christmas Mass celebrated by the Pope in St Peter's. A four-night Christmas stay is also arranged at the Company's hotels in Venice, at the Danieli, Gritti Palace and Europa and Regina. Details: Ciga Hotels, 67 Jermyn Street, London SW1 6NY (tel. 01–930 4147).

Public Holidays

1 December, Independence Day, Portugal
6 December, Independence Day, Finland
8 December, Feast of the Immaculate Conception; Italy, Portugal, Spain
24 December, Christmas Eve, Switzerland (afternoon only)
25 December, Christmas Day, Belgium, Denmark, France, Finland, Germany, Italy, Luxembourg, Netherlands, Norway, Portugal, Ireland, Spain, Sweden, Switzerland, Greece, UK
26 December, Boxing Day/St Stephen's Day, Denmark, Finland, Luxembourg, Germany, Italy, Netherlands, Norway, Ireland, Greece, UK
27 December, Public Holiday, UK
31 December, New Year's Eve, Switzerland (afternoon only)

USEFUL ADDRESSES

National Tourist Offices

Austria, 30 St George's Street, London W1R 0AL (01–629 0461)

Belgium, 38 Dover Street, London WIX 3RB (01–499 5379)

Cyprus, 213 Regent Street, London W1R 8DA (01–734 9822)

Denmark, 169–173 Regent Street, London W1R 8PY (01–734 2637)

Finland, 66 Haymarket, London SW1Y 4RF (01–839 4048)

France, 178 Piccadilly, London W1V 0AL (01–491 7622)

Germany, 61 Conduit Street, London W1R 0EN (01–734 2600)

Greece, 195–197 Regent Street, London W1R 8DL (01–734 5997)

Hungary, Danube Travel Agency Ltd, 6 Conduit Street, London W1R 9TG (01–493 0263)

Iceland, 73 Grosvenor Street, London W1X 9DD (01–499 9971)

Ireland, 150 New Bond Street, London W1Y 0AQ (01–493 3201)

Italy, 1 Princes Street, London W1R 8AY (01–408 1254)

Luxembourg, 36–37 Piccadilly, London W1V 9PA (01–434 2800)

Malta, College House, Suite 207, Wrights Lane, London W8 5SH (01–938 2668)

Netherlands, 25–28 Buckingham Gate, London SW1E 6LD (01–630 0451)

Norway, 20 Pall Mall, London SW1Y 5NE (01–839 6255)

Portugal, 1–5 New Bond Street, London W1Y 0NP (01–493 3873)

Spain, 57–58 St James's Street, SW1A 1LD (01–499 0901)

Sweden, 3 Cork Street, London W1X 1HA (01–437 5816)

Switzerland Swiss Centre, New Coventry Street, London W1V 8EE (01–734 1921)

Yugoslavia, 143 Regent Street, London W1R 8AE (01–437 2118)

British Tourist Authority and English Tourist Board, Thames Tower, Black's Road, London W6 9EL (01–846 9000)

Northern Ireland Tourist Board, River House, 48 High Street, Belfast BT1 2DS (0232 231221/246609)

Scottish Tourist Board, 23 Ravelston Terrace, Edinburgh EH4 3EU (031 332 2433)

Wales Tourist Board, Brunel House, 2 Fitzalan Road, Cardiff CF2 1UY (0222 499909)

Jersey Tourist Information Office 35 Albermarle Street, London W1 (01–493 5278)

Regional Tourist Boards in England

Cumbria Tourist Board, Ashleigh, Holly Road, Windemere, Cumbria LA23 2AQ (096 62 4444)

Northumbria Tourist Board, Aykley Heads, Durham DH1 5UX (0385 46905)

North West Tourist Board, The Last Drop Village, Bromley Cross, Bolton, Lancs, BL7 9PZ (0204 591511)

Yorkshire and Humberside Tourist Board, 312 Tadcaster Road, York, N. Yorkshire YO2 2HF (0904 707961)

Heart of England Tourist Board, 2–4 Trinity Street, Worcester, WR1 2PW (0905 29511)

East Midlands Tourist Board, Exchequergate, Lincoln LN2 1PZ (0522 531521)

Thames and Chilterns Tourist Board, 8 The Market Place, Abingdon, Oxon. OX14 3UD (0235 22711)

East Anglia Tourist Board, Toppesfield Hall, Hadleigh, Suffolk IP7 5DN (0473 822922)

London Visitor and Convention Bureau, 26 Grosvenor Gardens, London SW1W 0DU (01–730 3488)

West Country Tourist Board, Trinity Court, Southernhay East, Exeter, Devon EX1 1QS (0392 76351)

Southern Tourist Board, Town Hall Centre, Leigh Road, Eastleigh, Hants SO5 4DE (0703 616027)

South East England Tourist Board, 1 Warwick Park, Tunbridge Wells, Kent TN2 5TA (0892 40766)

British Arts Festivals Assocation, 23 Orchard Road, London N6 5TR

Information on Wine

Food and Wine from France, Nuffield House, 41–46 Piccadilly, London W1V 9AJ (01–439 8371)

German Wine Centre, 121 Gloucester Road, London W1H 3PJ (01–935 8164)

Italian Wine Centre, 37 Sackville Street, London W1X 2DQ (01–734 2412)

English Vineyards Association, The Ridge, Lamberhurst Down, Kent TW3 8ER (0892 890734)

English Wine Centre, Valley Wine Cellars, Drusillas Corner, Alfriston, E. Sussex BN26 5QS (0323 870532)

Portuguese Government Trade Office, New Bond Street House, 1–5 New Bond Street, London W1Y 9PE (01–493 0212)

Wine (and food) from Spain, 23 Manchester Square, London W1M 5AP (01–935 6140)

INDEX